D0998480

12-30-15

Hoover Institution Publications 145

Egypt's Young Rebels

About This Book

Begun in the early 1930s as a youth movement working for patriotic goals by paramilitary methods, Young Egypt reached its zenith of impact and influence in the late 1930s, when it became a full-fledged political party and its message was a dominant influence on younger Egyptians. Suppressed by the authorities because of its involvement in anti-British activities during World War II, it resurfaced after the war and enjoyed a brief period of importance in the early 1950s under the name of the Socialist Party of Egypt.

The movement left its mark on both pre- and post-war Egypt. Its dramatic and often violent political methods helped to erode Egypt's fragile parliamentary monarchy, and its emphasis on the politics of confrontation and populist and nationalist programs heavily influenced the generation which has ruled Egypt since 1952.

The author is Associate Professor of History at the University of Colorado. He is co-author of The Middle East: A Social Geography, second edition (London: Duckworth/ Chicago: Aldine-Atherton, 1970). He has done research in Egypt in 1964-65, 1969, and 1974-75, and he is a frequent contributor to scholarly journals in the field.

EGYPT'S YOUNG REBELS
"Young Egypt": 1933-1952

James P. Jankowski

Hoover Institution Press
Stanford University
Stanford, California

The Hoover Institution on War, Revolution and Peace,
founded at Stanford University in 1919 by the late President
Herbert Hoover, is a center for advanced study and research
on public and international affairs in the twentieth century.
The views expressed in its publications are entirely those of
the authors and do not necessarily reflect the views of the staff,
officers, or Board of Overseers of the Hoover Institution.

Library of Congress Cataloging in Publication Data

Jankowski, James P   1937-
  Egypt's young rebels.

  (Hoover Institution publications ; 145)
  Bibliography: p.
  Includes index.
  1. Hizb Misr al-Fatah. 2. Egypt--Politics and
government--1919-1952. I. Title. II. Series: Stanford University. Hoover Institution on War, Revolution,
and Peace. Publications ; 145.
JQ3898.H5J3   329.9'62   75-8654
ISBN 0-8179-1451-X

Hoover Institution Publications 145
International Standard Book Number 0-8179-1451-X
© 1975 by the Board of Trustees of the
    Leland Stanford Junior University
All rights reserved
Printed in the United States of America

1888356

Contents

Acknowledgements

This study was made possible only through the assistance and encouragement of many institutions and individuals. The bulk of the research on the movement in the period from 1933 to 1944 was carried out in Egypt in 1964-1965, with financial support provided by a Fulbright-Hays pre-doctoral fellowship. The assembling of the data on the movement over this early period of its history into a doctoral dissertation for the Department of History, University of Michigan, was greatly facilitated by a graduate fellowship from the Rackham Graduate School of the University. Most of the research on Young Egypt in the postwar period was done in Egypt in 1969, through financial assistance provided by the National Endowment for the Humanities, the American Philosophical Society, and the Council on Research and Creative Work of the University of Colorado. I wish to thank all these institutions for their support. The views expressed in the study are, of course, my responsibility.

On a personal level, my debts are legion: space allows for but the most important to be acknowledged. Makram Neguib Girgis and Salim Gneiber, both of whom assisted in the collection of data in Egypt, made my task an easier one through their industry and their friendship. Dr. S. M. El Sheniti, Under-Secretary of the Ministry of Culture in charge of libraries and archives, deserves thanks for his encouragement of scholarship through facilitating access to the Egyptian National Library. Dr. George Kent of the Department of State and Dr. Khalil Helou of the Library of Congress provided valuable assistance in the obtaining of archival materials in Washington, and Dr. Charles D. Smith was a gracious friend in letting me see data he had gathered in the Public Record Office, London.

In regard to those Egyptians connected with Young Egypt or with Egyptian student politics during the period of the parliamentary monarchy who were kind enough to share their memories with me, I hope that this study accurately reflects their activities at that time. To those teachers who guided and counselled me in the early stages of this work, I give my thanks. A special debt of gratitude is owed to my major advisor at the University of Michigan, Professor Richard P. Mitchell, for the time he gave to my education and for the invaluable assistance which I have received from him.

To my mother goes my thanks for all, over the years. My debt to my wife - and the depth of my appreciation - are known best to her.

Youth and Politics in Egypt
under the Parliamentary Monarchy

The subject of this study, the Young Egypt (misr
al-fatah) society and party, was first and foremost a youth
movement. Instituted as a patriotic association for youth in
1933, throughout the 1930's its leadership was composed of
young men in their twenties; its following was predominantly
made up of men of the same or a younger age; and its propaganda had as one of its major themes that of the "new
generation" being a distinctive and a hopeful force in
Egyptian politics and society. Even in the post-World War II
period when the movement's leadership had aged, Young Egypt
and its successor the Socialist Party of Egypt continued to
direct much of its appeal to Egyptian youth and to echo the
idea of itself as the representative of the Egyptian younger
generation. Because of this abiding orientation towards
youth, the development and history of the movement cannot be
understood without prior reference to the environment of
youth in Egypt during the period of the parliamentary
monarchy.

The inauguration of the Egyptian parliamentary monarchy
in 1922-1923 brought with it considerable changes in the
educational, cultural, and political circumstances of younger
Egyptians. In the sphere of education, the most important
change was the rapid expansion of the school population. The
men who ruled Egypt from 1923 to 1952 made a veritable cult
of education, seeing in it the only sure cure for Egypt's
problems and the only way of consolidating the Western
parliamentary system in which they believed.[1] Correspondingly,
they reversed the previous cautious educational policy which
had marked the period of British dominance, undertaking a
rapid expansion of the state educational system. As the
table on page 2 shows, the number of students in the state
educational system showed a dramatic increase during the
parliamentary period.[2] When secondary school and university
students are added together, one reason for the political
activism of Egyptian youth under the parliamentary monarchy
becomes apparent; there were a great many more of them being
educated, with all that education implies for political
awareness and involvement.

What kind of education was being offered to the
burgeoning number of Egyptian youth on the secondary and
university levels? The curricula of the secondary schools

SCHOOL YEAR	PRIMARY AND ELEMENTARY SCHOOL ENROLLMENT	SECONDARY SCHOOL ENROLLMENT	UNIVERSITY ENROLLMENT
1925/26	193,144	16,879	3,368
1930/31	373,888	38,809	4,247
1935/36	661,025	45,203	7,515
1940/41	1,080,333	58,867	8,507
1945/46	964,081	75,096	13,927
1950/51	995,676	152,552	31,774

and universities of Egypt during the period of the parliamentary monarchy have often been criticized for their predominantly Westernized orientation in which foreign languages and foreign models formed the basis of study.[3] The five-year Egyptian secondary schools, which were rigidly centralized and which followed the same curriculum throughout Egypt, placed their students in an overwhelmingly European academic environment.[4] Up to 1935, the course of study during the first three years of secondary school (where a common set of courses was taken by all students) allotted only twenty periods per week to the traditional subjects of religion and the Arabic language as opposed to forty-one periods of foreign languages, twenty-six of mathematics and the physical sciences, and thirteen of history, geography, and civics. A revision of the curriculum in 1935 which created a uniform set of courses for the first four years of secondary school maintained much the same proportions; twenty-five periods per week of religion and Arabic, but fifty periods of foreign languages, thirty-six of mathematics and the physical sciences, and seventeen of history, geography, and civics.

On the university level, even the traditional theological university of al-Azhar began to be influenced by the trend to Westernization so prevalent in education in the early twentieth century: a reform law of 1911 had introduced such subjects as mathematics, history, geography and the natural sciences into the curricula of the elementary and secondary schools attached to al-Azhar, another law of 1925 provided for their more effective teaching, and further legislation in 1930 and 1936 revamped the curriculum in a more Westernized direction, making mandatory such subjects as physics, chemistry, biology and civics on the secondary level and the study of a foreign language for students in two of the university's three college faculties.[5] Perhaps most indicative of the Westernizing trend in higher education under the monarchy are the degrees obtained by students in Egypt's secular universities. Between 1925 and 1959, dates extending beyond the period of the monarchy but indicative of the current established under it, Egypt's secular universities produced 7,859 doctors, 9,996 engineers, and 4,722 graduates of faculties of science – but 15,936 graduates from faculties of commerce, 17,433 lawyers, and 18,136 graduates from faculties of letters.[6] In fine, whereas the traditional educational system of premodern Egypt had produced theologians, lawyers of the Shari'ah, and mystics, and the new state system in nineteenth-century Egypt had generated soldiers, administrators and technicians, the educational emphasis in Egypt under the parliamentary monarchy was on churning out businessmen, modern lawyers (i.e., erstwhile politicians) and inspired generalists.

Both the expansion of education and the pell-mell Westernization of the curricula of schools undoubtedly contributed to the politicization of educated youth during the period of the parliamentary monarchy. With increasing numbers of youth gathered together and in contact with each other in the schools came an increasing potential for activism of any kind, once other factors could set it in motion. Educational expansion may have promoted political involvement in another way as well. Although definitive statistics are missing, it seems probable that a large proportion of the students in the expanding school system came from less prosperous backgrounds than the relatively wealthy landowner's and umdah's sons who bulked large among the notable products of the state schools in the late nineteenth and early twentieth centuries.[7] Economic issues were a major concern of educated youth by the 1930's: the world depression sparked a wave of economically oriented activities by students, and the youth movements of the 1930's and 1940's were acutely sensitive to questions of economic opportunity. It seems fair to say that, for many of the youth being educated in Egypt during the parliamentary period, their education was their only passport to a better future, and thus they were attuned to taking action on the political and economic conditions which were likely to affect their personal prospects after graduation.

In terms of the curricula's effects upon politics, civics had become part of the curriculum in the secondary schools, with the ideas of a citizen's rights and duties being included in the formal education of younger Egyptians who went to school. The Egyptian Constitution of 1923 made the nation "the source of all power," and the textbooks of the period reinforced for young Egyptians concepts of popular sovereignty and participation in government. Moreover, they did so in a fashion which, in its "formal idealism" and its tendency to "consider political rights and obligations as ethical values," may have intensified a drive to political activism as educated youth saw the principles which they were learning to regard as "self-evident ethical imperatives" being flouted by their elders.[8] Given the increasingly

3

malfunctioning nature of the actual political process in
Egypt in this period (Royal ousters of the majority party,
rigged elections, etc.), it seems likely that educated
younger Egyptians progressively experienced an intellectual
dichotomy between what they were learning should occur and
what they saw occurring in reality. While one result of the
frustration resulting from this gap between the ideal and the
real could have been the withdrawal of some youth from a
political game in which practice was so divergent from theory,
for other youth the result was undoubtedly a desire to correct
these evils through their own involvement in politics.

From the 1920's onwards Egyptian youth, both students
and non-students, had more youth-oriented organizations in
which to group themselves than had their predecessors in
earlier periods. Prior to World War I, there seem to have
been no permanent organizations for youth in Egypt other than
the "Higher Schools Club" (nadi al-madaris al-'ulya) formed
in 1905 as a social and cultural body for students and
recent graduates of the schools of the state educational
system and youth clubs of the Nationalist Party (al-hizb
al-watani) created in some schools in the decade before the
war.9 This organizational vacuum was increasingly eliminated
in the interwar period, when a variety of organizations
oriented primarily towards youth made their appearance in
Egypt. The Egyptian Boy Scout movement (jam'iyah al-kashafah
al-ahliyah) was organized on a national scale in 1920;10
branches of the Y.M.C.A. were set up in Egypt in the early
1920's;11 and by the later 1920's the more politically
significant Young Men's Muslim Association or Y.M.M.A.
(jam'iyah al-shubban al-muslimin) and the Muslim Brotherhood
(jam'iyah al-ikhwan al-muslimin) had emerged.12 Individual
schools (particularly the more prestigious) also began to
generate their own permanent student associations. According
to the memoirs of figures prominent in youth politics after
1930, such school clubs had been the forum where they first
found an opportunity for cultural and political self-expres-
sion.13 Several of these school clubs published periodicals,
with one catalog listing a dozen different secondary school
yearbooks or periodicals produced in the 1920's and another
fifteen for the 1930's (compared to only two in the period
prior to 1920).14 On the university level, the Egyptian
University had a Student Union (ittihad al-jami'ah) by the
late 1920's. Thus on both the national and school levels,
outlets for self-expression and leadership by youth, as well
as potential centers for political activism, were in existence
in Egypt by the interwar period.

The broader setting of Egyptian society and politics in
which the youth of this period found themselves also contributed to involving them in politics. To a degree unknown in

Egypt previously the political system itself, with its
various political parties, enthusiastic press, periodic
elections and appeals of politicians to the electorate,
encouraged public participation in politics, youth participation included. At least three of the political parties
of the parliamentary period - the Nationalists, the Wafd,
and the Liberal Constitutionalists (hizb al-ahrar
al-dusturiyin) - had somewhat-organized youth groups
affiliated to them in the 1920's and 1930's. The Nationalists continued to have student clubs in operation at some
schools,[15] although the degree of support they received is
dubious in view of that party's declining popularity by the
interwar period. The Wafd's network of local committees had
youth sections through the 1920's, and in 1931 the party
formed a national association for its younger supporters, the
"General Confederation of Young Wafdist Committees"
(rabitah lijan al-shubban al-wafdiyin al-'ammah).[16] The
Liberal Constitutionalists had their "Youth of the Liberal
Constitutionalists" (shubban al-ahrar al-dusturiyin) by the
later 1920's, as well as organizing various ad hoc youth
committees to propagandize for their party on specific
issues such as support for Muhammad Mahmud's treaty negotiations with the British in 1929.[17]

Nor was it merely the political parties which encouraged
youth participation in politics. In addition, the general
cultural environment of Egypt during the parliamentary
period provided an atmosphere conducive to the same end. In
many ways the 1920's were the heyday of Westernization in
Egypt. From the now-impressive group of Egyptian literati
and their multiplying journals came incessant discussion of
the benefits of Western ideas, Western social and economic
arrangements, and Western political forms - including the
concept of popular participation in politics.[18] Even in the
1930's and 1940's, when a growing disillusionment with
parliamentary and representative government manifested itself
in Egypt, the newer elitist, populist and/or quasi-revolutionary
doctrines which came into fashion (but which never totally
displaced liberal political concepts) nonetheless still
encouraged youth participation in politics, indeed often
positing youth and the "new generation" as the only pure force
capable of amending or overthrowing the discredited
parliamentary system.

Several aspects of the socio-psychological milieu of
Egyptian youth during the parliamentary period may also have
provided a personal prod to political involvement. Perhaps
most important in this respect were what may be termed the
imbalances of adolescence in Egypt. As Raoul Makarius has
observed in his insightful study of Egyptian youth after
World War II (the more general data of which applies to the

5

years before the war as well),[19] "teen-age" was not a recognized stage of life in Egyptian society. In the eyes of his elders, a young man passed abruptly at puberty from being a child to being a young adult, one who was expected to act the part of a man. In addition, many of the activities regarded as normal for the adolescent in Western culture were still largely absent in Egypt. Egyptian attitudes in regard to personal relations, including the relationship which should obtain between adolescents of different sexes, had changed much more slowly than political forms or abstract thought. Schools were overwhelmingly segregated by sex, thereby preventing the usual exploration of male-female relationships which occupies so much of the time of Western teen-agers. In general, the panoply of extra-curricular activities - dating, parties, athletics - were still missing from the environment of Egyptian youth. And yet, the older concerns which had made such personal activities unnecessary for youth before them - long hours at work in fields or shops, the sureties of traditional family and village life - were no longer there for the students in Egypt's schools. Moreover Egyptian youth, at least those in the cities, were exposed to newer patterns of personal behavior vicariously - in the cinemas which burgeoned in this period, in novels and translations, not least in the actions of the foreigners resident in Egypt whom they observed in Cairo or Alexandria - while unable to indulge in that behavior themselves.

The psychic results of this erosion of older personal ties, of being aware of newer and apparently more liberating ones and yet of being unable to engage in the new behavior because of the constraints of family and society, must have been profoundly upsetting for many younger Egyptians. While it would be reductionism to state that the political activism of Egyptian youth during the parliamentary period was merely the result of personal frustrations due to growing up in an environment whose component parts were out of joint, these socio-psychological factors cannot be totally disregarded in considering what drove younger Egyptians, particularly educated younger Egyptians, to political involvement with such a passion during the period of the parliamentary monarchy. Put simply, politics was one of the few spheres of personal involvement and collective activity open to them.

Finally, Egypt's recent past acted to impel youth to political activism by the period of the parliamentary monarchy. In the interpretation of Egypt's contemporary history being developed by Egyptian historians of the period, a glorified image of the political role of youth was presented: it had been an inspired youth, Mustafa Kamil, who had revived Egyptian nationalism in the early twentieth century; it had been youth who had been the most vigorous opponents of the British in the period before and during World War I; and it had been students who sparked the demonstrations which became the "revolution" of 1919.[20] Reinforcing the impact which this image of the role of youth made was the mark left on many younger Egyptians by their own experiences during the hectic events of 1919 and after. For at least some youth, the demonstrations and violence of the 1919-1924 period seems to have given them a vision of patriotic struggle and sacrifice which they later tried to emulate. Later recollections are interesting here: regardless of their factual accuracy, they present an image of how youth should act which indicates the politicization of this generation of younger Egyptians. Thus Ahmad Husayn (b. 1911) of Young Egypt claims to remember the demonstrations of 1919 "vividly" and to have "participated" - at age eight - in some of those in the Sayyidah Zaynab area;[21] Nur al-Din Tarraf (b. 1910) of Young Egypt recalls his older brothers, who were members of a secret society engaged in anti-British terrorism, as having to send him from Cairo to the family seat in Upper Egypt in order to prevent the enthusiastic pre-teen youth from being drawn into their activities;[22] and Mahmud Yunis (b. 1912) of the Wafdist Blue Shirts similarly claims to have participated in demonstrations in this period and eventually to have become so imbued with patriotic fervor as to have acquired a pistol for use against the British.[23] Ahmad Husayn's later rhetoric about the effects of growing up during a time of violent nationalist struggle may reflect a wider feeling among those of his demi-generation who were in primary school in the 1919-1924 period and who came to political involvement in the 1930's: "we are the sons of the Revolution [of 1919], believers in the glory of our country, and therefore we can do what the old generation is incapable of."[24]

With the political role of youth thus reified in both nationalist legend and personal memories, youth became, in Gustave von Grunebaum's graphic phrase, "the shock troops upon which the future seems to hang."[25] While their elders may not always have believed in this mythic image of the political significance of youth, younger Egyptians of the parliamentary period often did. For educated youth in particular, drawn from a similar background, marked by similar social and economic concerns, linked together by a network of youth associations and periodicals, inculcated with an official ideology which taught them to regard themselves as active participants in the political process, and inspired by an interpretation of their country's recent history which developed the view that they were the potential saviors of Egypt, both a desire for political involvement and a basis

for collective activism existed. By the 1930's, the desire
and the basis bore fruit in specifically youth-oriented
political organizations, of which Young Egypt was one of the
most important.

The Young Egypt Society
1933-1936

In the 1930's, the two preeminent individuals in Young Egypt were Ahmad Husayn and Fathi Radwan. The former was the only President which the movement had (both in the 1930's and later); the latter was the organization's Secretary-General from shortly after its inception until the early 1940's; and both were Young Egypt's most prolific public spokesmen throughout the 1930's, between them substantially articulating its leading concerns and ideas. Because of their dominance within the movement, it is not inappropriate to begin an examination of the history of Young Egypt with biographical sketches of Ahmad Husayn and Fathi Radwan.[1]

Husayn and Radwan show great similarities in background. Both were born in 1911 (Husayn on March 8, Radwan on May 7 or 14),[2] the fathers of both were government employees (Mahmud Husayn in the Ministry of Finance, Radwan 'Uthman in the Irrigation Department), both came from moderate landowning families from Lower Egypt (Husayn from Kafr al-Batikh near Damietta, Radwan from Sharqiyah Province), but both spent their early years in Cairo because of their fathers' occupations.[3] The two first met each other in primary school in Cairo, but were separated after a few years when Radwan's family moved to Upper Egypt.

By their years in secondary school in the later 1920's, each was demonstrating the personal activism and leadership which were to mark their later careers. Radwan involved himself in dramatic and journalistic activities, becoming president of his school's oratorical and dramatics club, editing one of the first secondary school periodicals published outside of Cairo, and having one of his articles published in the prestigious al-Siyasah while still in secondary school.[4] Husayn first became active in student dramatics as well, serving as president of his school's dramatics club.[5] By his last year in secondary school Husayn also became politically involved, joining the youth group of the Liberal Constitutionalist Party and helping to organize an ephemeral "Society of Liberal Youth in Support of the Treaty" (jam'iyah al-shubban al-ahrar ansar al-mu'ahadah) which tried to garner public support for Premier Muhammad Mahmud's treaty negotiations with the British of 1929.[6] Husayn's first reported political speech, delivered at a meeting of Liberal Constitutionalist Youth in August 1929, already used two of the phrases which were to mark the movement he was to lead in the 1930's and 1940's: "speaking in the name of liberal youth, in the name of young Egypt (misr al-fatah), I summon you to be the leaders of the youth [of Egypt]. . . . Long live Egypt. Egypt over all (misr fawqa al-jami')."[7]

These secondary school activities were but prologue to the political involvement which Husayn and Radwan were to demonstrate in their college years. Reunited in the autumn of 1929 when both entered the Faculty of Law of the Egyptian University, they were almost immediately drawn into politics. In November 1929 the two attempted to found a patriotic society for youth. Only a handful of students responded, however, and, disillusioned for the moment, they allowed the idea to lapse.[8] Soon they ventured into journalism. In March 1930 they became associated with the journal The Cry (al-Sarkhah), hoping to make it a platform for the expression of their views and the possible focal-point of a youth organization. For three months both men wrote for al-Sarkhah, the theme of their articles being a patriotic monotone recalling the past achievements of Egypt and summoning Egyptian youth to study and find inspiration in that glorious past. By June 1930, however, with public response to their message apparently being very poor, the publisher of al-Sarkhah terminated their relationship with the journal.[9]

Perhaps not coincidentally with their departure from al-Sarkhah, June 1930 was a major turning-point in the history of the Egyptian parliamentary monarchy. In that month the ministry of the Wafd was ousted from office (for the third time in six years) by Royal maneuvering, to be replaced by one headed by Isma'il Sidqi, the anti-Wafdist "strongman" of Egyptian politics.[10] Although the period from June 1930 to September 1933, the Premiership of Sidqi, was one of autocratic rule and political repression in Egypt (the dismissal of the Wafdist-dominated parliament; the enactment of a more authoritarian constitution and electoral law; stricter censorship and control of the press) which severely limited political activism in Egypt, both Husayn and Radwan succeeded in finding outlets for their political inclinations in the early 1930's.

Fathi Radwan became a youth of note through travel and journalism. In 1931, a group of faculty and students at the Egyptian University developed the idea of convening an annual "Conference of Eastern Students" (mutamar al-talabah al-sharqiyin) in Cairo.[11] Radwan and another student (Kamal al-Din Salah) were chosen to visit Turkey, Syria and Lebanon in order to promote the idea of the conference. Their visit to Turkey was uneventful, but French security

10

forces expelled them from Syria and refused to let them enter
Lebanon. Although the plan as a whole proved abortive when
the Sidqi government, apparently regarding the scheme as a
front for the Wafd, dissolved the organizing committee and
prevented the convening of any conference, Radwan's involvement and his journey served to bring him to public attention.
He wrote several articles about the proposed conference and
about his and Salah's trip on behalf of it for such respected
journals as <u>al-Siyasah al-Usbu'iyah</u> and <u>al-Risalah,</u> and by
1933 was contributing articles on diverse subjects to perhaps
the most famous Egyptian literary magazine of the day,
<u>al-Hilal.</u>[12]

The extra-curricular activities of Ahmad Husayn while in
Law School were more germane to the history of Young Egypt,
for they involved being one of the founders and leaders of
the direct predecessor of Young Egypt, the "Piastre Plan"
(<u>mashru' al-qirsh</u>). The world depression of the early 1930's
had made educated Egyptians all too aware of their country's
dependence on agricultural products and their export, and
this awareness spurred a variety of state and private activities aimed at the expansion of Egyptian industry. Significant
tariff protection for nascent Egyptian industries was enacted
in 1930; Egyptian journalists agitated for the boycott of
foreign manufactures and their replacement by domestically
produced goods; and on the popular level a variety of campaigns
for the encouragement of Egyptian manufactured goods were
undertaken, with educated youth playing a major role in the
promotion of many of them.[13]

One of the most important of the predominantly youth-
organized economic movements was the Piastre Plan. In late
1931 a committee of Egyptian University students headed by
Ahmad Husayn was formed to organize a national collection
drive to gather funds for the development of Egyptian
industry. The Piastre Plan received considerable support
from influential elements in Egyptian society: 'Ali Ibrahim,
Dean of the Faculty of Medicine at the Egyptian University,
became its official chairman; leading figures in Egypt's
economic life - including Tal'at Harb, the Head of Bank Misr -
endorsed it; and many of Egypt's great literary figures -
Ahmad Shawqi, Hafiz Ibrahim, Khalil Mutran, and 'Abbas Mahmud
al-'Aqqad - wrote in support of it.[14] The Plan also gave
Ahmad Husayn ample opportunity to make himself known. He
was the Secretary-General of the Executive Committee of the
Plan, and as such he came in contact with numerous public
figures and delivered public speeches promoting the Plan.

The first public collection drive for the Plan occurred
in January-February 1932, and was an impressive success for
a nation then in the midst of a depression.[15] Organized on a
nation-wide basis, with student committees extending from

Alexandria to Aswan and with the fundraising culminating in a two-day festival at al-Azbakiyah Gardens in Cairo at which an attendance of 85,000 was estimated, a sum of ŁE 17,000 was collected. Eventually, the funds gathered in this campaign were used to construct a factory for the manufacture of tarbushes (the fez). After a government donation of public land as the factory's site, the foundation-stone was laid in October 1932, and a year later the production of tarbushes began.[16]

The Piastre Plan continued in existence through most of the 1930's. A second collection drive in early 1933 raised ŁE 13,000.[17] After 1933, however, as the novelty of the idea wore off, as the effects of the depression abated, and as the original student activists involved in the Plan turned their attention to direct political involvement, the Piastre Plan declined. In 1935, the annual collection was down to 5,000 pounds; in 1937, only 1,500 pounds were raised; and by 1939 the Piastre Plan had faded from the Egyptian scene.[18] The tarbush factory which the Plan had established fared better, however: functioning as a non-profit concern, in the 1960's the value of this enterprise begun by Egyptian youth back in the 1930's was reported to be in the vicinity of a million Egyptian pounds.[19]

The Piastre Plan was not only a movement of economic significance; in addition, it also had a political spin-off of considerable importance. For it was the youthful leaders of the Piastre Plan who, after their organizational success in the Plan, turned from economic to political activity through the establishment of Young Egypt. The "Young Egypt Society" (jam'iyah misr al-fatah) was founded on October 12, 1933, in a meeting at the Piastre Plan headquarters on the Opera Square, Cairo. Its founders were a dozen of the student activists of the Piastre Plan, including Ahmad Husayn (who was chosen as the society's President), Nur al-Din Tarraf, Muhammad Subayh, and Kamal al-Din Salah. They were soon joined by Fathi Radwan, who became the society's Secretary-General by the end of 1933.[20] The youths involved in the society soon terminated their connection with the Piastre Plan, some under duress (e.g., Ahmad Husayn was forced to resign as its Secretary-General at the end of October, the Administrative Council of the Plan "accepting his resignation because it was impossible for any of its members to be connected with any political activity"),[21] and concentrated their attention on the new and more explicitly political organization.[22]

The reasons for Young Egypt's founding are not difficult to see. As early as 1929-1930, Husayn and Radwan had attempted to create a patriotic organization appealing primarily to Egyptian students. Whereas this had not been possible either then or during the politically repressive

12

years of the Sidqi regime, by 1933 it was. The Sidqi ministry had been dismissed in September 1933, being replaced by a Palace-dominated but weaker and therefore less repressive one headed by 'Abd al-Fattah Yahya. Equally important was that Husayn and Radwan had become young men of some renown by 1933, the former as the leading figure of a quite successful economic campaign by youth, the latter as a budding journalist. On another level, the economic activities of younger Egyptians in the early 1930's may have made these youth more conscious of their organizing capabilities and their power to influence public affairs. Finally, the setbacks to the parliamentary regime of the early 1930's (the royal coup of 1930, the autocratic Sidqi regime which ensued) had produced disillusionment among educated Egyptian youth not only with the government but also with the established political parties which were failing either to create effective representative institutions or to terminate the continuing British presence in Egypt. Fathi Radwan's later recollection may stand not only for his own position by 1933, but also for that of other youth involved in the founding of Young Egypt:

> I suggested to my friends that we begin nationalist activity by standing far removed from all the political parties, not favoring any of them, considering all of them an old school following traditional methods in politics which did not agree with the tendencies in our political thought which aimed at trying a new path. . . .[23]

This "new path" was formally defined in the society's program drafted in October 1933. Almost exclusively the product of Ahmad Husayn and endorsed virtually without change by the other founding members,[24] the 1933 program was to remain the official platform of the movement until 1940.[25] It was addressed to the youth of Egypt, telling them that Egypt had "slumbered too long" and that "ten years of work" were necessary to restore Egypt to her past "glory." It gave as the society's slogan the phrase "God - Fatherland - King" (Allah - al-Watan - al-Malik) and defined its goal as being ". . . that Egypt become over all (misr fawqa al-jami'), a mighty empire composed of Egypt and the Sudan, allied with the Arab states, and leading Islam." Thirty-eight articles detailed the specific measures for whose achievement Young Egypt would work. These included the promotion of a specifically "Egyptian nationalism"; the restricting of the privileged position of foreigners within Egypt; the expansion of Egyptian agriculture and industry, but particularly the latter; the improvement of education, of rural and urban living conditions, and of family life; the elimination of

"immorality, alcoholic beverages, and effeminacy"; and
finally the promotion of "the martial spirit" among Egyptian
youth. In line with the society's formal position as a
non-partisan association, the program did not mention Egypt's
political parties or endorse any of them. Young Egypt is
reported to have distributed as many as 100,000 copies of
this program in its first few years.[26]

From its founding in October 1933 until the beginning
of 1937, Young Egypt was not a formal political party but
rather was a patriotic society working primarily for the
achievement of certain reforms in Egyptian politics and
society. As such, it was not too different from other
voluntary associations in Egypt such as the Y.M.M.A., the
Muslim Brotherhood, or the Piastre Plan. But there were
certain distinguishing features to Young Egypt which made it
a unique association. One was the fact that, unlike most
of the "youth" organizations in Egypt, it was actually headed
by young men. Its President and Secretary-General were both
only twenty-two years old when it was founded; its other
leaders were also in their early or mid-twenties; and it had
no notables of the older generation in either honorary or
truly effective positions at the top of its hierarchy. It
was, in short, not only an organization for youth, but one of
and by youth as well. Secondly, it was the first paramilitary
organization organized for younger Egyptians, with many of its
symbols and techniques influencing later Egyptian paramilitary
groups such as the "Blue Shirts" of the Wafd or the "Rovers"
of the Muslim Brotherhood. Thirdly, Young Egypt differed
from the various associations which preceded it by its
relatively greater attention to politics. Although it was
not a political party at its inception, in practice it
directed much of its propaganda, agitation and direct
action to explicitly political matters.

The structure of Young Egypt, as evolved in the first
few months of its existence, expressed "the martial spirit"
which its program had emphasized as necessary for Egyptian
youth. The movement's Organic Law of March 1934 distinguished
two levels of membership in the society.[27] To become an
ordinary "member" ('udw), one needed only to apply, be
approved, and pay the membership dues of five piastres per
month. There were no duties enjoined on ordinary members
other than the general one of "supporting the principles of
the society." Above the ordinary member was the "fighter"
(mujahid), conceived of as the activists of the movement. He
was to be an "active participant" in the paramilitary formations of the society, was to give "complete obedience to the
leaders" of his formation, and was to carry out whatever orders
were given to him "without debate or delay."

The formal structure of the society provided for an

elaborate hierarchy of paramilitary formations. These ranged
as follows: a "section" (qism) composed of twelve mujahids
was the basic unit; a "squadron" (katibah) was composed of
four sections; a "troop" (firqah) was made up of four squadrons; a "brigade" (liwa) was formed of four troops; and the
highest formation, a "corps" (faylaq), was made up of four
brigades. Above the society's paramilitary formations there
was to be a "General Staff Council of the Struggle" (majlis
arkan harb al-jihad), composed of the commanders of brigades
and corps and headed by the society's president, which was
to function as the legislative body of the movement.

Along with a paramilitary structure went the trappings
of militarism. The mujahids of the movement wore a uniform
consisting of a dark green shirt, gray trousers, and a red
tarbush (all of which should be "made in Egypt of Egyptian
materials"). The society's flag was a green banner with a
white circle in the center and the three pyramids of Guizeh
outlined within the circle. Mujahids had a distinctive
salute; an outstretched right arm, palm open and fingers
pointing to the sky.[28] Mujahids were also bound to the
society by an oath of allegiance. Taken in a formal ceremony,
with old "fighters" standing in a triangle around the flag
and honoring their new comrade with the salute, the new
mujahid recited the following:

> I swear by God, by the Fatherland, and by the King,
> that I shall dedicate my person, my efforts, and my
> wealth for the sake of the achievement of the
> principles and the program of the society, that I
> shall not draw back from any sacrifice which the
> struggle may demand of me, and that I shall be sub-
> ject to the military law of the society, doing
> honor to my leaders, executing whatever orders I
> may receive without debate or delay, within the
> limits of the law.

While the symbols of militarism were an integral part
of the society, the formal paramilitary structure outlined
above had very little reality. The relatively small membership of the society in its early years meant that its
activities - distribution of propaganda, meetings, camping
trips, demonstrations - were undertaken on a more informal
basis. The true functional unit of the movement was the
local "branch" (shu'bah). These were established by any
group of young men who wished to become part of the movement.
They elected their own officers (a president, a secretary,
and a treasurer) and applied for affiliation to the society's
main office in Cairo.[29] Although they would from time to
time receive directives from the center, they were

substantially in control of their own recruiting, meetings, and local activities. The unit for carrying out group activities was the shu'bah itself, with ordinary members and mujahids participating side by side.[30] The ties between the society's leadership and its following seem to have been largely personal and ideological rather than rigidly hierarchical, based on personal contacts while in school or in the Piastre Plan, on a shared attitude towards the problems of the country, and on the bond provided by the journal which expressed their views.

At the center, the dominant figure in the Young Egypt Society was its President Ahmad Husayn, with its Secretary-General Fathi Radwan as his closest collaborator. Whenever Husayn was temporarily unable to function (i.e., when he was under investigation by the police or actually in jail), Radwan exercised day-to-day direction of the society. Around these two was a cadre of equally young men, often former veterans of the Piastre Plan and fellow-founders of the society, who staffed the movement's journal and participated in its meetings and demonstrations. The actual executive organ of the movement was its "Council of the Struggle" (majlis al-jihad), an ad hoc body whose membership fluctuated, generally being composed of the founding members, the most active contributors to the society's press, and some of the heads of local shu'bahs.[31] The actual direction of Young Egypt in its early years was handled largely by personal ties and contacts rather than through institutionalized lines of communication and authority.

Journalism was the movement's primary means of propaganda in the mid-1930's. In October 1933, the new society arranged with the publisher of the weekly journal al-Sarkhah (with which Husayn and Radwan had been connected in 1930) to have it serve as Young Egypt's press outlet in exchange for a financial subsidy of 200 pounds, raised by Husayn from an unnamed "friend."[32] Al-Sarkhah was the only journal expressing Young Egypt's views in the mid-1930's, with the brief exception of Valley of the Nile (Wadi al-Nil). This was a daily newspaper published in Alexandria with which Husayn contracted in the spring of 1935 in order to obtain a daily press outlet for the society. Public response proved poor in Alexandria, however, with less than one-tenth of the printed copies being sold each day, and by June 1935 Husayn declared the failure of his effort to produce a daily and terminated his and the society's connection with Wadi al-Nil.[33]

In accordance with the youth orientation of the movement, the material published in al-Sarkhah was directed towards the educated youth of Egypt. While national political affairs received considerable attention, generally being the subject of each issue's lead article, material aimed at the cultural

enlightenment of Egyptian youth (articles on the moral uplift
to be found in Islam; patriotic pieces glorifying Egypt's
past and praising her historical figures; contributions of
didactic analysis on other countries and what might be
learned from their history) bulked quantitatively larger.
Although most of the society's inner circle wrote for
al-Sarkhah from time to time, the two most prolific contributors to the journal were Husayn and Radwan. Al-Sarkhah's
journalistic style was usually passionate and often inflammatory, with the journal, its editors and its contributors being
the subject of numerous investigations resulting from what
the authorities felt to be defamatory and/or dangerous
material. Issues of the journal were frequently confiscated,
the offices of al-Sarkhah (which also served as the headquarters of the society) were searched and the records of the
society examined more than once, and the editors and journalists of the periodical were brought before the courts on
charges of slander several times.[34]

Young Egypt supplemented its journalism with a variety
of additional and equally modern propaganda techniques.
Pressure was brought on public officials through the publication of open letters and the collection of signed petitions
calling for such things as British evacuation of her military
forces from Egypt and the Sudan, the abolition of the
Capitulatory system and the Mixed Courts, or the introduction
of universal military conscription in Egypt.[35] The society
frequently enjoined its followers to undertake direct action
against that which it felt to be reprehensible, mounting
boycotts of foreign-owned tobacco manufacturers and cinemas
and listing the "approved" Egyptian-owned firms, calling on
its followers to abstain from the use of alcoholic beverages,
and sending its activists to picket foreign and "prohibited"
forms of entertainment such as a French circus visiting Cairo
in 1934.[36]

The most visible activity undertaken by Young Egypt was
the frequent marches and rallies of its uniformed members.
In addition to the regular meetings of the local branches of
the society, Young Egypt periodically called on its supporters
to march en masse to the Pyramids for a day of sports and
military drill followed by an evening of singing and oratory.[37]
Such marches and assemblies occasionally resulted in clashes
between the Green Shirts and Young Egypt and the police, with
members of the society sometimes being arrested.[38]

From its inception, Young Egypt was always strongest in
Cairo, where its headquarters was located, where its journalistic activities were centered, and where its most important
meetings were held. The society did expand to Alexandria
quite early, having an active branch there by mid-1934 which
undertook what al-Ahram called ". . . agitated demonstrations

against the various communities of foreign traders in
Alexandria."[39] The movement also had branches in some of
the larger provincial cities of Lower Egypt such as Tanta,
al-Mansurah, al-Zaqaziq, and perhaps Banha and Port Sa'id.[40]
It did not rely only on its student associates from the
University to carry its message to the provinces, but also
sent speakers and organizing teams to various provincial
cities, particularly in the Delta.[41] The society was stronger
in the Delta than in Upper Egypt, the only attested branch
in the latter region prior to 1936 being at Aswan.[42] The
formal membership of the society in the 1933-1936 period
probably never exceeded a few hundred. In the later 1930's,
looking back on its early years, the movement claimed the
following attendance figures for its annual major assembly
at the Pyramids; thirty in 1934, about fifty in 1935, and
ninety in 1936.[43] This would have been composed primarily
of the Cairo members of the society, from which smaller
figures could be estimated for the membership of the few
local branches in other cities.

    That Young Egypt's formal support in its early years was
small is indisputable. But two other factors need to be
cited in this respect. First, the propaganda of the movement
certainly reached many more people than the few who became
affiliated with it. It did have organized branches in several
cities, thus assuring a geographical diffusion of whatever it
did; its journal continued in existence, thus giving its
message diffusion over time; and its open letters, its
demonstrations, its boycotts and its marches of uniformed
Green Shirts were very visible forms of activity which
received frequent coverage in the establishment press of
Egypt. Secondly, its active supporters were predominantly
educated youth, the products of at least a secondary school
education and primarily from the modern educational system.[44]
In short, those who it did reach and convince were part of
the future elite of Egypt, a group whose influence would be
disproportionate with their numbers in the future.

    The relationship of the society with the major political
forces in Egypt in the mid-1930's is a subject of some
complexity. Its critics accused Young Egypt of being the
instrument of the Egyptian Palace, of being covertly
financed by King Fuad as a non-Wafdist and pro-monarchical
youth organization.[45] While no conclusive evidence of Palace
support has come to light, it is quite probable that Young
Egypt did receive Palace support in its early years. The
movement's spokesmen were generally laudatory of the monarchy
in their views; at least for the first year of its existence,
the society avoided any agitation on the question of the
restoration of the Constitution of 1923 or the holding of new
parliamentary elections, measures which the Palace was

opposed to; finally, Young Egypt was an alternative rallying-point for youth apart from the Wafd, and their being active in the society would indeed divert them from working for the return of the Wafd to power. The later testimony of Ahmad Husayn strongly implies Palace support for the movement, claiming that the King had read and approved of the society's program and that he had ordered the Minister of the Interior "to give them every possible assistance."[46] That such assistance included financial aid is a distinct possibility.

Young Egypt's relationship with the leading political party of Egypt, the Wafd, was generally a negative one. In the mid-1930's (as later in the decade) the Wafd opposed Young Egypt, considering it a Palace-sponsored, divisive, and "extremist" element in Egyptian politics.[47] For its part, although Young Egypt was not consistently opposed to the Wafd in practice (e.g., after the dismissal of the ministry of 'Abd al-Fattah Yahya in November 1934, Young Egypt called on the King to have the Wafd form a new ministry "for it alone is the leader of the people"),[48] in general Young Egypt did operate as an anti-Wafdist force, refusing to subordinate itself to the Wafd, supporting policies opposed by the Wafd, and by 1936 its uniformed Green Shirts engaging in street clashes with the newly formed "Blue Shirts" (al-qumsan al-zarqa) of the Wafd.

The society's closest political ties in the mid-1930's were with the non-Wafdist political parties and independent politicians of Egypt. Both of the dominant figures in the movement had been connected with the Liberal Constitutionalist Party prior to Young Egypt's founding, Ahmad Husayn having taken part in youth activities connected with the party in 1929 and Fathi Radwan having written for the party's journal al-Siyasah. Later testimony by Ahmad Husayn claimed that the society had received occasional financial support and even "monthly allowances" from such political figures as Muhammad Mahmud of the Liberal Constitutionalists, Muhammad 'Ali 'Allubah of first the Liberals, later the Nationalists, and the independent (i.e., pro-Palace) 'Ali Mahir.[49] The party with which Young Egypt was most intimately linked in the mid-1930's was the Nationalists. In many of the early libel cases of the journalists of al-Sarkhah, the defense lawyers were Nationalist politicians such as 'Abd al-Rahman al-Rafi'i and Fikri Abazah.[50] The first public meetings of Young Egypt had been held at the clubhouse of the Young Men's Muslim Association, the President of which was the Nationalist Party deputy 'Abd al-Hamid Sa'id.[51] From 1935 onwards, Young Egypt scheduled annual meetings commemorating the death of the Nationalist founder Mustafa Kamil.[52] Of greatest importance, Young Egypt's policy on the decisive problem of Egyptian politics - Egypt's relationship with Great Britain - was very close to that of the Nationalists. The Nationalist slogan had long been "no negotiation except after evacuation" (la mufawadah illa ba'da al-jala), and the Nationalist Party was one of the few groups in Egypt opposing the ratification of the Anglo-Egyptian Treaty of 1936. Young Egypt also attacked the idea of any agreement with the British prior to the evacuation of all their forces from Egypt and the Sudan, and it also opposed the ratification of the Treaty of 1936.[53]

In regard to the society's possible connections with foreign powers, the records of the German Embassy in Cairo (available up to mid-1938) show only one contact between the society and the German government. As the German ambassador Dr. Eberhard von Stohrer described it, Ahmad Husayn paid a call on him in June 1934 "in order to express his sympathy for the new Germany" and to request a visa to visit that country. The Ambassador refused to see the young man when Husayn asked for a second meeting, and also reported their one conversation to the Egyptian Department of Public Security. His own evaluation of the movement at the time was that it was "extremely weak in terms of its finances" and "of no great significance."[54]

Although the full Italian diplomatic record is not available, there was one authenticated "contact" - of sorts - between the Italian government and Young Egypt in the mid-1930's. From 1933 onwards, the spokesmen of Young Egypt vigorously attacked Italy's Middle Eastern policies in general and her activities in her Libyan colony in particular. Italy was accused of having colonized Libya "in the most brutal manner"; her educational efforts were criticized as "a policy which only paves the way for Imperialism"; and she was denounced as "the worst sort of economic and cultural Imperialist."[55] The culmination of this anti-Italian campaign was reached in August 1934, after Husayn had visited Italy. Upon his return he wrote a series of articles in al-Sarkhah, the burden of which was that "Italy has failed to live up to my opinion of it, and that in only four days."[56] He described Italy as still being a backward country, stated that Italian claims of a glorious new Roman Empire were "so much propaganda," described Fascism as only "the boasting of Mussolini pouring over the Italian people," and predicted that "the privileged position which Italy assumes at the present time, or rather which it has deceived the world into believing it has assumed, will all collapse suddenly when Mussolini dies."[57] In reaction to these articles, the Italian Embassy brought charges of the slandering of a friendly state against al-Sarkhah and Ahmad Husayn.[58] The case dragged on for years, the subject of repeated postponements before the courts, and was not completed until May 1946 when Husayn was acquitted.[59]

Thus Young Egypt's earliest contact with the Italians was not one of serving their interests, as has often been suspected, but rather one of attacking Italy's imperialist activities and belittling Fascism's internal achievements.

From the society's formation late in 1933 until the end of 1935, Young Egypt's actual impact upon Egyptian national politics was minimal. The society's journalistic propaganda and its occasional marches, rallies and demonstrations produced periodic libel cases and arrests of demonstrators, but they generated no major repercussions in Egyptian politics. Perhaps because of the latter, perhaps because of Palace sympathy for the society, the authorities seem to have regarded Young Egypt rather tolerantly in this period: al-Sarkhah always resumed publication after its temporary suppression, the police observed Young Egypt's marches and rallies but only infrequently interfered with them, and the followers of Young Egypt arrested in the few Green Shirt-police clashes which did occur were either acquitted or received light penalties in the courts.[60]

Only in 1935 did the society begin to meet with what may be termed as significant repression. On March 16, 1935, thirty-three members or sympathizers of Young Egypt were arrested after a violent demonstration in Alexandria.[61] In May, Husayn and Radwan were brought before the courts on the most serious charge yet levelled against them; that of "inciting revolution" in the pages of al-Sarkhah.[62] Although the case was subsequently dropped, it temporarily cost the movement its journal, the publisher of al-Sarkhah breaking the journal's connection with Young Egypt from May until November 1935.[63]

A major turning-point both in the fortunes of Young Egypt and in Egyptian politics generally occurred in late 1935, however. Throughout that year, popular discontent with the past few years' Palace ascendancy in Egyptian politics steadily accumulated. In November 1935 large-scale demonstrations erupted in Egypt's cities, to last, on a diminishing although still considerable scale, until January 1936. Along with maneuvers among Egypt's political parties and a changing British position due to the looming Italo-Ethiopian crisis (which necessitated a more secure British position in Egypt), the demonstrations produced major changes in Egyptian politics. In December 1935 a united front of most of Egypt's parties was formed and the Constitution of 1923 (abrogated in 1930) was restored; in January 1936 the Palace-inclined ministry of Tawfiq Nasim was replaced by a caretaker government under 'Ali Mahir authorized to hold new parliamentary elections; in May Wafdist victory in those elections returned Egypt's grand old party to office; and by August 1936 the Anglo-Egyptian Treaty of Alliance of 1936 had been concluded.[64]

Young Egypt appears to have been only marginally involved in the demonstrations of late 1935 - early 1936. Without a press outlet from May to November 1935, it could not have played a direct role in the rising level of discontent prior to the demonstrations. Nor was the society involved as an organized group in the earliest and largest demonstrations in mid-November 1935.[65] Young Egypt's spokesmen later claimed that they had played a role as individuals, as an "elite" whose individual agitation helped produce and maintain the protests.[66] There is some evidence for this. Nur al-Din Tarraf, a leader of Young Egypt at the Egyptian University, was a member of the "Executive Committee of Students" which coordinated student protests, and one of the slogans shouted by demonstrators was the distinctive motto of the society, "Egypt over all."[67] The latter is probably the best indication of Young Egypt's role in the demonstrations; that its previous propaganda had helped to produce the general mood of discontent which led to the demonstrations.

However limited its role in the demonstrations, Young Egypt wasted no time in attempting to capitalize on them. Late in November 1935, the society announced that it was sending a delegation composed of Husayn and Radwan to London and other European cities in order to "raise the voice of Egypt before English public opinion."[68] Husayn and Radwan left Egypt on December 5, 1935. They spent the majority of their time abroad in Great Britain, where they met with various British parliamentarians, addressed meetings of Egyptians resident in England, spoke at a Labour Party youth conference, and produced a pamphlet (of which they claimed to have distributed several thousand copies) outlining the Egyptian case against Great Britain.[69] Husayn and Radwan left England late in January 1936, the latter returning to Egypt while the former proceeded to Geneva, where he presented a written memorandum on Egypt's position to the Secretary-General of the League of Nations, before returning home.[70] The trip was of considerable value to Young Egypt as an organization. It resulted in the society being given more attention in the Egyptian press, and the size of the receptions greeting Husayn and Radwan upon their return to Egypt - particularly the one in Alexandria for Husayn which several hundred people are reported to have attended - indicate a significant increase in the following of Young Egypt when compared to the period before the demonstrations of 1935-1936.[71]

Young Egypt received a further boost in its fortunes during the tenure of the ministry of 'Ali Mahir (January to May 1936). 'Ali Mahir has been credited as being the first

Egyptian politician who realized the political potential to be had from building a pro-Palace alliance based on the non-Wafdist and primarily youth-oriented associations which had emerged in Egypt in the late 1920's and early 1930's (the Y.M.M.A., the Muslim Brotherhood and Young Egypt),[72] and his ministry's treatment of Young Egypt would bear this out. The society was able to hold large public meetings and marches by its Green Shirts without any police interference or harassment.[73] New branches of Young Egypt were established in several provincial cities.[74] According to Husayn, the sympathy given Young Egypt by the Mahir ministry allowed him to "put the administrative and financial affairs of Young Egypt in order," a phrase which, along with other testimony by Husayn, indicates the probability of financial aid to the movement.[75] Ahmad Husayn's first official meeting with an incumbent Prime Minister came in April 1936, when he visited Mahir and presented a petition outlining the society's "patriotic" reform measures.[76] All of this - freedom of publication, movement and assembly; probable financial aid; and an official meeting between the President of Young Egypt and the Prime Minister - indicates the legitimization of the society in Egyptian political life, its arrival as a political force with which leading politicians were willing to be associated. As Husayn said at the time, "the government has recognized Young Egypt as an organization worthy of respect and consideration. . . . It is the proclamation of a new age for Young Egypt."[77]

This "new age" also brought about changes in the attitude of Young Egypt itself. It was during the ministry of 'Ali Mahir that the leaders of Young Egypt decided to broaden the society's activities in order to appeal not only to youth, but also to propagandize and recruit among the urban and rural adult working population of Egypt. Thus the society announced that it was beginning "the organizing of workers who are sympathetic to its principles into organized sections, the members of which will also wear the Green Shirt," and organizational meetings to recruit workers into the society were held in Cairo and in the textile center of al-Mahallah al-Kubra in March 1936.[78] By May, Young Egypt announced its first attempt to proselytize among the rural population of Egypt by means of a walking-trip by Husayn and a group of his colleagues from Aswan to Cairo. The stated objectives of this march make the broader orientation of Young Egypt clear: the marchers intended to visit as many villages as possible, mixing with the peasantry in each, "associating with them, exchanging opinions with them on anything which pertains to their interests or the interests of the country, and giving them lessons in patriotic education. . . ."[79] In fine, the journey through Upper Egypt was to be the first step in an

23

attempt to transform Young Egypt from a youth group into a
political movement appealing to all segments of Egyptian
society.

The attempt, however, soon ran into opposition from the
new Wafdist ministry which had assumed power in May 1936. The
Wafd had always regarded Young Egypt as an organization hostile
to it, and the Wafdist ministry engaged in a campaign of
harassment against Young Egypt's marchers in Upper Egypt
(prohibiting the wearing of the Green Shirt by the group;
police cordons around their camps; a police "escort" as they
marched).[80] On June 22, 1936, in reply to a question by an
opposition member in the Chamber of Deputies inquiring as to
the ministry's justification for this harassment of the society,
Premier Mustafa al-Nahhas made a dramatic charge against
Young Egypt:

> It has been proven to the Ministry of the Interior
> that the Young Egypt Society is working in the
> interests of a foreign power against the interests
> of the country. Therefore, the Ministry decided
> it was in the best interests of the state to
> prohibit the members of this organization from
> travelling through the villages in a special
> uniform.[81]

This accusation made Young Egypt a subject of national
controversy in 1936. Although questions in Parliament from
opposition deputies as to the government's evidence for the
charge were not answered by Nahhas on the grounds of the
necessity for secrecy for national security reports, the
press did not hesitate to identify Italy as the foreign power
which Nahhas had in mind.[82] On its part, Young Egypt denied
the accusation and asked for a full investigation by Public
Prosecutor, which was refused. Later it attempted to bring
legal action for slander against Nahhas but the case, after
several postponements, was never heard.[83]

The most immediate result of Nahhas's accusation was the
first outbreak of large-scale violence between rival youth
organizations. The Wafd had formed its own paramilitary
organization, the "Squadrons of the Blue Shirts" (firaq
al-qumsan al-zarqa) early in 1936.[84] Immediately after
Nahhas's statement, the Blue Shirts mounted several attacks
on the offices and public meetings of Young Egypt. Newspaper
accounts leave little doubt that the adherents of the Wafd
were responsible for the initial clashes.[85] The Blue Shirts
gained the upper hand in most of the street scuffles, to the
point where Husayn had to order his Green Shirts not to wear
their uniforms in public "in order to restore calm in the
country."[86] But the followers of Young Egypt were not

innocent of aggression. The most serious incident instigated
by Green Shirts came in August in Damanhur, when one Blue
Shirt was killed and several injured in an attack provoked by
Green Shirts.[87] The government used this incident to close
down many of the clubhouses of Young Egypt and to suspend the
movement's journal, at which time the publisher of al-Sarkhah
decided to permanently disassociate himself from the
society.[88] When this first major round of violence between
the two rival paramilitary youth organizations died down in
the fall of 1936, the victors on one level were the Blue
Shirts; Young Egypt had been temporarily intimidated from
public demonstration, many of the society's branches had been
closed, and the movement had lost its journal. But on another
level, Young Egypt made a major gain through Nahhas's accusation
and the violence of the summer of 1936; the society was now
identified as the chief youth group opposing the Wafd, and as
such was ". . . receiving a fair amount of unsolicited support
and becoming a rallying-point for Wafdist dissatisfaction...."[89]

    As 1936 neared its end, Young Egypt gradually regained
much of its freedom of activity. With the violence between
Blue and Green Shirts abated by the autumn of the year, the
government allowed the society's branches to be reopened. In
November 1936, Young Egypt contracted with the journal The
Light (al-Diya) and thus acquired a press outlet again.[90] Most
importantly, the end of 1936 saw Young Egypt formally acknowledge the new orientation it had taken in 1936 by converting
itself from a "society" (jam'iyah) to a formal political
"party" (hizb), thus beginning a new period in the history of
the movement.

The Young Egypt Party
1936-1940

Young Egypt became a formal political party at the end
of 1936. At a meeting of the society's Council of the
Struggle on December 31, 1936, Ahmad Husayn delivered a
three-hour speech to his colleagues calling for the change
from society to party on the grounds of Egypt's "deteriorating"
position under the rule of the Wafd and the need for "the
youth of Egypt" to "set things right." He then presented to
the Council the charter for such a party, which it accepted
without demur.[1]

The structural differences between the society and the
party were largely formal.[2] The name of the reorganized body
became the "Young Egypt Party" (hizb misr al-fatah), and Young
Egypt's original 1933 program was designated as the program of
the party. Whereas the society had had only two categories
of membership, "member" and "fighter," the new party recognized
a third level of affiliation, the "follower" (nasir), "any
Egyptian who is sympathetic to the party. . . and who votes
for the party or its candidates in elections." The Council
of the Struggle which had been the society's informally
appointed executive body was now designated as a primarily
advisory body, with its executive functions taken over by a
new, smaller, body, the "Administrative Council" (majlis
al-idarah). Its membership, usually around ten in number in
the later 1930's, were selected by the party's President, and
it assumed the major administrative, financial and policy-making
functions which had previously been exercised either informally
or by the Council of the Struggle. The movement's local
branches or shu'bahs were recognized as the functional lower
units of the party, and new provisions were set down for their
supervision by the Administrative Council. The new party's
charter made only one reference to paramilitary bodies, but
that reference made clear the continued paramilitary orientation
of the movement: "absolutely the most important duty of the
shu'bah is the preparation of the greatest possible number of
its young members to be mujahids in the organized formations
[of the party]."

The paramilitary features of Young Egypt lasted only
until 1938, however. In March of that year, after the
prolonged violence between Blue and Green Shirts which had
occurred in 1936 and 1937, legislation was enacted by the new
ministry of Muhammad Mahmud which prohibited paramilitary

organizations in Egypt.[3] Although it vigorously protested
the legislation, Young Egypt adjusted rather well to this
ban on paramilitary groups. A party decree soon stated that
"the special organized formations of the Green Shirts are
disbanded" and told former Green Shirts to "do what you will"
with their uniforms.[4] But at the same time the party created
a special class of membership for all former Green Shirts,
dropping the name of "fighter" (mujahid) but calling anyone
who had previously borne that title a "founding member"
('udw muassas) of the party.[5] However inaccurate the new
name was as a descriptive term, nonetheless a certain sense
of exclusiveness and esprit de corps was thus retained for the
party's activists.

Continuity in structure was paralleled by a considerable
continuity in leadership between the Young Egypt Society of the
mid-1930's and the Young Egypt Party of the later 1930's.
Through the later 1930's, Ahmad Husayn remained the party's
President, Fathi Radwan its Secretary-General, and several of
the members of the party's central executive body, the
Administrative Council, were men who had been either
co-founders or leaders of the society in the mid-1930's. The
educational background of the members of the Council in 1937
throws an interesting light on the nature of the party's
leadership:[6] of the ten members listed in 1937, four had been
educated as lawyers, one held a degree from the Faculty of
Letters of the Egyptian University and another from its
Faculty of Commerce, two were graduates of British universities, and only one had been educated at al-Azhar. At least
eight of the ten were contemporaries of Husayn and Radwan in
age, being either in their late twenties or early thirties in
1937. These two characteristics of Young Egypt remained
constant throughout the 1930's; the secular background of its
leadership, and the youthfulness of that core.

But major changes in Young Egypt's leadership were
occurring by 1938-1939. While Fathi Radwan remained the
party's Secretary-General, his political orientation
progressively diverged from that of Ahmad Husayn in the later
1930's. According to his own testimony, Radwan felt that
Young Egypt should have no connection with the politicians of
the older generation. He thus disagreed with the party's
alliance with the non-Wafdist parties and with 'Ali Mahir and
the Egyptian Palace in 1937-1939. Because of these differences
with Husayn, Radwan gradually withdrew from playing an active
role in the party (although formally remaining its Secretary-
General), by the outbreak of World War II having "little" to
do with Young Egypt.[7]

Radwan's place as Young Egypt's second-in-command was
taken by Mustafa al-Wakil. A boyhood friend of both Husayn
and Radwan, Wakil had not been connected with Young Egypt in

the mid-1930's since he was then studying at the University of London.[8] He joined the party upon his return to Egypt in 1937, and early in 1938 became its Vice-President (naib al-rais).[9] From mid-1938, it was usually Wakil who served as Husayn's closest advisor and who directed the affairs of the party and wrote the lead articles in its journal when Husayn was unable to do so (i.e., on trips abroad or in jail).

This withdrawal of Radwan and elevation of Wakil was only part of a broader change occurring in the quality of Young Egypt's leadership by the later 1930's. In Young Egypt's phase as a society in the mid-1930's, one has the impression that the movement's leadership was genuinely a collegial affair, with Husayn and Radwan, although the two most important figures in the organization, nonetheless working closely with the group's leading activists and being amenable to influence from them. If this had been the case in the mid-1930's, it was not so by 1938 or 1939. By 1938, with the considerable growth of the movement, Ahmad Husayn was Young Egypt's unchallenged leader. Now referred to as "the leader of the new generation" (rais al-jil al-jadid), enormous attention was given to his pronouncements: "the rais was speaking, and it was as if God Almighty had sent a heavenly spirit into him."[10] In fine, Young Egypt was increasingly becoming an autocratic organization with but one real leader, its President.

The later 1930's were the highpoint of Young Egypt as an organized movement. In this period the party reached the height of its growth as an organization and the zenith of its influence within Egyptian politics and society. Because this was the period of its greatest strength and impact, it is worth examining its activities and its influence in some detail.

The one area where Young Egypt had no success in the later 1930's was as a political party competing for votes in Egyptian elections. The only parliamentary election between when Young Egypt became a political party (December 1936) and its wartime dissolution (May 1941) occurred in March 1938, and Young Egypt did not formally contest for seats in it. The party wished to present some of its leaders as candidates in several constituencies, but suffered from a peculiar disability; that none of its leaders were old enough to run for the Chamber of Deputies in 1938. Its repeated demand of the ministry to lower the minimum age of deputies from thirty to twenty-five was rejected, and in the end the party boycotted the elections, neither participating through older candidates nor giving its support to the candidates of another party.[11] It was not until 1950 that Young Egypt, under its new name of the Socialist Party of Egypt, succeeded in seeing one of its leaders elected to Parliament.

One major area of activity by Young Egypt in the later 1930's (as earlier) was journalism. The volume of its journalistic output increased considerably as the decade progressed. In March 1937, the party replaced al-Diya with the periodical The Mouth (al-Thaghr) as its journal, installing new equipment for printing the latter and expanding it into a thrice-weekly publication.[12] In January 1938, after the fall of the hostile Wafdist ministry, Ahmad Husayn was granted a license to publish his own journal, thus obviating the movement's previous need to contract with established publishers.[13] The result was the publication of The Newspaper of Young Egypt (Jaridah Misr al-Fatah) as the party's press outlet. At first a weekly, by September 1938 it was publishing three issues each week. In September 1938, the party also established The Evacuation (al-Jala), a short-lived weekly published in Alexandria.

The party published more than periodicals in the later 1930's. By 1937 it had its own publishing house, Dar al-Thaqafah al-'Ammah, the most notable publication of which was a monthly series of books entitled "Book of the Month." Biographical in orientation, with each month's offering devoted to the study of either an Islamic figure or some political personality of the modern world, the series has been credited with having been a forerunner of later Egyptian book-series aimed at the diffusion of historical and political awareness in Egypt.[14] The "Book of the Month" series continued to be published through 1938 and 1939, being joined in 1939 by a second series entitled "Summary of European Thought."[15]

Young Egypt's internal activities for its membership and following show a great expansion in the later 1930's.[16] The party had local branches organized in most of the provincial cities of Egypt by 1937-1938. At least several local shu'bahs had rented clubhouses or clubrooms, often including a library and occasionally with printing facilities. Weekly meetings of the party's branches were the rule, with the normal content of a meeting consisting of a reading from the Quran, speeches by members or local notables on such topics as the duties of a member of Young Egypt, the message of Young Egypt for workers and/or peasants, or Islamic morality, followed by poetry readings and the singing of anthems. On Fridays, the members of local branches would often assemble for weekly prayer, then spend a portion of the afternoon in athletics or military drill.

The activities of the party's Cairo branches (of which there were several in different quarters or suburbs of the city by the later 1930's) exceeded those of the party's provincial shu'bahs. In late 1938, the following disparate activities could be found occurring at the party's Cairo headquarters or "Green House" (al-bayt al-akhdar): instruction in music and civil-defense measures against air attack; bi-weekly gymnastic sessions; a "flying school" (of unknown quality) for selected members; and a free consulting clinic for members and their families.[17] But not all of Young Egypt's major activities took place in Cairo. Perhaps its most ambitious service program for its members was centered in Alexandria, where in the summer of 1938 it opened a summer camp where members could spend twenty-five days in athletics, agricultural labor, and cultural/educational activities.[18] Thus the local branches of the party performed useful functions of social integration for its primarily urban membership, many of whom may be presumed to have broken some of the ties of family and village through education and/or migration to the cities.

Following the orientation which the society had taken in 1936, the party in the later 1930's attempted to appeal to both the peasantry and urban workers of Egypt. In August 1937 another walking-tour of party activists through Upper Egypt occurred in order to propagandize for the movement among the peasantry.[19] In the summer of 1938, the party attempted to organize its student followers into cadres capable of going out into the countryside for part of their summer vacation "so that by the end of the summer the message of Young Egypt will have been publicized before every Egyptian in every place, far and near."[20] But the party seems to have had little success with this program, eventually allowing it to lapse, and thereafter Young Egypt made no major initiatives directed at proselytizing among the peasantry.

The party seems to have given more attention to and to have been more successful with urban labor. It had branches in the industrial centers of al-Mahallah al-Kubra and Shubra.[21] Night classes to teach literacy were set up in the Green House in 1938, and seem to have been successful in attracting urban workers to that site.[22] In October 1938 Husayn and Radwan were called on to defend in the courts a group of workers from al-Mahallah al-Kubra who were on trial for an illegal strike, and the party did give legal assistance to strikers in both 1938 and 1939.[23] By mid-1939 it was attempting to set up workers' committees associated with the party and to host a "workers' conference" (eventually prohibited by the government), as well as planning to organize a one-day general strike as a protest against the government's policies towards labor.[24]

By the late 1930's Young Egypt was no longer primarily a student movement as it had been in its early years. While it did continue to recruit among secondary school and university students, and while a considerable proportion of its most active followers were students (e.g., one of its

largest branches was in Guizeh, the site of the Egyptian
University),[25] by the later 1930's much of the membership and
following which it had been building up since 1933 had
graduated from school. The membership and following of Young
Egypt continued to be largely composed of the Egyptian younger
generation, as the press testified in evaluating the composi-
tion of those attending the party's major public meetings;
but it was now composed at least as much of some workers and
more teachers, government bureaucrats, and other recent
graduates of the Egyptian state educational system as it was
of students proper.[26]

The extent of the party's popular support in the later
1930's is a difficult question to answer with any degree of
certainty. In June 1937 the party claimed a membership of
1536 mujahids in Cairo alone, 384 in Alexandria, "approximately
the same number" in Lower Egypt, and gave no membership
figures for Upper Egypt.[27] Interviews with former party
leaders indicate that these claims were inflated, the estimates
of those leaders pointing to a core membership of perhaps one
thousand dues-paying activists at the movement's peak in
1937-1938. Ahmad Husayn calculated that a figure of 500 active
members for Cairo (always the heart of the movement) "would
be exaggerated."[28] Fathi Radwan's recollection was that the
movement's active membership in the 1930's "never exceeded
one thousand in all Egypt in any one year."[29] A former
journalist for Jaridah Misr al-Fatah gave the following
estimates for the movement at its peak; "not more than 300
members" in Cairo, perhaps another 200 in Alexandria, with the
size of provincial branches varying widely.[30]

But Young Egypt certainly had a much larger passive
following - those Egyptians, mainly younger ones, who
occasionally attended meetings, periodically sampled the
party's propaganda, and were influenced by what the party had
to say about Egyptian politics and society - than its
relatively small membership in the later 1930's. In regard
to students, this is evidenced by the results of the elections
to the Student Union of the Egyptian University. In the
elections of October 1937 (admittedly a time of great
dissension within the Wafd), Young Egypt's candidates in both
the Faculty of Law and the Faculty of Arts outpolled those
of the Wafd.[31] A year later, however, Wafdist candidates were
victorious.[32] Going beyond students, Young Egypt's major
meetings in 1938 drew attendances estimated by non-party
observers in the thousands,[33] and its varied publishing
activities reached a broader population than merely the
party's formal membership. Press reports of the meetings of
provincial shu'bahs indicate that some of the branches in the
cities of the Delta and the Canal Zone drew an attendance in
the hundreds (the meetings of branches in Upper Egypt were

much smaller). Ahmad Husayn has reasonably claimed that some
people who were sympathetic to Young Egypt may have been
intimidated from formally affiliating with it because of
dangers to their careers in the bureaucracy by the frequent
police seizure of party records at times of clash between
the government and the party.[34] As an author who was himself
a student in Egypt in the 1930's put it (in a passage quite
antagonistic to Young Egypt), "a huge group of youth" were
influenced by Ahmad Husayn and his movement in the 1930's, and
it took them "many years to free themselves intellectually
from this leader."[35]

Corresponding to Young Egypt's increased scale of
activity and larger following in the later 1930's, there was
a great difference between the political role and importance
of the minuscule Young Egypt Society of the mid-1930's and
the Young Egypt Party of later in the decade. Whereas the
society had had only a minimal impact upon the course of
Egyptian politics in general from 1933 to 1936, the party
was a more significant force in Egyptian public life in the
period from 1937 to the outbreak of World War II.

Young Egypt's political links in the later 1930's were
similar to but not identical with those which the movement had
developed in the mid-1930's. The generally hostile relationship
between it and the Wafd which had crystallized in the mid-1930's
was maintained through the later years of the decade, Young
Egypt being one of the most vehement opponents of the Wafdist
ministry which ruled Egypt in 1936-1937, with the party playing
a major role in the fall of that ministry in late 1937.[36] With
the smaller non-Wafdist parties Young Egypt's relationship
vacillated from cooperation with them in 1937 (when both they
and Young Egypt had a common interest in bringing down the
Wafdist ministry) to opposition to them, at least to those
parties which formed the coalition ministries headed by the
Liberal Constitutionalist leader Muhammad Mahmud in 1938-1939
(when Young Egypt found them to be insufficiently nationalist
and "reformist" in power and also when the party's own
militance inevitably brought it into conflict with any ministry
responsible for maintaining law and order in Egypt).[37] Young
Egypt's closest political ties in the later 1930's were with
the Egyptian Palace and with the Royal advisor who was perhaps
the most powerful Egyptian politician in the years immediately
before World War II, 'Ali Mahir. Financial support for the
movement via Mahir is highly probable: as Ahmad Husayn put it
in mid-1939, "he [Mahir] was the man who never failed to
support us fully, giving us money for six years and opening
his door to us night or day."[38]

Contrary to what has sometimes been suspected of Young
Egypt since Nahhas's charge of 1936 that the movement was
"working in the interests of a foreign power," Young Egypt

does not seem to have been involved in clandestine collaboration with the Axis powers in the later 1930's. The incomplete
German Foreign Ministry archives and published Italian
diplomatic documents which are available make no mention of
any link between the movement and Germany or Italy. While a
relationship with other Axis agencies besides their Foreign
Ministries is possible,[39] no primary material bearing on such
a connection in the years prior to the war has come to light.
Although the former leaders of Young Egypt have denied any
prewar connection with Italy or Germany,[40] there is one
tentative indication that Young Egypt may have tried to
establish some sort of link with Italy in the later 1930's
but was turned down by the Italians. Muhammad Subayh (head
of the party's publishing activities in the later 1930's) has
written that "Mussolini refused to cooperate with the Young
Egypt movement before the war, out of respect for the
'Gentleman's Agreement' which he had made with England in order
to calm down the state of tension in the Mediterranean."[41]
Subayh says no more on the subject, but the phrasing of this
passage could imply that an approach was made by Young Egypt
to Italy sometime after the Anglo-Italian Pact of April 1938
but was rejected by the Italians.

The publicly expressed attitudes of Young Egypt's spokesmen towards the international crises of 1938 and 1939 which
eventually led to World War II indicate that the movement was
not acting as an Egyptian propaganda outlet for the fascist
powers. At the time of the Munich crisis, the party's journal
placed the blame for the crisis on Hitler, and Ahmad Husayn
wrote that "if war breaks out now, after all the efforts and
sacrifices which England and France have made and which
Czechoslovakia has accepted, the meaning of all that is that
Hitler is a madman who wishes to destroy the world in order
to satisfy his arrogance and his desires."[42] The breakup of
Czechoslovakia in March 1939 was called "beyond a doubt a
flagrant act of aggression,"[43] and the Italian occupation of
Albania a month later was also condemned: "Italy has
aggressed on Albania, occupying it by fire and sword."[44] The
latter article generalized about the recent actions of Germany,
Italy and Japan in unquestionably hostile terms: "The hysteria
of conquest and aggression is becoming prevalent in Germany
and Italy and in Japan as well, and this hysteria is steadily
increasing because the weak nations faced with this aggression
have not resisted or stood up to the forces of the aggressors."
Finally, the Polish crisis in the summer of 1939 which led to
war saw Young Egypt at first officially pass a resolution
calling on Egypt to enter the war "at the side of Britain until
final victory is achieved,"[45] a decision modified, however,
with the last-minute neutrality of Italy which prompted
Husayn to issue a "clarification" of party policy which

altered its stand to one of neutrality for the time being,
but preparedness for possible Italian aggression in the
future.[46] All of this should not be taken to mean that Young
Egypt was totally negative towards the fascist states; as
we shall see in the next chapter, fascist ideas had a
considerable impact on the movement, particularly in the
later 1930's. But it does show that Young Egypt was not
acting as an apologist for the Axis powers in the tense year
before the war.

In 1937, the party's political activities were
overwhelmingly directed to opposing the Wafdist ministry which
ruled Egypt throughout that year. The main arena of opposition
was in the press, where the party's journals constantly
attacked the ministry on a variety of issues ranging from the
alleged personal corruption of Wafdist leaders to the
ministry's insufficiently nationalist stance in regard to the
termination of foreign privilege in Egypt. The tenor of Young
Egypt's attacks on the government was such as to involve the
party in numerous press investigations and trials on charges
like "defamation and calumny of ministers, of the dignity of
the Prime Minister, and of the dignity of other public
agencies" or "openly arousing the peasants and the workers
against the wealthy, against officials, and against foreigners
resident in Egypt."[47] In April 1937 alone, Young Egypt had
six such cases pending before the courts, the majority
involving articles written by Ahmad Husayn.[48] Husayn spent
four weeks in jail in 1937 as a result of these trials.[49]
On its part, the government used the inflammatory journalism
of Young Egypt as a justification for the occasional confiscation of issues of the party's journals, for seizing the records
of the party, and for prohibiting many of the party's public
meetings.[50]

Compared to this propaganda struggle between Young Egypt
and the Wafd, public violence between Green and Blue Shirts
was desultory through most of 1937. Although Blue Shirts
attacked the offices of opposition newspapers and the Cairo
headquarters of Young Egypt in March, and although smaller
clashes between the two paramilitary groups occurred in the
al-Azhar area in April, these were the only significant
incidents of violence reported prior to the massive unrest
which developed in the fall of 1937.[51]

In the summer of 1937, two parallel developments prompted
a major political crisis in Egypt which lasted for the
remainder of the year and which ended only with the fall of
the ministry of the Wafd.[52] The first of these was the
determination of King Faruq and his advisors to eliminate
the Wafdist ministry which they regarded as a barrier and a
threat to the power of the Egyptian Palace. The second was
a serious schism in the Wafd Party itself in which the popular

34

1888356

Wafdist leader Mahmud Fahmi al-Nuqrashi publicly broke with
the party's dominant figure, Prime Minister Mustafa al-Nahhas,
and led his supporters out of the Wafd. In brief, the schism
within the Wafd, the charges of corruption and "dictatorial
tendencies" against Nahhas levelled by Nuqrashi and his
supporters, and not least the widespread violence which
developed from September 1937 onwards between loyalist Blue
Shirts, dissident Wafdist youth loyal to Nuqrashi, and
various anti-Wafdist youth groups (Young Egypt included)
greatly eroded the ministry's public position and eventually
were used by the Palace as the justification for dismissing
it from office (December 30, 1937).

In this general political crisis Young Egypt played an
appreciable role. From August, when the split within the Wafd
became apparent, it called on the King to dismiss the ministry;
by October, it was expressing the opinion that only a coalition
government of anti-Wafdist parties could "save the country."[53]
More important was its physical participation in the crisis.
Young Egypt was one of the forces (from press reports, perhaps
the major force) engaged in violence against the supporters
of the Wafd in late 1937, its supporters in the schools
demonstrating against the ministry and its uniformed Green
Shirts repeatedly battling with Wafdist Blue Shirts.[54] The
climax of the anti-Wafdist struggle for Young Egypt occurred
on November 28, 1937, when a former member of the party, one
'Izz al-Din 'Abd al-Qadir, unsuccessfully attempted to
assassinate Prime Minister Nahhas. Not unexpectedly, the
government promptly set out arresting members of Young Egypt.
The party's entire leadership and many of its members were
arrested and interrogated, the offices of the party and the
homes of many members searched, and the party's records
seized.[55] With its leadership and many of its activist
followers in jail through December 1937, Young Egypt was
effectively eliminated as a political force in the struggle
against the Wafd. But it had already contributed its share:
thanks partially to its journalistic attacks but more to its
physical opposition to the Wafd, the party had helped to
create the climate of opinion which enabled the Palace to
dismiss the Wafd from office at the end of the year.

In 1938 and 1939, Young Egypt's main activity in relation
to other political forces in Egypt was in acting as a staunch
supporter of the position of the Egyptian Palace and its
leading advisor 'Ali Mahir. The party championed 'Ali Mahir
personally, several times addressing petitions to the King
calling for the dismissal of the incumbent ministries of
Muhammad Mahmud and asking for the formation of a "national
ministry" headed by Mahir.[56] More importantly, Young Egypt's
spokesmen were enthusiastic backers of King Faruq. In the
later 1930's a now seemingly inconceivable (given our

hindsight about Faruq's public and private careers after
World War II) campaign was mounted by the Egyptian Palace
to gain recognition of Faruq as Caliph of the Muslim world.[57]
Young Egypt's propaganda firmly endorsed this idea. In June
1938, Ahmad Husayn declared himself to be in favor of the
restoration of the Caliphate and stated that he felt Faruq
to be "the proper man" for the position.[58] When the agitation
over the Caliphate reached its peak in early 1939, Young
Egypt's journal came out solidly for Faruq as Caliph: "we
call for Egypt to be the leader of Islam, and for Faruq to
be its Caliph."[59]

But Young Egypt's political position in the later 1930's
was not merely one of the party serving as a pliable instrument
of 'Ali Mahir and the Egyptian Palace. Beyond support for
Palace policies and for Mahir, the party also undertook major
new initiatives of its own aimed at enhancing its position in
Egyptian politics.

In 1938, there are several indications that Young Egypt's
leaders and some outside observers seriously considered that
the party would have a formal role to play in ruling Egypt
in the near future. In March, the party established a special
"Office of Foreign Affairs" (maktab al-shuun al-kharijiyah) to
study the subject of Egypt's foreign relations and to prepare
reports on it for the party's leadership.[60] In May, this idea
was greatly expanded by the party creating twelve other such
offices to study various aspects of Egyptian life and politics
and how the party's program might best be implemented in each
area.[61] As James Heyworth-Dunne has observed, this was no
less than a "shadow cabinet," ready to step into power if
Young Egypt should be called upon to do so in the future.[62]

The optimism reflected in the establishment of the shadow
cabinet was to some extent justified, for in 1938 the party
began to receive consideration as a potential competitor in
the struggle for political office. An independent journal
interviewed Ahmad Husayn and asked him "What would be your
program if you assumed power?", and the party's own journal
claimed that "His Majesty has ordered his August Royal
Cabinet to prepare a list of young men who could be intrusted
with positions of power [in the state]."[63] Young Egypt itself
set its sights on achieving some share of political power by
1940: this was its prediction in May, and in August the
party's journal confidently asserted that "the year 1940 shall
not pass before Young Egypt has come to a position of power."[64]

However, if these optimistic predictions by a party which
had not as yet placed any of its leaders in Parliament were
indeed a sincere reflection of the expectations of its
leaders in 1938, they came to have much less possibility of
being realized by 1939. Young Egypt underwent a fundamental
process of reorientation in both its propaganda and its

activities in 1938-1939. From the movement's enlargement of
its own conception of its role in 1936 until about mid-1938,
Young Egypt had generally tried to operate within the
permissable limits of the Egyptian parliamentary system. In
the intellectual sphere, the movement's propaganda upheld the
Egyptian Constitution and Parliament and declared the party's
intention to work within the system by eventually competing in
elections.[65] In the physical sphere, it concentrated the bulk
of its activities in peaceful organizational work aimed at
increasing its following. Although there were major incidents
of violence between its adherents and the Blue Shirts, in 1936
and 1937, these were often instigated by the Blue Shirts,
there were few acts of violence by Young Egypt's supporters
in 1938 (after the Wafdist ministry had been ousted and the
Blue Shirts suppressed), and, as the preceding pages have
shown, street brawling was by no means the only thing which
Young Egypt encouraged its followers to do in 1936, 1937 or
1938.

But from mid-1938 onwards, Young Egypt's previous
concentration on peaceful organizational work and its general
acceptance of the parliamentary and party system was replaced
by increasingly vehement denunciations of parliamentary
government and by an emphasis on militant activism. The
movement's intellectual shift will be explored in detail in
the following chapter: here it is sufficient to note that
Young Egypt's propaganda in 1938 and 1939 progressively
questioned the existing Egyptian parliamentary system,
denounced its shortcomings in solving Egypt's economic and
social problems, and came to call for more authoritarian but
more "efficient" rule as the only way for Egypt to progress
in the future.[66]

The emphasis of Young Egypt's physical activities also
shifted appreciably by the end of 1938. Through most of
1938, there had been very little in the way of militant or
violent activity by Young Egypt's adherents. But in the
autumn of 1938, Young Egypt abruptly reorganized itself and
implicitly turned away from attempting to build up a mass
following through peaceful techniques of organizational
growth, deciding instead to devote its energies to militant
campaigns of agitation on selected political and social issues.

There were signs of dissension within Young Egypt by late
1938. In September, the party's Office of Propaganda decreed
that all publications by local branches of the party must
receive its approval because some shu'bahs had been issuing
material "which differed from the political orientation of
the party."[67] In October, party members in Luxor seceded
from the party's branch in that city, setting up their own
shu'bah in opposition to the established one.[68] There also
seems to have been a split in the leadership of the party:

37

at a meeting of the Council of the Struggle in September 1938, Husayn proposed that that body double its membership, only to have the Council table the proposal (an action which contrasts vividly with that body's usual procedure of approval of the President's suggestions).[69]

Ahmad Husayn reacted vigorously to all this. On November 5, 1938, he declared that all the party's local branches and the Council of the Struggle were dissolved, calling for the party to be reorganized "on a sound basis and with a youthful spirit."[70] The ensuing reorganization demonstrated a more autocratic and militant ethos within the movement. Although the party's Administrative Council remained in existence, its membership was somewhat altered during the reorganization.[71] The relationship between the party's leader and his followers also changed: at a meeting of the party's activists on November 14, 1938, Husayn had those assembled make a personal "pact and covenant" ('ahd wa mithaq) with him, swearing to such questions as "are you confident in me as your leader?" and "are you prepared to proceed with me until the end?"[72] Most importantly, the reorganization was accompanied by a new spirit of militant activism within the movement. From November 1938, Young Egypt's publications began carrying a new set of Ten Goals of the party. The emphasis in these was on militance: the set was entitled "Overthrow is Inevitable, Force is Inevitable" (la buddah min inqilab, la buddah min quwwah), and each specific goal was prefixed by the phrase "Force is Inevitable" for the achievement of the goal.[73] Ahmad Husayn's speech to his followers of November 14 similarly placed great emphasis on militant activism: "overthrow," "revolution," and "force" appear repeatedly in the text, and Husayn stressed more than once that Young Egypt would now resort to direct action to achieve its aims; "it is now necessary that our revolution be by deeds, not by words."[74]

The first specific object of the party's intensified militancy was the Western and "unIslamic" social practices prevailing in Egypt's cities. In the past Young Egypt had sporadically demonstrated and petitioned on such issues as the use of alcoholic beverages, prostitution, or the negative moral influence of "prohibited entertainments" imported from the West. But from late 1938 onwards the party gave these socio-religious subjects a great deal more of its attention. After repeated injunctions by Ahmad Husayn to his followers to "abolish the existing laws and to return to the Sacred Law" or to "wage war against wine, and against gambling, and against prostitution, and against all forms of sin,"[75] Young Egypt's militants began what seems to have been a concerted campaign of attacking taverns. In January and February 1939, there were more than a dozen attacks on bars in Cairo, Alexandria and provincial cities, ranging from youths entering a cafe and destroying its stock of liquor to actual arson against taverns.[76] At the same time bar owners began to receive anonymous letters promising similar destruction if they did not cease selling alcoholic beverages.[77] Prostitution was denounced and demonstrated against. A "protest march against prostitution" sponsored by Young Egypt occurred in February 1939 and in April, when an Azharite student was killed in the course of another demonstration against prostitution, the party organized a funeral ceremony for the "martyr" and sent a petition to the King requesting the abolition of licensed prostitution as well as demanding "the review of all the country's laws and regulations which might be contrary to religion, morals and virtue."[78]

Somewhat later in 1939, a similar campaign of direct action was undertaken in relation to the Palestine problem. Articles defending the cause of the Palestinian Arabs and attacking Zionist intentions and British policy in Palestine had been published by Young Egypt's journals since at least 1938,[79] but in mid-1939 the party turned to attack Egypt's native Jewish population through organizing a boycott of Jewish merchants in Egypt. A "Committee for the Boycott of Jewish Commerce" was formed by Young Egypt in July 1939.[80] It established local boycott committees, printed and distributed application forms for volunteers who wished to assist in this "patriotic" undertaking, opened a public subscription drive to finance itself, and asked the local shu'bahs of Young Egypt to do the "statistical work" of determining exactly what were the Jewish commercial activities in their localities.[81] By the end of August 1939, this Boycott Committee had published three lists of Jewish merchants in Cairo who should be boycotted, with further lists promised.[82] The agitation surrounding the boycott soon had effects beyond mere boycott: in Asyut, a cache of bombs was found by the police along with pamphlets advocating the boycott; two members of Young Egypt were arrested for distributing anti-Jewish literature in Tanta, two more in Kafr al-Shaykh, and six in al-Mahallah al-Kubra; in the last city, two others were arrested on the charge of placing a bomb in the Jewish district.[83] The boycott campaign and its potentially violent spinoffs were only terminated by the imposition of press censorship and martial law which accompanied the outbreak of World War II in September 1939.

Young Egypt's militant campaigns of 1939 were accompanied by a very interesting political gambit; the promotion of a merger between itself and the Muslim Brotherhood (whose phenomenal growth into the premier mass organization in Egypt was well underway by the late 1930's) in order to form a new political party. An amalgamation of these two implicitly anti-parliamentary groups was probably desired by the Palace and 'Ali Mahir (Mahir's associate General 'Aziz 'Ali al-Misri is reported to have been urging such a merger at the time),[84] and eventually Young Egypt turned towards promoting the idea. Articles emphasizing the commonality of concern between the two movements and advocating cooperation between them in the defense of Islamic mores and in aiding the Palestinian Arabs appeared in the party's journal in late 1938 - early 1939,[85] and by June Young Egypt's Vice-President Mustafa al-Wakil declared his party's "complete readiness" for "absolute cooperation" between the two groups, calling for a "composite organization" to be created from Young Egypt and the Brotherhood.[86] No merger between the two groups was ever achieved, however: Hasan al-Banna of the Brotherhood was facing serious dissent and eventually secession from a segment of his following by 1939 over the precise issue of the growing connection of the Brotherhood with partisan politics,[87] and the outbreak of the war put a damper on the militant activities of both groups which had been the rationale for suggestions of merger between them.

Considered in conjunction, Young Egypt's militant campaigns against "sin" and Jews and its overtures to the Brotherhood mark a turning-point in the history of the movement. There are several indications that the movement was a fading force in Egyptian politics by 1939. One sign of this would seem to lie in Young Egypt's having mounted its militant campaigns in the first place. These were directed into the two areas - the vigorous defense of Islamic mores and the championing of the cause of Palestine - in which the Brotherhood had gained prominence in the later 1930's and which were important, if not central, factors in its rapid growth in those years. On both these issues Young Egypt had not been totally inactive in previous years, but, with its more overtly political orientation, it had done much less than the Brotherhood prior to 1939. In that year, however, it attempted to do more, indeed to out-Brotherhood the Brotherhood. This conscious aping of the activities of the Muslim Brotherhood, taken in combination with Young Egypt's suggestions of merger with the Brotherhood, would seem to indicate that the party was being eclipsed by the Brotherhood by 1939. The Brotherhood seems to have been successful in attracting to itself some of the youth who had previously followed Young Egypt by this time, as well as making serious inroads into those segments of the population which Young Egypt regarded as its natural clientele if it was indeed to become a truly competitive party - the government functionary, the artisan, the urban laborer.[88] Young Egypt's renewed militance of 1939 thus appears to have been a defensive measure as much as anything else, an attempt to regain the initiative from a rival organization through campaigning on the same issues which had contributed to the success of that rival.

This interpretation of Young Egypt's declining position vis-à-vis the Muslim Brotherhood by 1939 is reinforced by the major internal event within the party in 1940. In March of that year, Young Egypt formally changed both its name and its program, becoming "The Islamic Nationalist Party" (al-hizb al-watani al-islami) and adopting a new program which gave the movement a much more Islamic orientation than it had had in its earlier years.[89] Thus Young Egypt, originally a patriotic society emphasizing Egypt and its needs, by 1940 had become a religious party devoted to the promotion of Islam and its demands.

But not too much significance should be attached to the new name and the new program of the movement. However great an intellectual reorientation they seem to suggest, they seem best interpreted as a tactical maneuver by the party, one necessitated by the movement's desire to combat the Muslim Brotherhood on its own ground, that of the defense of Islam. The new name was not even used consistently by Young Egypt's leader, Ahmad Husayn sometimes signing official party pronouncements as "President of the Islamic Nationalist Party," but at other times with his older title, "President of the Young Egypt Party" – an indication perhaps of how little real change he saw in his movement's formal alteration of its name.[90] As we shall see later, both the name and the religious orientation of the movement proved to be ephemeral, disappearing after World War II when concerns other than the defense of Islam came to dominate Egyptian public life.

If Young Egypt's militant campaigns of 1939 were an attempt to compete with a burgeoning Muslim Brotherhood on its own ground, the attempt failed. Leaving for the next chapter the intellectual weaknesses of Young Egypt which made it a feeble rival for the Brotherhood, one practical political reason for the failure needs to be noted here. This is simply that Young Egypt's militance of 1939 met with severe repression by the government, repression which both cut into the party's existing following and greatly restricted its ability to attract new supporters.

Whereas in 1938 the Muhammad Mahmud ministry had given Young Egypt considerable freedom of activity, in 1939 it prevented the party from holding many of its public meetings, occasionally confiscated its journal, and closed several of the party's clubhouses for varying periods of time. Young Egypt's publicists, whose articles in 1939 unquestionably did incite attacks on taverns and agitate against other "prohibited" forms of entertainment, were repeatedly brought before the courts on charges ranging up to "publicly inciting the overthrow of the Egyptian Constitution by advocating before the people a violent revolution against the Constitution and Parliament."[91] By June 1939, eleven separate court cases

concerning articles published in Jaridah Misr al-Fatah were
scheduled for trial.[92] The verdicts in these press trials
were often more severe than those handed down against Young
Egypt in the period of Wafdist rule in 1936-1937: Ahmad
Husayn spent the period from January 12 to March 23 in jail,
and fines ranging from ten to one hundred pounds were imposed
against the party's journalists several times, creating a
serious drain on the party's treasury.[93] The government's
treatment of the militants of Young Egypt who expressed
their piety by the destruction of property was still more
severe. Beginning with the first attacks on taverns in
January 1939, the police began apprehending members of Young
Egypt. Each new incident was accompanied by the arrest of
suspects from the party, with Young Egypt claiming that
"several hundred" of its followers had been arrested by
mid-February 1939.[94] For some of these, the penalties were
originally detention without bail and eventually sentences
of up to a year in prison.[95]

There seems little doubt that both Young Egypt's abrupt
reorganization of late 1938 and its militancy of 1939 had
effects which were counterproductive for the organizational
strength and growth of the movement. There are no figures as
to the scope of the discontent within the party in late 1938
which in part produced its reorganization, but it seems
reasonable to assume that at least some of its following was
either purged or voluntarily left the party at that time.
Certainly the evidence which is available - reports in the
party's press on the meetings of its local branches - indicate
that many of these were only resuming activity by mid-1939,
more than half a year after Husayn had dissolved existing
shu'bahs in November 1938.[96] More definite is that the party's
militant campaigns in 1939 brought severe repression down upon
it, and did so at a time when its most immediate rival, the
Muslim Brotherhood, was developing still unhampered by
government restrictions (thanks to its employment of legal
methods in pursuing its goals in the prewar period).
Repression is not always harmful, at least not always to a
dynamic movement. But in 1939, with an alternative outlet
available to the discontented younger generation of Egypt,
its own militance and the subsequent crackdown of the government did prove injurious to Young Egypt as an organization.
By the beginning of World War II, having consciously
sacrificed its passive following by its recent insistence on
activism, suffering from the harsh government treatment
accorded its militants, and presumably having alienated more
secular-minded youth with its heightened religious orientation,
Young Egypt seems to have been becoming what many originally
promising youth movements develop into - a permanent fringe
group of visible but ineffectual activists. Even before the

war, the restrictions, and the eventual dissolution which
it brought, the decline of Young Egypt was under way.

The Ideas of Young Egypt in the 1930's

In the realm of ideas as well as that of action, Young
Egypt played its most important role in Egyptian history in
the 1930's. After World War II, the movement was to be but
one of many groups claiming to speak for the younger generation of Egyptians and offering solutions for the by-then-
obvious ills of the parliamentary monarchy. But in the 1930's,
with the Muslim Brotherhood still largely a-political, the
Blue Shirts of the Wafd dominated by the party's leadership of
the older generation and thus not really an autonomous voice
of youth and its concerns, and the socialist movements of the
1940's not yet in existence, Young Egypt was the major
organization of younger Egyptians which offered a "new"
program for the reformation of Egyptian politics and society.
In fine, in the 1930's Young Egypt was both a movement
speaking for the Egyptian younger generation and an organization speaking particularly to that generation. Being partial
representative of and preacher to Egyptian youth in the 1930's,
the movement's ideas in this period deserve to be considered
in some detail.

THE QUESTION OF LOYALTIES: "EGYPT OVER ALL"

As its name would indicate, Young Egypt was a primarily
Egyptian nationalist organization, one asserting and promoting
ideas of Egypt's past glory, its present separate existence,
and its right to future greatness. Emotional pride in being
an Egyptian was a dominant theme in the movement's propaganda
throughout the 1930's. As the first article of the new
society's program of 1933 put it,

> It is incumbent on us to occupy ourselves with the
> advancement of Egyptian nationalism (al-qawmiyah
> al-misriyah), and with filling ourselves with faith,
> confidence and pride in it. It is necessary that
> the word "Egyptian" become the highest ideal. . . .
> It is necessary that Egypt become over all (misr
> fawqa al-jami').[1]

The depth of the identification of the men of Young Egypt
with their country can be seen from their interpretation of
Egyptian history. One of the fullest treatments of Egypt's

history offered by a spokesman for Young Egypt in the 1930's was that given by Ahmad Husayn in the first few chapters of his autobiography Imani ("My Faith"). Published in 1936, at a time when Young Egypt was just beginning its first few years of significant growth, Imani may be considered as an organizational as well as an individual document, the view of history presented in it providing both the emotional drive and the intellectual rationale for many of the movement's activities.

Husayn begins his discussion of Egyptian history within an account of a secondary-school trip to Upper Egypt which he took in 1928. In visiting the Valley of the Kings, Husayn was overwhelmed with the artistic and technical achievements of the ancient Egyptians. After reflecting on the arts of wall decoration and embalming, he compared the skills of his ancestors with the achievements of contemporary science, and found the former to be more impressive: "these forefathers of ours knew the secrets and the arts of nature in a manner which we do not even know today."[2] At Karnak, the young man was similarly impressed by the military power of Pharaonic Egypt. In his eyes, Karnak was a ". . . place which had witnessed the triumphant armies of Egypt departing filled with strength and zeal. . . [and] the place which had seen kings coming from the ends of the earth, all shackled in chains, to pay their obeisance to the Egyptian Emperor."[3] Thus ancient Egypt had been the scene of unparalleled grandeur in both the spiritual and material realms.

But to Husayn the greatness of Egypt was not restricted to the Pharaonic period. Rather, his account protested against the idea which he said he had been taught in school, that "the golden age of Egypt was limited to the age of the Pharaohs," maintaining instead that "the golden age has repeated itself two and three and four times."[4] This is the theme underlying Husayn's treatment of post-Pharaonic Egyptian history. He identified several other periods in which he credited Egypt with playing a key role in human development. In the Hellenistic era, Egypt was cited as having held "the leading position among the nations of the world," Egyptianizing her Greek conquerors and giving birth to cultural institutions such as the library at Alexandria which were the "pride" of the civilized world.[5] The next era in which Egypt deserved recognition greater than that which she usually received was that of Rome and Christianity. In Husayn's view, Egypt could have defeated the Roman Empire militarily, had she chosen to, but instead she opted for a "spiritual struggle" against Rome, with her people adopting Christianity, suffering martyrdom for its sake, and through their sacrifice playing the most important role in the conversion of the Roman Empire to that "higher religion."[6]

The third post-Pharaonic era of Egyptian greatness was that
of Islam. Here Husayn asserted categorically that "Egyptians
played the leading role in the history of Islam,"[7] offering
as evidence of this such disparate developments as the lead
taken by Muslims from Egypt in the revolt against the Caliph
'Uthman in 656, the glories of the Shi'ah Fatamid Caliphate
and the place of its university al-Azhar in Muslim culture, and
the prominent role played by Egypt during the Crusades.
After this survey of the history of Egypt from the Pharoahs to
Saladin, Husayn's conclusion comes naturally: "Egypt has
always remained the pulsating heart of the world, the source
of its knowledge and culture everywhere."[8]

But this story of glory ended in the nineteenth century.
Although Egypt made "a sudden leap forward," after the
generally retrogressive periods of Mamluk and Ottoman
domination, in the early 1800's under Muhammad 'Ali when
"she became a splendid empire, the possessor of any army
which was able to vanquish the Turks (the masters of warfare
in Europe),"[9] this last flicker of greatness also marked the
beginning of Egypt's modern decline. For Muhammad 'Ali's
military successes had "frightened all of Europe," and so
"Europe banded together against her."[10] Europe was held
responsible for the majority of Egypt's setbacks and problems
since the reign of Muhammad 'Ali; the military defeat of
1840, the loss of her overseas empire, the British Occupation
of 1882, and the economic, social and cultural domination of
Egypt by Europe and European civilization. Husayn's
conclusion to his portrayal of Egyptian history in the modern
era shows not only his primarily negative interpretation of
Egypt's recent past, but also the emotional effects of his
perception of the developments of the modern period upon him:

> These incidents [of the nineteenth century] had a
> profound effect upon me. They filled me with
> bitterness and anger and made me comprehend the
> extent of the injustice which we endure. For here
> we are, the masters of the world in previous times,
> we who taught mankind the sciences and knowledge, we
> who carried the torch of culture, here we are a
> retarded nation because of the deeds of the English.[11]

Ahmad Husayn's treatment of Egyptian history in his
autobiography is representative of the portrayal of Egypt's
past offered in much of Young Egypt's propaganda in the
1930's. From a broader perspective, it is similar to much
nationalist history-writing. Its details specific to Egypt
are akin to the portrait of Egypt as "the dispenser of
civilization throughout the lands of the East" and as the
nation which "brought forth civilization and culture to the

entire human race" being propounded for the edification of
youth by Young Egypt's nationalist predecessor Mustafa Kamil
a generation earlier;[12] in its general features, it is
typical of the highly selective and highly pragmatic manipu-
lation of the past in order to build confidence for the future
which characterizes much nationalist historiography, both in
the Arab world and beyond. In W. C. Smith's classic summary
of this "apologetic" genre, "it seeks not to analyze or to
understand the past, but to glorify it; that is, to glorify
oneself. The purpose is not investigation but aggrandizement,
not intellectual accuracy but emotional satisfaction."[13] But
whether we must also conclude (with Smith) that such interpretations are "of necessity self-defeating" because they force
one's confidence to rest on an imaginative picture which lacks
"outer support" and therefore "ends by making one the more
insecure" is open to question.[14] David Gordon has suggested
that such apologetics may be a necessary stage through which
a people must move, the assertion of psychological certainty
being a prerequisite to later intellectual certainty.[15] If
the latter is the case, then Young Egypt's simplistic and
glorifying interpretations of Egyptian history may have
played a positive role in developing an Egyptian sense of
pride and dignity after the humiliations, both personal and
national, to which educated Egyptians had been subjected to
in the modern period.

It is their image of Egypt's recent past which is most
important for understanding the nationalist attitudes and
positions of the men of Young Egypt. As we have seen, Egypt's
last period of greatness was the reign of Muhammad 'Ali. But
glory came to an end in 1840, and since then Egypt has counted
for little on the world scene. The blame for this termination
of Egypt's playing her proper role in the world rested
primarily with Great Britain: "were it not for English
policy, intervening and inciting against us, we would be over
all today."[16] This view of nineteenth-century Egyptian
history provided the rationale for one of the most
frequently expressed themes in the propaganda of Young Egypt;
opposition to the British position in Egypt.

What is of greatest interest in Young Egypt's view of
the British position in Egypt is the variety of levels upon
which the men of Young Egypt saw the hand of perfidious
Albion operating in Egypt. To them, the British position
was not just one of the Residency interfering in Egyptian
politics and British troops stationed in Egyptian cities:
they also saw British machinations in Egypt's administrative,
legal and economic arrangements as well as in her social and
cultural life. In terms of politics, it was the British who
were credited with having "broken the unity of the nation"
which had existed during the revolt of 1919 by "creating a

number of parties";[17] since then, the British had succeeded in "domesticating" Egyptian politicians "to go about in awe and veneration of them."[18] But the British had not only perverted Egyptian politics: Britain was also responsible for sapping the moral fibre, the "virtue" of the Egyptian people. Britain's presence in Egypt as an interfering power "deprived it [the Egyptian people] of all its spirit," instead "instilling it with doubt in its own capabilities and the capability of the country."[19] On another level, Britain was accused of deliberately working to corrupt the Egyptian people. In a 1933 speech, after reviewing the moral laxity which he found so prevalent in Egypt, Husayn declared:

> All that is due to the despicable policy of the English. For the English know how to rule this country. They know that the path by which to do it is by separating the young generation from religion and its principles. . . . So they allow wine and usury, prostitution and gambling, all on the pretext that this is the "civilizing" of Egyptians.[20]

Not all of Egypt's contemporary problems were solely the responsibility of Great Britain, however. There was another crucial factor behind Egypt's modern decline to the men of Young Egypt, one which supplemented and reinforced the effects of British domination. This was the influence of the European communities resident in Egypt and of their Western and "materialist" civilization which had come to permeate Egyptian life.

The spokesmen of Young Egypt accepted two notions which had become commonplace with many Arab intellectuals of the previous generation. These were the concept of European civilization as being "materialist" in its essence while the ethos of Eastern civilizations (the Arabo-Islamic included) was "spiritual," and the idea that the good features of Western civilization were not unique to it but could be found in Eastern civilizations as well.[21] But they carried their aversion to Western civilization one step further, seeing it as having negative characteristics which far outweighed its positive features. Ahmad Husayn's autobiography makes these points in the context of discussing his first trip to Europe (to France in 1930).[22] While he had found some good aspects in the civilization of the West as represented by France, particularly the promotion of individualism ("the feeling of each individual for his own personality and his own freedom"), on the whole he claims to have been unfavorably impressed by European traits and values. Europe's "virtues and good characteristics" were only "the fruits of mature humanity generally," with all of them to be

found in "the East in general and in Islam in particular."
Moreover, European civilization had in his view an abundance
of negative qualities which made it a poor exemplar for other
peoples: its development of "godless, materialist principles
which do not recognize truth, virtue, religion, customs or
traditions"; its promotion of "the desire for liberation from
morality and law, the wish for the gratification of material
lusts"; and (if more were needed) its encouragement of "the
spirit of domination over weaker peoples, the tendency to
quarrel, to aggress, to envy each other in what they possess."

Given this negative view of Western civilization in and
of itself, it is not surprising that Husayn decried the
penetration of Western morals and mores into Egypt. His
attitude towards what the intrusion of Western customs meant
is best illustrated by two complementary articles written in
1938. In the first article, Husayn discussed the breakdown
of the extended family in modern Egypt. In his view, the
traditional Egyptian family had been a self-help unit within
which the weak were protected, the sick cared for, the
unemployed given aid. It was the opening of Egypt to modern
European civilization - "the 'civilization' of hunger, greed
and egoism, the 'civilization' of selfishness, lust for
wealth and exploitation" - which was destroying this beneficial
family structure to the point where "they [the people] die
and no one cares, they become sick and no one pays any
attention."[23] The second article extended this analysis from
the family to society as a whole, claiming that the people's
previous "honorable character, with religion filling their
souls" which had led them to "cooperate with one another"
had been destroyed by Western civilization, the result being
that "cooperation has disappeared, confidence has faded, and
today the peasantry endures calamity alone and thus are
overwhelmed by it."[24] To Ahmad Husayn, there was no doubt
as to where the blame for this state of affairs rested: it
was due to the replacement of old and beneficial institutions
by alien and "materialist" Western ones. The depth of Husayn's
antipathy to Western civilization comes out best from a
passage in another article of 1938, one attacking the French
role in modern Egypt:

> As for what France has done in regard to Egypt's
> social system, this is the calamity of calamities,
> something for which we hate her [France] a hundred
> times. For this ill-starred state is the one which
> proclaimed French law in this country, that law
> which has destroyed religion. . . . Religion will
> continue to be rare in this country until we can
> exterminate French law.[25]

Thus Young Egypt's opposition to the West was fueled by more than just the West's political and economic hegemony over modern Egypt. Jacques Berque's at-first-sight extreme statement, that "colonization and expansive capitalism seem to have played in the Arab world. . . the part played amongst ourselves by original sin,"[26] finds confirmation in these attitudes in the propaganda of Young Egypt.

The specific proposals advocated by Young Egypt for the elimination of this foreign hegemony over Egyptian life will be examined in the sections which follow. Here we may conclude the account of Young Egypt's attitude to the West by discussing the general themes which the propaganda of the movement emphasized concerning Egypt's relationship to the West. The first of these was that the movement's opposition to the Western position in Egypt was not directed to obtaining merely utilitarian benefits for Egyptians through the reduction of European influence, but that is also aimed at a more profound psychological transformation of Egyptians as well. In fine, British political interference, European economic privilege and Western cultural hegemony were not only a material liability - they were at the deepest level a stain upon the self, what Berque has so elegantly termed an "ontological insult" which violated the educated Egyptian's conceptions of the worth of his country, his religion and his civilization.[27] Because the men of Young Egypt regarded "any assent to the privileges of the foreigner as servitude, oppression, and dishonor,"[28] not only the actual foreign privilege or influence had to be eradicated; in addition, the manner in which these were removed had to be consistent with Egyptian honor and dignity.

Young Egypt's emphasis on the manner in which Egypt and Egyptians should behave vis-à-vis the foreigner can be seen from a consideration of the movement's position towards the Montreux negotiations of 1937 for the abolition of the Capitulatory system in Egypt. Whatever the pragmatic political reasons for the party's attacks on the position of the Wafdist ministry negotiating at Montreux, its opposition was justified primarily on grounds of national dignity and honor. At first, Premier Nahhas and his colleagues were denounced for going to Europe to resolve this essentially Egyptian affair:

> If he [Nahhas] had a spark of patriotism, he would
> prefer to remain in his own house, strong, and to
> invite the foreigners to come to him. The
> Capitulations must be abolished. The Mixed Courts
> must be abolished. But their abolition should
> occur in Egypt, not in Switzerland, because Egypt

is the competent authority, the deciding element,
the master in its own house.[29]

After the signing of the Montreux Convention the party opposed
it, arguing that it was deficient because it did not provide
for the "immediate abolition of the Capitulations, abolition
by the stroke of the pen by one side alone, the side of the
Egyptian government. This is the only solution which every
state wishing to achieve its sovereignty has followed, because
this is the only solution fitting for a people who wish to
call themselves 'independent' and 'sovereign.'"[30] The party's
official proclamation on the Convention thus considered it to
be a "worse insult" to Egypt than the Anglo-Egyptian Treaty
of 1936 had been, for whereas the Treaty had seen a strong
nation (Great Britain) dictating to a weak one as "the law
of life" required, the Montreux affair was "the weak imposing
their will" on Egypt. "We cannot be pleased by that or
agree to it. If we do [agree], we are a base and wretched
people."[31]

The second general theme found in the propaganda of Young
Egypt concerning the relationship of Egypt with the Western
world was the repeated assertion that Egypt could revive her
past "glory" and that she could indeed surpass the achievements
of modern European states. Egypt's potential superiority over
European states was emphasized again and again in the propaganda of the movement, with the indispensible prerequisite
for Egypt surpassing them in actuality being held to be the
degree of "faith," "determination" or "self-confidence" of
the Egyptian people themselves.[32] By 1938, after returning
from a lengthy trip to Europe, Ahmad Husayn was presenting
a comparison between Egyptians and Europeans which came close
to being a doctrine of innate Egyptian supremacy, a supremacy
based on the belief that the millenia over which the Egyptian
people had possessed a civilized way of life had raised them
to a more potent level of human capability than that of
Europeans. In reviewing the traits of different categories
of Egyptians versus their European counterparts, Husayn
found his countrymen to be the more qualified. The Egyptian
peasant was "stronger and more patient" than the farmers of
Europe; Egyptian soldiers were better military men than
European soldiers; Egyptian students were "more capable
intellectually" than European students.[33] The reason for
this Egyptian superiority was attributed to history:

I will tell you, gentlemen, a reality which I
discovered in Europe. It is that most of its peoples are close to the primitive, primal stages of
life. The only thing responsible for their progress
in life is the great amount of learning which they

51

receive all over Europe. Their knowledge, their
character, their virtues, their peculiarities –
all of these have been acquired by striving and
only by that. This means that if you strip from
them this learning and this knowledge which they
have won through striving and study, you will
find Europeans close to the barbarism of prehis-
toric times.[34]

Given this denigration of European capabilities, it is not
surprising that the men of Young Egypt should summon their
compatriots to end the foreign domination of Egypt and to
regain for Egypt her "proper" place as a great state.

It should be clear from the preceding that the primary
allegiance of the men of Young Egypt in the 1930's was to
Egypt per se. Egypt, however, was not the only sphere in
which they lived. There are still to be considered the
(for Young Egypt, secondary) questions of what Egypt's
relationship should be to the Arab and Islamic worlds.

In its early years, the movement had very little to
say about the allegiance of Egyptians to any community
broader than Egypt itself. Its attention was concentrated
on Egyptian issues; its concern with cultural or religious
questions dealt with these primarily as specifically
Egyptian problems rather than as broader issues of concern
to the whole Arab or Muslim community; and its propaganda
paid little attention to the affairs of Muslims or Arabs
except for their struggles against the same European domination which was oppressing Egypt. In terms of its official
position, the movement's program of 1933 (which remained in
force until 1940) made but a few references to the Arab and
Muslim worlds. Thus the society's goal was stated to be
that "Egypt become over all, a mighty empire composed of
Egypt and the Sudan, allied with the Arab states, and leading
Islam," and the program called for Cairo to be made "the
capital of the East" and for al-Azhar to become "the chief
spokesman for the Islamic nations."[35] As these references
made clear, the original focus of Young Egypt was upon
Egypt's greatness, its primary goal being to assert Egypt's
position "over all other states," with alliance with the
Arabs or Egypt's leadership of Islam being advocated as two
of the manifestations of Egyptian revival.

In the later 1930's, however, with the growth of Islamic
sentiment within Egypt (as illustrated in the rapid growth
of the Muslim Brotherhood) and with rising Egyptian concern
with Arab affairs sparked by the Palestinian Arab revolt of
1936-1939, Young Egypt's propaganda began to show a greater
concern with Egypt's relationship with the world around the
Nile Valley. The movement's shift in position in regard to

Egypt's connection with the rest of the Islamic world was only a slight one. Two of the "fundamental goals" of the Islamic Nationalist Party's new program of March 1940 dealt with the Muslim world, but in terms which show little change from the vagueness of Young Egypt's 1933 program:

> The goals of the party are. . .
> 3) To fight imperialism in the Islamic countries
>   and in all parts of the world, and to completely
>   liberate the Islamic lands;
> 4) To realize spiritual Islamic federation, to
>   revive the glory of Islam, and to spread its
>   message to all parts of the world.[36]

Whereas the new program gave the movement an "Islamic Nationalist" name and stipulated an "Islamic" set of provisions for internal reform within Egypt,[37] its passages on the outer Islamic community spoke only of the goal of liberation from imperialism (an aim with which Marxists as well as "Islamic" nationalists could concur) and paid a vague lip-service to Muslim unity without attempting to define or elaborate upon its nature. Young Egypt may have become the Islamic Nationalist Party in 1940; but it was a party whose concern with Islam was directed primarily to the status of Islam within Egypt, not to the condition of Islam throughout the whole Muslim world.

Young Egypt's evolving attitude towards the relationship of Egypt with the surrounding Arab world was more involved. A significant concern with Arab affairs on the part of the movement seems to have developed only in the later 1930's, with the Palestinian Arab revolt and the implications of the Zionist enterprise for Egypt being the catalyst.[38] An official party proclamation of solidarity with the Palestinian Arabs of May 1938 (apparently the party's first official statement on the subject of Palestine) emphasized pragmatic, Egypt-centered reasons in calling for greater Egyptian involvement in the Palestine problem: the economic danger of Jewish industry stifling nascent Egyptian industries and "closing Eastern markets to us"; the socio-economic disability that a neighboring state composed primarily of European Jews would be an encouragement to the European communities in Egypt to maintain their own privileges; and the political threat which such a state would pose, encouraging repeated European intervention in the Middle East in order to protect it.[39] It was on the basis of these issues of Egyptian self-interest that the movement originally came to be involved in championing the Palestinian Arabs in the later 1930's, stating that "it is necessary for us to work with all our power to help our Arab brothers in Palestine by every possible means. . . ."40

Soon, however, Young Egypt's spokesmen began to
express sentiments pointing in the direction of some
measure of unity among the states of the Arab East. By
August 1938, Ahmad Husayn was voicing a commitment to Arab
unity which, although it still envisaged a leading role for
Egypt, was much more Arabist than anything in Young Egypt's
previous propaganda:

> You must realize that the unity of any people is
> based on five factors; language, religion, culture,
> a shared past, and common aspirations, that is,
> interests. These factors are all found in their
> entirety in the Arab states, in Egypt, Syria, Iraq,
> and without a doubt the day will soon come when this
> unity will be realized and ties forged. I cannot
> at present define the form of association between
> these states, for this is something which only time
> and circumstances can determine. But Egypt, as is
> only natural for it, will be the mainspring of this
> union.41

The movement's increased commitment to the idea of Arab unity
was spelled out in detail with the drafting of its new program
of March 1940. In that document, one of the "fundamental
goals" of the Islamic Nationalist Party was stated to be
"to realize Arab unity (al-wahdah al-'arabiyah) among all the
Arab states," and the final section of the program specified
six measures which should be taken by Arab governments to
achieve a measure of unity: (1) "fighting imperialism, in
all its forms, in all parts of the Arab lands"; (2) the
lowering and eventually the elimination of customs duties
between Arab states; (3) agreement on preferential trade
pacts; (4) the coordination of educational policies in order
to produce a common culture; (5) agreement on "a unification
of fundamental laws, based on the Islamic Shari'ah"; (6) the
conclusion of a mutual defense treaty among all Arab states.42
Considered as a body, these proposals were an appreciable
commitment to Arabism by the movement, a greater one than
those made by most Egyptian political groups of the period
and certainly a considerable shift from the movement's
concern with Egypt alone earlier in the 1930's.

Yet the Islamic Nationalist Party's position on Arab
unity by 1940 should not be taken to mean that the movement
had abandoned Egyptian nationalism. There is, for example,
no provision for common citizenship nor any of the post-World
War II phraseology concerning the Arabs as "one nation" in
the 1940 program, and the framework of Arab unity which it
proposes is clearly that of greater cooperation between

54

separate Arab states. The spokesmen of Young Egypt still conceived of Egypt as a distinct entity and still considered themselves as Egyptians before all else. These considerations appear from a new set of principles drafted by the Islamic Nationalist Party for the edification of its followers in 1941.[43] In that list, a clear distinction is still made between the Nile Valley on the one hand and the Arab and Islamic worlds on the other: "Your country (biladuka) is Egypt and the Sudan, which cannot be separated or divided, and your fatherland (watanuka) is all the Arab and Islamic lands." The last of these principles of 1941 expressed the proper goal of a member of the Islamic Nationalist Party in terms altered in detail but not in essence from the goal of a follower of the Young Egypt Society in 1933: "Your goal is that Egypt become an extensive state, composed of Egypt and the Sudan, allied with the Arab states in a unified front which will liberate the Islamic fatherland, returning glory to Islam and raising its banner on high everywhere." Thus the place of Egypt in the propaganda of the movement remained what it had been in 1933, the object of the basic allegiance of the men of Young Egypt, and the Arab and Islamic worlds, although given greater attention by the movement, were still largely theaters of Egyptian self-realization rather than centers of identity in which Egyptianism had been dissolved.

THE QUESTION OF POLITICAL METHODS: TOWARDS "REVOLUTION"

Young Egypt's attitudes concerning methods of political action show considerable ambivalence in the mid-1930's. On the one hand, the movement demonstrated unmistakable inclinations towards autocratic political concepts. We have already seen this in its paramilitary organization and in its frequent resort to direct means of pressure and sometimes to violence in order to attain its goals.

Underlying this militarism and activism, on the intellectual level the movement's propaganda demonstrates a consistent tendency towards a strife-oriented view of human events. The language employed by the movement from its inception reeked of the vocabulary of conflict, its members being called "fighters," its uniform being termed "the emblem of the struggle," its program speaking not of the society's "economic platform" or its "social platform" but rather being subdivided into sections entitled "Our Economic Struggle" (jihaduna al-iqtisadi) or "Our Social Struggle" (jihaduna al-ijtima'i).[44] Tied in with these phrases, indeed underpinning them, was a mental construct which made them more than verbal conventions. This was the idea of human existence as a perpetual "struggle." The

nineteenth-century concepts of survival of the fittest and
life-as-struggle had been absorbed into Arabic thought by
the previous generation of Arab intellectuals,[45] and the men
of Young Egypt seem to have been echoing these already-trans-
mitted ideas rather than being influenced originally by
twentieth-century European extensions of Social Darwinism
(although European movements of the 1930's undoubtedly
reinforced their tendency to see the world in Social-
Darwinist terms). Thus concepts of struggle were perhaps
the dominant single theme running through the writing of
Ahmad Husayn in the 1930's. From his first published
literary piece, written when he was only seventeen, which
quoted Nietzsche and which referred to life as "this race in
which all created beings participate,"[46] Husayn consistently
interpreted human existence in terms of the struggle. The
most unequivocal expression of this comes from a speech of
1935:

> There is no way for us to achieve all that [the
> goals of the nation] except by force, physical
> force. Indeed, nature teaches us that there can be
> no accord between the ruler and the ruled, nor
> between the strong and the weak. Agreement can
> only be reached by struggle and strife. The con-
> queror is the worthy one, because he continues to
> exist; the conquered is weak, so he is exterminated.
> Life knows no restraint or leniency. He who is
> strong, lives; he who is weak, dies.
>   In vain does a weak people imagine that they
> can ever reach an amicable accord with a strong
> people. For that is an "accord" like the accord
> of the wolf and the lamb, which is always ended
> by the wolf eating the lamb. So, if you desire
> your independence, dream of it and wish to achieve
> it, there is but one path before you - to be strong,
> to be strong first and last.[47]

On the other hand, Young Egypt's propaganda in the
mid-1930's did not apply this vision of life-as-struggle to
Egyptian internal affairs. Rather, the society was generally
loyal to the Egyptian parliamentary system, advocated
national unity among all groups of Egyptians rather than
class struggle between them, and called for a struggle of
the united Egyptian people against the nation's external
opponents - the British and the foreigners generally.
Thus the movement's program deplored the fact that
Egyptians were divided into antagonistic political parties,
calling instead for the mutual cooperation of all Egyptians
"aloof from partisan squabbling."[48] When attacked by the

Wafd as a divisive force, Young Egypt denied the charge and
declared that "we will cooperate with anyone who is working
for the good of Egypt."[49] That these declarations of the
need for national unity were more than political persiflage
can be seen from some of Young Egypt's actions in the
mid-1930's: in 1934, the movement asked the King to call
on the Wafd to form a ministry, "for it alone is the leader
of the people";[50] in 1935, it supported the idea of a
patriotic front of all the political parties in order to
bring about the restoration of the Constitution of 1923;[51]
and in 1936, when the Wafd did take office, Young Egypt
originally called on its followers to support the ministry
because it had come to power constitutionally and "it is
necessary for every Egyptian to support this Constitution."[52]
In the communal sphere, at first Young Egypt similarly
preached harmony between religious groups in Egypt,
presenting itself as a non-sectarian organization and
accepting Copts within its ranks, extolling the past
"patriotic union between Muslims and Copts" as a model to
be maintained, and calling on both religious groups to
continue to be "brothers in the cooperative struggle for the
sake of the Fatherland."[53]

But Young Egypt's original vision of internal national
unity for the sake of opposing the external enemy was eroded
and eventually destroyed as the 1930's progressed. It first
began to be shaken significantly during the period of
Wafdist rule in 1936 and 1937. The change of Young Egypt
from a patriotic society to a formal political party at the
start of 1937 itself implied a new view of internal competition, and was justified on the grounds of Egypt's
"deteriorating" position under the Wafdist ministry and the
need for "the youth of Egypt" to "set things right."[54] The
brawls of Blue and Green Shirts in this period must have had
their psychological effects on those involved. Certainly
Young Egypt's propaganda had a much harsher tone by 1937
than it had had earlier, being marked by charges of personal
corruption against Wafdist leaders as well as by the new
accusation of "Coptic domination" over the Wafd.[55] By early
1938, when the Wafd had been dismissed from office, Young
Egypt was denouncing the Wafd in much stronger terms than
it had used for domestic opponents in the past. "Ninety
percent" of the Wafd's supporters were claimed to be Copts;
the Wafd was repeatedly termed a "Coptic clique"; and the
arrest of the dismissed Wafdist ministers was demanded by
Husayn, because "they are responsible for the spreading of
crime in the country and for inciting our youth to go beyond
the law. . . . "[56] Thus the political and physical struggle
against the Wafd had had its effects upon Young Egypt: by
1938, the Wafd and its Coptic element were well on the way

to being excluded from any concept of national "unity."

It was only in 1938 and 1939 that Young Egypt's propaganda became hostile to the entire parliamentary and party system in Egypt. There would seem to be two major factors underlying the increasingly authoritarian content of Young Egypt's propaganda in the later 1930's. One was the party's connections with anti-parliamentary forces in Egyptian politics. In 1938 and 1939, with the eclipse of the Wafd and the dominance of the Palace in Egyptian public life, ideas generally hostile to parliamentary government were being promoted by the Palace and those politicians associated with it.[57] As we have seen, Young Egypt supported the initiatives of the Palace aimed at enhancing the prestige of the monarchy and diminishing that of the political parties (i.e., the agitation surrounding the Caliphate), and was almost certainly receiving financial assistance from the Palace or from politicians aligned with it. Given this, it is reasonable to assume that the movement's evolving ideas on political methods were influenced to some degree by the Palace or its allies. But the relationship between Young Egypt's position and the ambitions of the Egyptian Palace should not be conceived of as the movement's merely serving as an instrument of Palace policy. As we shall see shortly, Young Egypt's spokesmen had their own ideas about political life, and these, while in some respects paralleling ideas emanating from Palace circles, in other respects went considerably beyond what the Palace circle was advocating.

The other major factor behind Young Egypt's considerable shift in political attitudes was the growing impact of European fascism upon the movement. The ideas of the spokesmen of Young Egypt towards the utility of European fascist principles for Egypt were far from uniform in the 1930's. Unquestionably, some of the symbols (a uniform; a salute), organizational techniques ("absolute obedience" to one's leaders; military drills and assemblies) and ideas (the vision of a lost national "harmony" which must be restored; life-as-struggle) found in European fascist movements could also be found in Young Egypt from the movement's inception. Nevertheless, in the mid-1930's the spokesmen of Young Egypt demonstrated a definite scepticism about the internal achievements of fascist states and were unwilling to identify their movement with fascism on an ideological level. Ahmad Husayn's unfavorable views of Italy after his brief trip there in 1934 have already been mentioned. A 1937 biography of Mussolini by Fathi Radwan came to similarly negative conclusions, evaluating the man as one who "in spite of his stirring words yet has reformed nothing" and summarizing Italian Fascism as "not a new ideology, because it never goes beyond an 'armed-to-the-teeth'

patriotism, and this kind of patriotism is not beneficial to
mankind."[58] In general terms, the usual position of Young
Egypt's leaders on their own movement in the mid-1930's
was that it was an essentially "spiritual" movement different
from the basically "materialist" fascism of Europe:

> How different is our struggle from that of Mussolini
> or Hitler! How great is the difference between the
> struggle of Young Egypt and their struggle! For
> they began their struggle by gathering together
> soldiers and the unemployed, whereas Young Egypt
> has taught the new generation and prepared it for
> the struggle. They believe primarily in material
> force. We believe primarily in spiritual force,
> in faith in God and in religion.[59]

By the later 1930's, however, this reserve gave way to a
considerable admiration for the achievements of the European
fascist regimes. In a speech of April 1938, Husayn praised
Italy as "the greatest state in the Mediterranean, a model
and an example to be imitated," termed Germany "absolutely
the greatest state in Europe," and now attributed the
success of both to the "spiritual" aspect of their revolu-
tions: "This revolution from weakness to strength, from
nothingness to life, from the depths to the heights, was not
the result of new armies or new fleets. . . . What is the
secret, therefore, of these rebirths and revivals? The only
secret is profound faith. . . ."[60] Young Egypt became
willing to admit influence and/or borrowings from European
fascism, Husayn stating that Young Egypt "hopes one day to
achieve in its meetings what the Nazis have achieved in
theirs" and an article on the party's summer camp for youth
crediting the idea to the example of "reviving nations like
Italy and Germany."[61]
The peak of Young Egypt's adulation for European fascism
was reached during a trip to Europe in mid-1938 by Husayn.
His articles describing Germany were all highly laudatory of
Nazi achievements. The Nazi Party's summer work-camps were
praised for bringing together "people of all classes" in
labor for the benefit of the nation;[62] the German Labor
Front was characterized as a proper way to organize labor
with "no swindling of the working classes. . . for there is
no 'big' and no 'small' - all are members of one organization,
and every worker works for the public interest before he
works for himself" and termed "a return to true Islamic
society where there was no employer and no employee but
[where] all were brothers cooperating together";[63] and his
final article from Germany, in the form of an open letter
to Hitler, leaves no doubt as to the favorable impression

made on Husayn by both the social and the national aspects of German National Socialism:

> How much have you accomplished, oh leader, in the
> returning of spirit to this great people, putting
> them under one banner, one leadership, one plan,
> and then proceeding with them into the battles of
> life as one force, strong, able to hold its head
> high, filled with dignity, not accepting any wrong
> or insult to itself, its own master first and last,
> with no outside power having authority over it.[64]

Immediately upon his arrival in Italy from Germany, Husayn was willing to make a public declaration signifying European fascism as a proper example for Egypt - and his movement - to follow in the future:

> Ahmad Husayn declared that the principles of his
> party are made up of a combination of the princi-
> ples of Rome and Berlin, that he does not consider
> Hitler and Mussolini to be dictators but rather
> that they are reflections of their peoples, of the
> basis of their life and greatness, and that Germany
> and Italy are the two democratic states in Europe,
> the other states being capitalist-parliamentary
> organizations.[65]

Husayn's articles from Germany mark the highpoint of Young Egypt's intellectual enchantment with European fascism. From late 1938, with the developing international crisis in Europe, the movement's attitudes towards European fascism were progressively influenced by the German and Italian threat to world peace, and favorable views on fascist principles and achievements gave way in the movement's propaganda to attacks on German and Italian aggression in the international sphere.[66] But this reaction occurred only after Young Egypt's infatuation with fascism's seeming successes had served as the final catalyst for the movement's committing itself to a more authoritarian position towards Egyptian politics.

In the spring of 1938 (during the electoral campaign of that year in which Young Egypt had been unable to participate because of the youth of its leadership) the entire electoral process in Egypt began to be denounced by the party's spokesmen. Egyptian politicians were decried as being motivated only by "lust for office" and "desire for personal gain."[67] Elections in Egypt were belittled as "not at any time having revolved around principles or programs, but rather [as] having been campaigns motivated by and based on

partisanship for the tribe and partisanship for the family,"
and were denied any validity: "all the elections which have
occurred in the past and which are occurring today cannot be
considered as an expression of the will of the people."[68]
An official party proclamation of April 1938 saw the party
for the first time attack the Constitution of 1923:

> The entire nation is disgusted with the elections
> and with the present Constitution. The nation
> looks to you [parliamentary deputies] with
> indifference and unconcern. . . . The nation
> expects that, first of all and before anything
> else, you will be intent on the glory of being a
> deputy, and thus you will support the government
> whatever its form or composition. The nation
> expects that you will excel in debates, arguments,
> and personal quarrels. The nation expects that
> you will concern yourselves with your parliamen-
> tary salaries and with the prerogatives of member-
> ship. But the nation does not expect any serious
> reforms or saving of the country from you. All
> this will, after a while, cause the nation to cry
> out that it does not want deputies, or a parlia-
> ment, but that it wants work and bread and
> justice.[69]

It was also in 1938 that Young Egypt's spokesmen began
to postulate the existence of serious class cleavages within
Egypt. This soon led to a general assault on the rich of
Egypt for their way of life, their conspicuous and wasteful
consumption, and their lack of concern for their less
fortunate compatriots. The increasingly radical and yet
somewhat archaic (in the sense that a dismal present was
compared to an overly idealized past) tenor of the party's
propaganda can be seen in an article by Husayn entitled
"The People are Starving and Oppressed."[70] Husayn began
with an impassioned description of how "the people are
starving - without a doubt," how "fourteen millions out of
sixteen millions. . . take their nourishment from the
leftovers of the crop," how "there are also hundreds of
thousands of unemployed in the cities," and how "this can
have only one result: one day the people will explode,
screaming with one voice 'We want bread! We want bread!'"
After analyzing what he felt to be the novelty of this
situation, that Egyptian society had not been like this in
the past because the people, rich and poor, had "cooperated
with one another," he moved on to call the Egyptian upper
classes "the greatest criminals in Egypt" because "they
think that all this wealth which they have in their hands

is theirs to do with as they please." Husayn's conclusion
directly coupled the present miseries of the mass of the
Egyptian people with the failures of the Egyptian parliamentary system:

> The people are starving. The people are sick.
> But the rich squander their wealth on dancers
> and gambling. The rulers are busy with trifling
> political crises. A minister will exit, and a
> minister will enter; an official will be
> discharged, an official will be hired; formal
> dinners and dancing-parties, that is the life of
> our ministers. That is the life of our govern-
> ment, while the people under this system die, and
> the unemployed find no sustenance because bread
> has gone up in price.

It was not only Ahmad Husayn who spoke in these
increasingly radical terms by the later 1930's. The party's
Vice-President Mustafa al-Wakil similarly spoke of the
Egyptian Constitution as "one from which the country has
not received any benefit from its promulgation until the
present,"[71] and even the more moderate of the two dominant
figures of Young Egypt, Fathi Radwan, demonstrated a
radicalism similar to Husayn. In an article entitled "Are
We Propagandists of Dictatorship?",[72] Radwan flayed the
Egyptian political system in much the same terms as Husayn
was using: it was "the parliamentary system which prevents
and hinders action, which turns the country into a stage
for oratory and theatrics"; "the people are starving, yet
the deputies wax eloquent"; "while the people are in need
of productive action, of reform and renovation and bold
undertakings, Parliament does not advance or satisfy that
need." The article concluded with a series of rhetorical
questions which show that, for Fathi Radwan at least, the
issue of the necessity of another regime to replace the
impotent parliamentary one had been faced and decided:

> If it is dictatorship which will put a limit to
> the anarchy which has been disclosed about our
> high officials, then we will be among the suppor-
> ters of dictatorship, believers in it and propagan-
> dists for it. . . . If it is dictatorship which can
> fill youth with power, fill the nation with the
> military spirit, and fill the people with elec-
> tricity, vigor and dynamism, then we will be
> dictators to the bone.

The new strands of discontent with the Egyptian parliamentary system and with class inequalities in Egypt eventually led Young Egypt to demand internal revolution in Egypt. Party propaganda had begun to employ the word "revolution" (thawrah) or its equivalents by 1938, a party petition to the King of March calling for "a reforming revolution" in Egypt and a speech by Ahmad Husayn of June rather verbosely stating that "we believe that everything in Egypt today is grossly misarranged. . . . Everything must be destroyed, everything must be demolished, everything must be turned upside down."[73] A major speech by Husayn of August 1938, after his return from his European trip, was dominated by the themes of revolution and social upheaval in Egypt.[74] He attacked the parliamentary system, refusing to recognize any distinction between "democracy" and "dictatorship" and instead expressing his preference for "sound government. . . based on the service of the people." Forgotten was the idea of national unity, being replaced by declarations that "the rights of the peasant in this country have been usurped and stolen, stolen by a clique of foreigners, a small group of rich people, a band of high officials" or that "fifteen million Egyptians work like slaves for the benefit of the two million or less of foreigners, of the rich, of the high officials, ministers and pashas." The following passage draws together most of the themes discussed previously – disillusionment with the parliamentary regime, class divisions in Egypt, egalitarianism and populist protest – into a commitment to the transformation of Egyptian society by authoritarian methods:

> We have in this country fifteen million peasants
> who eat only mish and onions, who manage to subsist
> only with great difficulty, and who work as the
> hirelings of a tiny minority. We [Young Egypt] wish
> to liberate these millions, to give them the same
> type of homes as human beings live in, to give them
> the same type of education as human beings receive,
> to give them their fair share out of life as God
> wishes for them. This is what this country
> wishes. If the Constitution and Parliament are
> able to achieve this result for us, I will be
> content. Otherwise, say of me that I am an
> aggressor against the Constitution. Indeed, I am
> an aggressor against any system which keeps
> laborers in hard labor in exchange for only a few
> piastres. I am against any person, against any
> organization, and against any system which prevents
> the worker or the peasant from living in a house.
> And if the Constitution is an obstacle to this, well
> then I will fight the Constitution and eradicate it.

A speech of November 14, 1938, saw one further step taken by the leader of Young Egypt.[75] After speaking of how "we believe that there can be no prosperity for this country except by means of a general, complete overthrow (inqilab)," Husayn then went on to express his willingness to act against popular wishes if that should prove necessary to carrying out such an "overthrow": "We shall not wait, as some people believe, for twenty years, until all the people believe in the soundness of our views. . . . We shall not wait until the pashas and the beys and the foreigners and the English believe in us." Eventually he declared the purely elitist view that Young Egypt had the truth and that it would act to impose its views even if that ran against the desires of "the people":

Do you think that work like this [the party's program] can wait until the people are persuaded, one by one, of its necessity? Or is it sufficient that we believe in it and then struggle with all our ability to achieve it?. . . It is necessary that we be strong in order to impose our will — the will of the best — on this country.

In these speeches of 1938, Ahmad Husayn and the movement which he led had come a considerable distance from their earlier position that "we will cooperate with anyone who is working for the good of Egypt" or that "it is necessary for every Egyptian to support this Constitution." In the place of its original concepts of internal unity among Egyptians and their mobilization against an external foe, Young Egypt now advocated internal political upheaval and class conflict within Egypt. That the party's actual "revolution" of 1939 turned out to be a rather shabby affair involving attacks on taverns, prostitution and Jews rather than an assault on "high officials, ministers and pashas" matters little in terms of evaluating the ideas of Young Egypt. In essence, by the late 1930's Young Egypt had decided that representative government was unworkable in Egypt, that the economic and social needs of the country took precedence over representative government, and that these needs could best be met by authoritarian methods.

THE QUESTION OF REFORM (I): "SOCIAL JUSTICE" IN EGYPT

As passages in the preceding section have indicated, Young Egypt's disillusionment with the parliamentary monarchy and its eventual call for "revolution" in Egypt in the later 1930's were accompanied by the movement's showing a greater awareness of the problems of inequality, the distribution of

wealth, and the relationship between the upper and lower
classes within Egypt. The subject of "social justice" for
the mass of the population of Egypt is one of great interest
in the history of Young Egypt in the 1930's: it is a topic
about which the movement had very little to say in its
early years, but one which came to bulk larger and larger
in its propaganda as the decade progressed, until by the
end of the 1930's it was expressing concerns and demands
which foreshadow some of the post-1952 measures taken in
Egypt in regard to wealth and its distribution between
rich and poor.

In the mid-1930's, there was very little in Young
Egypt's propaganda in regard to class relationships and
inequalities in Egypt. Overwhelmingly concerned with the
foreign domination to which all Egyptians were subject and
wedded to a vision of national harmony among all elements of
the indigenous population, the movement's propaganda largely
limited itself to vague generalizations to the effect that
"it is necessary that we educate the peasant in order to
eliminate ignorance and illiteracy, to elevate his living
conditions, and to give him contentment and prosperity
once again" or that "our programme is directed at raising
the status of the Egyptian working classes, improving their
lot, and securing for them a healthy and happy life."[76]

In only two areas touching upon class relationships
did Young Egypt's spokesmen put forward specific proposals
for reform in the mid-1930's. The first was that of
industrial labor, where the movement supported attempts
aimed at organizing the urban labor force, where it called
for protective labor legislation such as the eight-hour
day and the passage of social security legislation, and
where by 1936 it was demanding that the government enact
a "Work Charter" defining the rights of labor and setting
down government-enforced safety standards for industrial
concerns.[77] The second was in regard to land distribution,
where Ahmad Husayn's autobiography of 1936 called for the
distribution of both foreign-owned large estates and
government-owned agricultural lands to "the starving
peasants" of Egypt.[78]

It was only in the late 1930's that Young Egypt came
to give significant attention to class differences in Egypt.
We have already surveyed how the movement came to condemn
not only the parliamentary system of Egypt but also the
division of the country into "two classes," one of which
was composed of "millions of people who do not enjoy the
rights of people, whose dignity is non-existent, and whose
activities are despised," the other of which was made up of
"wealthy people whose only thought is for the accumulation
of wealth by the thousands [of pounds] from the peasantry,

then for its squandering on the gaming-tables and in the dancehalls and bars of Europe."[79]   For the elimination of these economic inequalities in Egyptian life, Young Egypt's spokesmen eventually did propose a much fuller set of reforms than could be found in their propaganda in the movement's early years.

The movement's attitude towards the amelioration of the condition of the Egyptian lower classes was particularly influenced by Ahmad Husayn's European trip of 1938.   In Czechoslovakia (which Husayn visited before proceeding to Germany), Husayn was very impressed with that nation's Masaryk Institutes, promising that "the first thing" Young Egypt would try to establish in Egypt if it came to power would be similar social service and health units managed by workers themselves.[80]   As we have seen, in Germany both the Nazi Party summer work-camps for youth and the German Labor Front were praised by Husayn; in his articles on both, he called for similar arrangements to be instituted in Egypt.[81]   In his open letter to Hitler upon leaving Germany, Husayn voiced the general lesson which he had learned on his visit to Central Europe:

> Work has become honored in Germany, and the worker has become the most important unit within the state. Indeed, the state is the worker.   But that does not mean anarchy or destruction, ruin or chaos.   Rather, its meaning is that the state is obligated to ceaseless vigilance in the interests of the worker.[82]

In his first speech upon returning from Europe, Husayn laid down two principles which were to be the basis of Young Egypt's specific proposals concerning labor thereafter. The first was that "the government is obligated to set a limit beneath which the standard of living may not drop," the second that "it is the right of every worker in the state that it [the state] find a job for him when he is unemployed."[83]   From the first principle came a series of specific proposals for legislation to protect the standard of living of the mass of Egyptians; from the second came several suggestions for government intervention in the economy on behalf of the worker.   Since these various recommendations were expressed in their most comprehensive and official form in the movement's new program of March 1940, it is with that document that we shall deal in detail in summarizing Young Egypt's evolved attitude toward labor.[84]

The program's section on "The Working Classes" began by setting down the basic principle of the dignity of labor: "Work is an honorable thing for the Egyptian, and the

Egyptian who does not work has no honor." After defining "worker" broadly enough to explicitly include agricultural labor within the category, the program listed several specific recommendations for workers' legislation. A minimum wage of four pounds per month or fifteen piastres per diem was demanded for adult urban labor, and one of three pounds per month or ten piastres daily for adult agricultural labor. Legislation was requested guaranteeing an eight-hour day, one day of rest per week, and a ten-day annual vacation with pay for all labor. The program's social security provisions were very broad, stating that "every worker has the right" to "complete medical treatment" for himself and his family, to sufficient compensation if injured in the course of his employment, to a "suitable" pension upon retirement or if permanently disabled, and to unemployment insurance sufficient to provide for his family when unemployed. All this was to be guaranteed by government legislation, Young Egypt having adopted the example of "ceaseless vigilance" by the state in the interests of the worker which its leader had seen operating in Europe.

The state's duties towards the worker went beyond the passive function of enacting rules for his fair treatment by his employer. Several other provisions of the program demanded active intervention by the government in the economy to protect the worker. Thus the state was to inspect both factories and agricultural estates to see that they provided "clean and healthy dwellings" for their workers, and similarly the state was to regulate agricultural rents so as to "prevent injustice." In more general terms, the government was to "find work for every unemployed worker" and, failing that, its duty was "to feed every hungry person who presents himself to the police." In a proviso reflecting the movement's continuing nationalist orientation, the program demanded that the state give any worker a financial grant whenever a new child was born to him and provide a special grant for any worker whose family had more than five children. The result of both the legislative and the interventionist suggestions of the program would have been to establish an economy in which the government would not only regulate economic life for the benefit of the worker but also would intervene in economic affairs at any sign of the deterioration of the working or living conditions of the mass of Egypt's people.

Although Young Egypt saw the state as the predominant influence in guaranteeing the interests of Egypt's working population, the role of labor organizations and the European example of workers' institutes were not neglected in the movement's detailed program for the betterment of the conditions of the Egyptian worker in the late 1930's. As we have seen, the party supported organized labor in Egypt, giving legal aid to striking workers and attempting to organize various workers' committees and conferences.[85] In terms of specific recommendations concerning organized labor, the program of 1940 endorsed trade unionism: "it is necessary that there be a union for every profession. . . and it is necessary that every worker belong to a union."[86] Very broad functions were envisaged for unions, the program suggesting that adult education for workers could be provided through their unions and that unions could also serve to arrange the leisure-time activities of workers. Thus the European examples which Husayn had previously praised as "official organizations for the ordering of the free time of the worker, to aid him in achieving culture and enjoying life,"[87] were accepted by the movement as an example for Egyptian society.

The same principle of the promotion of corporative bodies linked with the government was found in the program of 1940 in regard to rural life. The program called for the establishment of a village council in every Egyptian village. Such councils, subsidized by the central government, were to supervise public hygiene, improve roads, help the poor, spread culture, and generally to "strengthen cooperation" (that cooperation which had been eroded by the impact of the West). On the individual level, every farmer was to be required to join the local agricultural cooperative which was to serve as the farmers' agent in marketing, purchasing, and providing loans at low-interest rates.

The various specific proposals being offered by Young Egypt concerning labor legislation, state supervision of the economy, and the encouragement of unions and cooperatives should not be allowed to obscure the significant omissions in the movement's ideas on the distribution of wealth in Egypt. For, while suggesting much which it claimed would be of benefit to the poorer strata of Egypt's population, the movement propounded little in the economic sphere which would take their already accumulated wealth from the rich of Egypt or which would inhibit Egypt's existing capitalist orientation.

The major exception to this was in relation to foreign economic privilege in Egypt. Opposition to the European economic dominance of Egypt was one of the leitmotifs of Young Egypt's actions and propaganda throughout the 1930's. As we have seen, many of the movement's early activities involved boycotts, picketing and propaganda campaigns against foreign firms, foreign products and the foreign economic position in Egypt.[88] On the programmatic level, from its founding Young Egypt called for a variety of governmental actions to reduce the foreign role in the Egyptian economy; the abolition of the Capitulations and the Mixed Courts, legislation to "Egyptianize"

68

foreign-owned firms, Arabic to be made the official language of commerce and Friday to become the official day of rest of businesses, internal commerce to be made the prerogative of Egyptian merchants only, government employees and students in government schools to "wear clothing made in Egypt," and the government's own purchasing "always to give preference to local products, whatever their price."[89] In terms of the individual, the movement's followers were constantly enjoined to "speak only in Arabic," to "eat only Egyptian foods," to "wear only Egyptian clothing," to "buy only Egyptian goods," and generally to "scorn anything foreign, each of you, and cling steadfastedly to your nationalism, making it an obsession."[90] Activities and injunctions directed against foreign economic dominance remained a constant with Young Egypt through the 1930's, the movement sponsoring occasional boycotts and protests against the foreign presence and telling its followers that "we summon you to boycott everything foreign. . . for that is the essence of the struggle of Young Egypt."[91]

The most detailed statement of the measures which the movement advocated to reduce the foreign position in Egyptian economic life was made in the Islamic Nationalist Party's new program of March 1940.[92] In addition to reiterating the demands made in Young Egypt's original program of 1933 concerning the Mixed Courts (the remainder of the Capitulatory system had been eliminated in 1937), the use of Arabic and the observance of Friday in business, the reservation of internal trade for Egyptian merchants, and state preference for local products in its own purchasing, the program of 1940 advocated several further measures aimed at reducing the foreign economic role in Egypt. In the agricultural sphere, it categorically demanded that "no foreigner will be permitted to own agricultural land under any circumstances" and insisted that the compensation paid for the expropriation of foreign estates should be reduced according to the profits which the foreign owner had reaped from Egyptian agriculture in the past. In regard to industry, the program stated that "foreigners will not be allowed to administer any monopolies in Egypt or any companies connected with the public interest such as water, light, communications and the like" and that "the government should take over all foreign monopolies" (the largest foreign monopoly in Egypt, the Suez Canal Company, was explicitly included in this demand). These proposals for nationalizing foreign-owned monopolies were accompanied by other demands for the "Egyptianizing" of those firms which would be allowed to remain under foreign ownership. Thus the program demanded that "all employees are to be Egyptians," stipulated that exports or capital should not be sent out of Egypt until the government was satisfied that Egypt had received adequate

recompense for their export, and set down the general principle
in regard to both commercial and industrial development that
"the aid of the foreigner should not be sought except in
exceptional circumstances."

In comparison with this sweeping opposition to the
economic role of foreigners in Egypt, Young Egypt's attitude
towards native Egyptian industry and commerce was very
favorable in the 1930's. While advocating that "Egypt be
restored to its old position as an industrial state" or that
Egyptians should "assume our proper place in world trade as
the entrepôt between East and West," the implication was always
that, although the government would aid in promoting industrial
and commercial development, the ownership and control of
industry and commerce would remain in the private sphere.[93]
The sections of the program of 1940 in regard to industry and
commerce, as opposed to that document's specificity and
frequent radicalism in other areas, were composed of vague
exhortations calling for the construction of a variety of new
factories, the fuller exploitation of power and mineral
resources, and the improvement of transportation facilities,
with all but the last area to be handled through the efforts
of private enterprise.[94]

But whereas the propaganda of Young Egypt showed no
antipathy to native commercial or industrial interests, the
movement did develop a definitely hostile strand of thought in
regard to vested agricultural interests in Egypt. By the late
1930's, it was a consistent demand of the movement's propaganda
that foreign-owned and government lands be distributed to the
peasantry.[95] The redistribution of privately held estates
was being suggested as well, an article of 1938 asking "cannot
the rich landowners see that both justice and necessity demand
that they renounce a part of their lands, giving them to the
poor peasants?", and the party's Ten Goals of November 1938
stating that "force is inevitable for us to distribute the
lands of the government to the peasantry, and to do the same
with other lands as well."[96] However, the movement's new
program of 1940 drew back from calling for the redistribution
of private, indigenously owned agricultural lands, demanding
only the distribution of foreign-owned estates, of uncultivated
government lands, and of reclaimed lands to the small farmer
in exchange for long-term payments.[97]

A similar hostility to agricultural interests comes out
in the proposals regarding taxation which the movement developed
in the late 1930's. The movement's basic suggestions in regard
to taxation in the later 1930's were two. The first was a
demand that the Islamic alms-tax be reinstituted in Egypt:
"the payment of the zakah is obligatory on every Egyptian."[98]
The second related only to the land: "it is necessary that the
system of taxation be made more equitable by lightening the

70

burden of the small farmer and by multiplying the share of the large farmer."[99] The program of 1940 spelled out the latter principle in some detail, calling for the small farmer to be exempt from any land tax while progressive taxation was to apply to the holdings of large landowners. Another provision of the program was punitive in regard to landed wealth, demanding the imposition of an extra tax on absentee landlords.[100] But, while landed wealth was thus to be brought under financial constraints, the program made no such suggestions in regard to wealth which had been accumulated in trade or industry.

Young Egypt's position by the end of the 1930's towards the problems of class relationships and the distribution of wealth in Egypt may be summarized as follows: "social justice" for the mass of Egypt's population was to be provided by protective legislation, by the strengthening of the labor union and cooperative movements, and above all by "ceaseless vigilance" by the state; foreign enterprise was to be significantly diminished or "Egyptianized"; the native industrial or commercial entrepreneur was to be encouraged by the state but was not to be subject to restrictions (other than a few relating to the fair treatment of his employees) which might hinder him; the small farmer was to be relieved of his tax burden and given more land; and the landed rich were to assume the burden of paying for most of the improvement in the condition of the small farmer by being subject to increased taxation. The explanation of Young Egypt's more negative attitude towards agricultural wealth, as opposed to its unrestrictive stance towards industrial and commercial wealth, may be found in the movement's belief in the necessity of the rapid economic development of Egypt. Basically an urban movement born in the great depression when the general current of Egyptian economic thought was directed towards industrialization as the cure for the country's previous dependence on agricultural exports, the movement's spokesmen saw the solution for Egypt's economic problems to be rapid industrial development. Correspondingly, they did not wish to hamper the commercial or industrial entrepreneur (particularly since these had the added burden of replacing foreign commerce and industry in Egypt), and therefore they suggested few restrictions on the untrammeled capitalist development of industry or trade. Placing no great hopes for the future in the (already developed) agricultural sector, and well aware of the poverty existing in rural Egypt, the movement's spokesmen advocated greater restrictions on landed wealth.

THE QUESTION OF REFORM (II):
THE "ISLAMIC" RESTRUCTURING OF SOCIETY

In its early years, Young Egypt had not been a particularly religiously oriented organization. Its early activities
were directed primarily to political or economic questions,
and its propaganda, although not totally neglecting the subject of religion, had less to say about it than about the
secular issues of Egyptian politics or the foreign domination
of Egypt. In the society's original program of 1933, only
four of thirty-eight articles were directed specifically to
the subject of religion. One stated that al-Azhar had a
"great role" to play in their hopes for Egypt's future, that
"it is necessary that it be reinvigorated and that it regain
its old position," while the other three summarized the
society's "Social Struggle - In Regard To Religion And Morals"
in very general terms:

> It is necessary that we accord total respect and
> veneration to higher religions.
> It is necessary that we elevate morals and that
> we struggle against immorality, drunkenness and
> effeminacy.
> It is necessary that we cultivate integrity, that
> we be virtuous in our striving, and that we continue
> to cooperate and to love one another.[101]

It is noteworthy that Islam was not mentioned by name in the
latter articles but that the society declared its "total
respect and veneration" for "higher religions" in general.
Thus Young Egypt originally presented itself as an organization
appealing to youth of any religious affiliation, subsuming
religious differences under the umbrella of its Egyptian
patriotism.

There are few detailed presentations dealing with Islam
in the writings of the men of Young Egypt during the movement's
early years. Ahmad Husayn, at least interpreted Islam in a
highly selective fashion, in terms of the attributes of social
utility and modernity which it had been given in the writings
of the previous generation of Arab intellectuals. Thus in a
speech of 1933 which discussed Islam, only a few paragraphs
were spent on its nature, and those emphasized its modernity:
it was a "democratic" religion, God having called for "consultation" (al-shura) among believers; it was egalitarian,
promoting "absolute equality" among its adherents through the
Quran's having said that all Muslims were equal; finally it
was a "socialist religion" through its alms-tax (zakah).[102]
In fine, Husayn was able to find in Islam whatever good
qualities he wished to find in it, and he seems to have wished

to find virtues relating to the affairs of this world rather than to the transcendent. As a speech of his of 1935 put it, "it [Islam] is that which teaches us the meaning of ruling, of consultation, democracy, equality, freedom, and brotherhood. It is that which teaches us the systematic and beneficial socialism of the zakah."[103]   From these characteristics there appears what was to be a persistent feature of Young Egypt's propaganda throughout the 1930's; the attributing to Islam of primarily utilitarian features, ones which would establish its suitability as a twentieth-century belief system through emphasis on its secular efficacy in comparison to contemporary schools of thought.

In the later 1930's, the movement came to give a much more prominent place to Islam than it had accorded it in its early years. We have already discussed the political factors behind the movement's changing public orientation which resulted in the Young Egypt Party becoming the Islamic Nationalist Party in 1940.[104] This shift in orientation was accompanied by a greater concern for Islam in the movement's propaganda, with the movement eventually coming to make the general demand that the laws of Egypt be made to correspond with Islamic principles and with it going on to advocate specific "Islamic" reforms which it felt would purify Egyptian life.

The idea of a return to the Islamic Sacred Law as the legislative basis of Egyptian life became a tenet of the movement's propaganda during 1938. Speeches and articles from early 1938 spoke of Islam as "taking first place in our struggle" or of the necessity for "Islamic legislation" to "reign supreme in this country."[105] But it was with the party reorganization of late 1938 the idea of the supremacy of Islamic law within Egypt became a fixed principle of the movement. A speech by Husayn of November 1938 set down what was to be the movement's public credo for the next few years: "We say that God and the Quran are the source of all authority. . . . It is the Shari'ah to which we are obedient. We wish, brothers, to abolish existing laws and to return to Islamic law."[106] A similar statement was given as one of the first of the movement's official demands in its new program of March 1940: "The laws of the state must all be based on the Islamic Shari'ah or on what is not in opposition to the Islamic Shari'ah."[107]

The leading characteristics of the Islam which the movement was now championing so assiduously remained largely what they had been in the occasional earlier references to Islam made by spokesmen for Young Egypt; attributes more secular and material than religious or spiritual. The egalitarian nature of Islam was perhaps its most important feature to the men of Young Egypt in the late 1930's. In their vision of Islam, "no discrimination is permitted between race and race, between a free man and a slave, between the high and the humble, between a king and a subject, between the ruler and the ruled, between rich and poor."108 The movement's spokesmen constantly postulated a link between this egalitarian religion and the attainment of social justice in contemporary Egypt, with a return to Islamic practices being the best way to correct the injustices of Egyptian society. In their desire to "exterminate the contradictions and marked disparities in Egyptian life" and to "restore equalibrium to Egyptian society," they held that such a ". . . restoration [should] be soundly built on the basis of Islamic virtue, cooperation, and brotherhood, [all of] which should become the foundation of Egyptian life."109 Finally, they found in traditional Islamic concepts like the alms-tax or the ban on usury the indispensible mechanisms for the restoration of social justice in Egypt, with medieval concepts like the zakah being seen as the rationale for a system of modern social justice:

> . . . the right of society to take from the rich,
> gentlemen, is not arbitrary, nor is it an invention
> of Europe or a result of the teachings of socialism
> or communism. Rather, it is based on the precepts
> of the higher religions. . . . What is occurring in
> Europe in the way of the imposition of taxes on the
> rich is nothing but a clear application of the
> Quran.110

Thus letting "the heterogenetic appear as orthogenetic,"111 the spokesmen of the movement went on to demand specific "Islamic" reforms which they wished to see enforced in Egyptian society. The most authoritative detailing of their religious demands was given in the new program of the Islamic Nationalist Party of March 1940.112 After setting down the basic premise cited above (that "the laws of the state must all be based on the Islamic Shari'ah or on what is not in opposition to the Islamic Shari'ah"), the program gave the essential elements of such a reconstruction of the laws of the state. The system of government was dealt with only briefly, the program demanding that Egypt's government should be "a constitutional one in which the people enjoy true freedom, equality, and consultation." To provide for that, it called for a special commission of Muslim scholars, legists and lay lawyers to draft a new set of fundamental laws for Egypt, one which would establish "a single court system and a single set of laws for all residents" with the exception of the personal law of the non-Muslim communities in Egypt. As part of this new legal system, the program itemized six specific reforms which it demanded should be made operative in Egyptian life: (1) the total abolition of "usury" and its replacement by a system of credit where interest was to be made dependent on the profits made by the borrower through his use of the funds lent to him; (2) the legitimization of inalienable endowments (awqaf) for "educational, social, and national" purposes only, as opposed to private awqaf established for the benefit of a family's private wealth; (3) the Islamic alms-tax (zakah) to be made "obligatory on every Egyptian"; (4) daily prayer (salah) to be practiced in all government offices; (5) the designation of Friday as the official day of rest; (6) Arabic to become the only official language of the state.

In addition to calling for the enforcement of these practices in Egyptian life, the program of 1940 also demanded the elimination of other practices which it felt to be contrary to Islam. Thus it asked that alcoholic beverages be banned from Egypt, that all forms of gambling be prohibited, that both licensed and unlicensed prostitution be stamped out, that all places of "prohibited amusements" be closed, that the arts and communications media be "purified" (presumably by government censorship), that the mixing of the sexes on bathing beaches and the like be forbidden, and that women be forced, by threat of "hard punishment," to maintain a decent and decorous appearance in public places.

These are the specifically "Islamic" reforms advocated in the Islamic Nationalist Party's new program of 1940. In addition, the program also made several other recommendations based on what were presented as traditional Muslim practice in regard to the areas of education and the family. Concerning education, the program made a radical distinction between the nature of male and female education:

The primary object of the education of the boy student is to implant in him the spirit of religion and to prepare him morally in such a way as to give him the characteristics of manliness, confidence in himself, the readiness to cooperate with the community, and the willingness to sacrifice for the sake of duty.
The object of the education of the girl student is to prepare her to be a wife capable of sharing with her husband the hardships of life and [to prepare her to be] a mother capable of raising her children and giving them the best preparation for serving the fatherland. . . .

In regard to the family, the main tenet of the 1940 program was that "the state must encourage marriage by every possible means," specifically by granting a stipend for each new child born into a family (with no limitation on number) and by eliminating barriers in the way of marriage such as exorbitant dowries, costly wedding celebrations and other "outmoded customs." Within the family, the traditional distinction between the roles of men and women made in regard to education was paralleled, the husband being termed "the master of the family" to whom "absolute obedience" was due ("within the limits of the Islamic Sacred Law") by other family members, the wife being cited as deserving of "respect and affection" from her husband but being placed in a position definitely subordinate to the male.

The most interesting question concerning this much greater commitment by the movement to religious reform in Egypt at the end of the 1930's is why the men of Young Egypt made "Islamic" reform such a major part of their program. Motivation is complex, of course: in most cases men are prompted to do what they do by a multiplicity of factors conscious and unconscious, calculated and emotional. In the case of Young Egypt's advocacy of religious reform, purely political factors undoubtedly played some role; the parallelism between Young Egypt's demands and the ideas of "an Islamic ordering of rule" emanating from Palace circles at the same time is considerable,[113] and the movement placed greater emphasis on Islam at precisely the time when it was beginning to feel the challenge of the even-more-Islamically-oriented Muslim Brotherhood. Nor can a genuinely moral concern be ruled out; the leaders of Young Egypt were Muslims, and their movement had always expressed a concern with the integrity of the Muslim values and customs which they saw as being threatened by the alien and "materialist" civilization of the West. In addition to these factors, however, it also seems that the heightened religious orientation of the movement in the later 1930's was produced by the perception that "religious" reform would help to satisfy two other, more worldly desires – first the movement's intense nationalism which wished to assert Egyptian worth, dignity, and autonomy in the face of an all-powerful West which had for so long belittled worth, destroyed dignity, and encroached on autonomy, and secondly its increasingly radical commitment to the realization of a greater measure of "social justice" in Egypt.

That the men of Young Egypt were using Islamic reform in this instrumental fashion is indicated by the highly selective nature of their discussion of Islam. Young Egypt's concern with Islam was quite shallow, with the movement's propaganda having very little to say in the way of interpreting the principles of the faith or of evaluating Islamic institutions. When the movement's spokesmen analyzed Islam, they did so largely in secular terms; that it was an "egalitarian," a "democratic," or a "socialist" religion. When they dealt with existing Islamic institutions such as <u>al-Azhar</u> or the

Shari'ah court system, they championed their existence and
called for their strengthening, but without offering any
critical reassessment of the institutions themselves. Thus
the section of the program of 1940 which dealt with al-Azhar
differed little from the section concerning Egypt's secular
schools, the main demand in regard to both being that they be
expanded and improved and that they do more work with foreign
students from other Arabic and Islamic countries. Nothing
was said about al-Azhar's problems, its reform or any
transcendental purpose which it might be serving; instead
it was viewed as a vehicle for expanding Egypt's influence
in the world around her. In fine, the men of Young Egypt did
not reinterpret: they reasserted - and that which they
reasserted involved either the reinstitution of practices or
the reinvigoration of institutions which would be useful in
the secular reform of Egypt internally or in the enhancement
of Egypt's prestige externally.

When we turn from what the movement did not say to what
it did say, there are sufficient statements made by spokesmen
of the movement which directly link its demands for Islamic
reform to the issues of nationalism and social justice to
indicate that a major factor producing Young Egypt's Islamic
orientation was that orientation's perceived usefulness as
an instrument in the material reformation of Egypt. Thus
Ahmad Husayn's speech of November 1938 which explained the
reorganization and new orientation of his party directly
coupled Young Egypt's heightened emphasis on Islam with the
evils of the corrupt upper classes: "We wish to abolish
wine, and to outlaw gambling and all forbidden things, at
this time when Egypt is filled with them and when they form
an indivisible part of the life of our ministers, our rulers,
and our rich."[114] Mustafa al-Wakil made the connection
between religious reform and social justice more explicit in
an editorial about Husayn's arrest for inciting the
destruction of taverns in 1939:

> He was arrested because he called for fighting
> against wine and for the combatting of bad things.
> He was jailed because he worked and struggled in
> the path of the Lord and for the teachings of
> Islam. . . . Indeed, he was jailed because many
> of the rulers and ministers are immersed in
> pleasure-seeking and depravity, in enjoying
> themselves at dances and parties, occupying
> themselves with wine, women, gambling and at the
> racecourses contrary to the interests of the
> miserable, starving people.[115]

The "fundamental goal" of the movement's new program of 1940 gave clearest expression to this linkage, specifically stating that the aim of the party's Islamic reforms was the achievement of Egyptian greatness externally and a just society internally:

> The program of the party undertakes to realize the greatest possible amount of moral and material strength for the country on the one hand, and to spread social justice among all classes of the people on the other hand, adopting as the basis for these achievements the exalted Islamic Sacred Law and its provisions.[116]

Thus the Islamic orientation of the movement at the end of the 1930's was as much a means as an end, a means to the achievement of the essentially secular concerns of reasserting Egyptian independence and autonomy vis-à-vis the foreigner and of improving the position of the peasant and the worker vis-à-vis the upper classes of Egypt. In a sense, the end returns to the beginning: the problem which had agitated the movement at its inception in 1933 was still its primary concern in 1940, except that in the intervening years its views of the dimensions of the problem had broadened. In 1933, the men of Young Egypt had viewed the major problem of modern Egypt as being the perpetual struggle between the oppressed Egyptian and the exploiting foreigner. By 1940, after the formal solutions of the problem of independence (in the Anglo-Egyptian Treaty of 1936) and of the problem of foreign privilege (in the Montreux Convention of 1937) had been achieved but Egypt still remained a nation where "fifteen million Egyptians work like slaves for the benefit of two million, or less, of foreigners, of the rich, of the high officials, ministers and pashas,"[117] the men of Young Egypt came to believe that the malady of their country was more indigenous than they had at first imagined, and consequently they came to include within the scope of their attack the Egyptian upper classes. To fight against both the foreign oppressor and his native ally, they adopted selected proposals from the contemporary exemplar of European fascism as the basis of an economic solution and an even more select set of social customs from the enormous tapestry that is Islam as the foundation of the social and moral reconstruction of Egyptian society.

Interlude: Young Egypt
During the Second World War

The tenor of Egyptian political life during the six long years of World War II was significantly different from what it had been in the preceding decade and a half of the parliamentary monarchy. Although Egypt did not become a belligerent until the closing days of the war (February 26, 1945), from 1939 onwards the country was deeply involved in the hostilities, serving as a major staging area for the Allied powers as well as being an occasional theater of combat. Internally, the massive British military presence and the need to maintain a secure Egypt as a base produced almost a moratorium on parliamentary politics as they had operated in the 1920's and 1930's. From one side successive Egyptian governments, through martial law and censorship, arrests and forced residency in the countryside, exercised greater control over potential internal opponents than before. From their side the British insured, by force if necessary, Egyptian ministries which would collaborate with the British war effort, then greatly reinforced the efforts of these ministries in controlling Egyptian political life. Competition between political parties, individual politicians and the Palace did not cease during the war; but Egyptian public life lost its more visible characteristics of vigorous public attack and counterattack, frequent public protest, and occasional violence, coming to be conducted in more subdued and conspiratorial conditions due to the exigencies of wartime.[1]

The constriction of Egyptian politics during the war years had particularly serious effects for a movement like Young Egypt, given its militant style of political operation and appeal. Martial law and press censorship were put into effect in early September 1939, and they terminated the party's 1939 campaigns on the issues of unIslamic practices and Palestine.[2] The boycott of Jewish merchants which had been sponsored by the party's press in the summer of 1939 was discontinued due to press censorship. Although it continued to call for restrictions on practices contrary to Islam, the party's newspaper no longer incited its readers to direct action in order to attain an Islamic society in Egypt. It adopted a much more muted tone in wartime, limiting itself to saying that it "regrets" the inaction of the government in moving against "forbidden things."[3]

But Young Egypt was able to continue its less disruptive
activities until well into the war years. Exactly at the
outbreak of the war, the party realized an old ambition: on
September 2, 1939, Jaridah Misr al-Fatah became a daily
newspaper. It functioned as such for only a few months,
however. On November 22, admitting that the production of
a daily consumed too much of its resources, the party made
its paper a bi-weekly.[4] From that point on, the journalistic
activity of the party showed a steady decline through the
early years of the war; by early 1941, a reduced-in-size
Jaridah Misr al-Fatah was appearing irregularly, on the average
of once a week. This decline was in large part due to the
emasculation of the party's journalistic content because of
wartime censorship, the once-vigorous and sometimes-scurrilous
journal being reduced to printing war news taken from standard
sources and general pieces on society and culture in place
of its former controversial attacks on individuals and
institutions. The government threatened the suspension of the
party's journal at least once, in November 1939, and apparently
the threat was enough to keep the publication in line.[5] From
March to June 1940 the journal had to sever its formal
connection with the party, a maneuver which allowed it to
continue publication while the party's book and pamphlet
publications were suppressed by the government.[6]

As the censorship circumscribed the propaganda activities
of the party, so the martial law in effect in Egypt from the
start of the war imposed limitations on the physical activities
undertaken by Young Egypt. The party was allowed considerable
freedom of assembly. Its clubhouses in Cairo, Alexandria
and other cities were able to continue to function, holding
meetings, giving lecture series, and hosting speeches by
party leaders. In late 1939, new provincial branches of the
party were still being formed, and in both 1940 and 1941 the
party was able to hold its annual overnight assembly at the
Pyramids.[7] But the subject of meetings and the content of
speeches or lectures, at least those which were published
and reported upon, were strictly a-political after the start
of the war, and martial law did effectively prevent the
holding of large public meetings by the party. The largest
public meeting reported for Young Egypt during the war years
was one attended by five hundred persons according to the
party's own estimate - a far cry from the thousands estimated
in attendance at Young Egypt's major meetings back in 1938.[8]

The most important public development within Young Egypt
in the war years was the party's formal change of name to the
Islamic Nationalist Party in March 1940. As we have indicated,
the change of name and the adoption of a new program which
accompanied it were the last step in the movement's defensive
effort to combat the appeal of the Muslim Brotherhood on its

own ground, that of the defense of Islam, which it had begun in 1938.[9] The success of the attempt seems to have been marginal, however, the movement's new religious emphasis not setting off any great groundswell of public support for the Islamic Nationalist Party. Both before and after the change of name, Ahmad Husayn and other party leaders were in some demand as speakers before other organizations of an Islamic orientation, delivering lectures on such subjects as "Islamic Unity," "Islamic Virtue," or "The Duties of a Muslim Youth."[10] In 1940 and 1941 Husayn made the pilgrimage to Mecca, in both years delivering public addresses while there, speeches non-political in the narrow sense but emphasizing the need for closer cooperation between Muslims for the sake of the defense of Islam.[11] But on the whole the early years of the war seem to have seen a continued drop in the movement's influence and following in Egypt. With its propaganda gutted by censorship, its militant activities and its ability to mount protests curtailed by martial law, and its new Islamic orientation presumably alienating some of its former clientele, the period between the beginning of the war in September 1939 and the total suppression of the movement in May 1941 was one of continued decline for Young Egypt/the Islamic Nationalist Party as an organized movement.

Beyond its public operations in the early years of the war, Young Egypt was also involved in clandestine political activities. The all-important new condition created for Egyptian politics by World War II was the threat of the invasion of Egypt by Italy and/or Germany and the resultant replacement of British hegemony by Axis domination. Faced with this possibility, a variety of individuals and groups in Egypt engaged in two types of secret activity. The first was in establishing contacts with the Axis powers, either to obtain their assistance in furthering internal resistance to the British or to assure Egypt or (more frequently) individual politicians in Egypt of the most favorable position possible if Axis armies should conquer Egypt. The second was in undertaking preparations for physical resistance to the British, when and if the circumstances of war should give violent opposition to the British any chance of success.

Egyptian contacts with the Axis powers is the best-known aspect of the sub rosa politics of the war years, thanks primarily to the availability of German archival materials and partially published Italian diplomatic records. Secret contacts with the Axis powers, particularly in the years 1941 and 1942 when Axis arms were having their greatest successes in North Africa, have been definitely established for two major Egyptian political groupings; first the Egyptian Palace and some of the politicians associated with it, secondly for nationalist circles in the Egyptian Army.[12]

In terms of Young Egypt/the Islamic Nationalist Party, there is as yet no evidence indicating direct contact between the movement and the Axis powers in this period. As in regard to the years before the war, such contact, particularly with Axis agencies other than the German or Italian Foreign Ministries, is not impossible; but the material currently available gives no indication of Young Egypt's having dealt directly with the Germans or the Italians.[13]

But external dealings with Germany and Italy were not the only form of activity directed against the British presence in Egypt during the war years. In addition, a variety of Egyptian groups undertook either preparations for eventual anti-British revolt or actual sabotage operations directed against the British military.[14] This is the aspect of clandestine Egyptian wartime politics more relevant for Young Egypt, for here there is no question that the movement was involved in such secret preparations for anti-British activity and that its actions in this respect were of great significance to the movement itself, indeed leading to its total suppression in May 1941.

There is considerable evidence of preparations for eventual resistance to the British presence in Egypt being undertaken by Young Egypt in the early years of the war. Young Egypt's leadership and some of its following were definitely involved in the illegal accumulation of arms in 1939 and 1940. Even before the war, arms caches had been discovered by the police and members of Young Egypt arrested in connection with them.[15] For the period after the war had begun, a British Intelligence report mentions the party's Vice-President Mustafa al-Wakil as having built up a supply of arms in his home,[16] and postwar books by Ahmad Husayn and Muhammad Subayh confirm that Wakil was the party's chief agent in buying and secreting black-market and stolen arms in more than one cache.[17] At least one party member was arrested in 1940 for possessing an illegal horde of explosives in his home.[18]

The first claim of specific anti-British activity being planned by Young Egypt refers to 1940, after the German Blitzkrieg in Western Europe and Italy's belated entry into the war (June 10, 1940) faced Great Britain with seemingly impossible odds. In his fictionalized memoirs, Husayn claims to have met with Hasan al-Banna of the Muslim Brotherhood in mid-1940 and to have tried to persuade the Brotherhood to join Young Egypt in an uprising which would first seize local centers, gather arms and momentum, and then proceed to try to drive the British from Cairo, this "revolt" to occur as soon as the Germans invaded the British Isles.[19] While much of what is contained in Husayn's al-Duktur Khalid is historically verifiable by other data, this tale is unmentioned in any other source, including the other postwar

82

writings of Ahmad Husayn, and as such it seems highly
unlikely that it accurately reflects the intentions of
Husayn and his movement in 1940.

But this account, while dubious as an accurate indication
of what Young Egypt may have been considering in 1940, may
bear some resemblance to what the movement was planning, in
conjunction with other forces, by 1941. It is for the spring
of 1941 that there is prima facie evidence of a possible
anti-British uprising being planned in Egypt. The only
non-ex post facto report of revolt against the British in
Egypt dates from April 1941, in a communication from the
exiled Mufti of Jerusalem, al-Hajj Amin al-Husayni, to the
Axis. The Mufti, at that time a leader of the pan-Arabist and
anti-British circle in Baghdad which was about to attempt an
Iraqi break with Great Britain, claimed that the Egyptian
Generals 'Aziz 'Ali al-Misri and Muhammad Salih Harb were
then in the process of organizing an anti-British revolt in
Egypt, "in agreement with some of King Faruq's closest
advisors, such as 'Ali Mahir, and with the help of part of
the Army and irregular forces."[20]

To what extent did this message from Baghdad reflect
Egyptian reality? While a definitive answer to this question
cannot be given, there is circumstantial evidence to indicate
that such an uprising may have been in the planning stages
in early 1941. Certainly the time was propitious for
anti-British action: Axis forces successfully went on the
offensive in the Western Desert and in the Balkans by April
1941, thereby beginning to put Britain's military position in
jeopardy and raising the possibility that the Axis might soon
be in a position to aid an internal Egyptian revolt against
the British. By early 1941, the individuals and groups
mentioned in the Mufti's report were in some degree of
contact with each other, this making plausible the organization of anti-British action. General Misri in particular
seems to have been the linchpin of communication between the
various anti-British elements in Egypt in the early years of
the war, being in contact with the Germans, with the
nationalist circles in the Egyptian Army, with the Egyptian
Palace through 'Ali Mahir, and with civilian organizations
which the Mufti may have had in mind in his reference to
"irregular forces"; i.e., the Muslim Brotherhood and Young
Egypt. Ahmad Husayn reports having met with Misri in the
early years of the war and being encouraged by him to "gather
arms and practice using them, for the hour [of revolt] is
coming, there is no doubt of it," and Misri took refuge when
a fugitive later in 1941 in the home of a member of Young
Egypt.[21] Postwar memoirs also claim that an anti-British
uprising was being considered in Egypt in early 1941. Anwar
al-Sadat has stated that the younger officers in the Egyptian

Army wished to attack the British at the time of the
Anglo-Iraqi hostilities (May 1941), although he also claims
that it was General Misri who dissuaded them from actually
doing so at that juncture.[22] Among civilians, Muhammad
Subayh of Young Egypt has written of "the Egyptian revolution
which was in preparation" at the time of "the Iraqi revolution" and asserted that the youths arrested in Egypt in May
1941 on suspicion of anti-British activities (a group which
included Subayh himself) "were in reality preparing for this
step [of revolt]."[23] From the other side the British
security officer Alfred Sansom claims to have received
information that a revolt, primarily by Egyptian Army
elements, was being planned early in 1941, and records his
feeling that "nothing could stave off an Egyptian Army
revolt, I thought, when I heard the news on May 2nd [1941]
that Iraqi troops had opened fire on the RAF base at
Habbaniya."[24]

Finally, the Mufti's report of a planned uprising in
Egypt may not have been merely speculation from a distance.
Hajj Amin was in contact with at least one of the groups
which had been preparing for anti-British resistance in
Egypt prior to 1941, namely Young Egypt. In November 1940
Mustafa al-Wakil went to Baghdad to assume a teaching post
at the Baghdad Teacher's College.[25] According to his
colleagues' later accounts, he had been sent to Iraq by Young
Egypt in order to establish contact with the galaxy of Arab
nationalist leaders assembled in Iraq in the early years of
the war.[26] This he did, meeting the Mufti and others and
contributing articles to the Iraqi press in the winter of
1940-1941.[27] Shortly after the coup of April 1-2, 1941 had
placed Rashid 'Ali al-Kilani and his colleagues in power in
Iraq, a telegram of congratulations from Young Egypt to the
new Iraqi regime appeared in the Baghdad newspaper al-Bilad.[28]
Whatever the telegram's provenance - whether it was actually
sent by the party from Egypt or whether it was the doing of
Wakil without the party's knowledge (as Husayn later claimed)[29] -
it was soon followed by a more serious declaration by the
Islamic Nationalist Party's Vice-President. On May 2, 1941,
the month-long war between British and Iraqi forces began;
on May 5, Wakil made a radio broadcast from Baghdad calling
on his Egyptian countrymen to rise against the British.[30]
Given Wakil's connection with the Mufti (which was to last
through the war years),[31] his party's known preparations for
anti-British action in at least the form of collecting arms
in 1939-1940, the later claims of contemporaries that some
sort of revolt was in preparation, and the Mufti's 1941
report of an uprising being planned in Egypt, Wakil's
broadcast appears not merely as the pious hope of a voluntary
exile but as a serious appeal from one group of anti-British

Arab nationalists (those in Iraq) to another such group
(those in Egypt) that the time for parallel anti-British
action had come.

There is yet one other factor which lends credence to the
Mufti's report of a revolt being planned in Egypt in the
spring of 1941; the action of the British. For Wakil's
summons to revolt was answered in Egypt not by an uprising,
but by a crackdown of unparalleled severity. By May 7 (only
two days after Wakil's broadcast from Baghdad), the Egyptian
and British security services began to take action against
potentially anti-British elements in Egypt. 'Ali Mahir was
ordered out of Cairo to his country estate by military order;
his associate 'Abd al-Rahman 'Azzam was dismissed as head of
the Territorial Army (a reserve force established at the
start of the war); and the two leading figures of the Muslim
Brotherhood, Hasan al-Banna and Ahmad al-Sukkari, were sent
out of Cairo.[32] On May 15-16 the architect of collaboration
between the various anti-British groups in Egypt, General
Misri, attempted to flee from Egypt to join the Axis, only
to fail and to be forced to go into hiding until his arrest
on June 6, 1941.[33] But security measures were most severe
in regard to the Islamic Nationalist Party: in May 1941 its
newspaper was suspended, and most of its leadership and many
of its members were arrested.[34]

The relative harshness of the authorities towards Young
Egypt/the Islamic Nationalist Party may have been a function
of its generally obstreperous past history and of the greater
excuse for repression given by the party's Vice-President in
his radio broadcast calling for revolt in Egypt. But it
also may have been prompted by British knowledge that something was underway in early 1941, and that Young Egypt was
part of it. From the vagueness of references to revolt in
1941 in the postwar memoirs of the younger nationalists
involved (men whose postwar writings have been eager to
stress their opposition to the British during the war), it
seems most likely that any uprising was in the talking stage,
with the groundwork between Army elements, the notables
linked to 'Ali Mahir and the Palace, and the "irregular
force" only in the process of being laid down, and with the
outline of a course of action (perhaps one similar to the
"plan" attributed by Husayn in his memoirs to 1940) only
being developed. Whatever action was in the process of
preparation, however, was forestalled by the countermeasures
of the authorities in May 1941.

From the security crackdown of May 1941 until late 1944,
Young Egypt or the Islamic Nationalist Party simply ceased
to exist as an organized movement. Its press was inoperative;
some two hundred of its adherents were taken into custody in
May 1941, with approximately thirty of the more important of

these being incarcerated until well into 1944;[35] and there are
no reports of meetings or other public activities by the
followers of the movement who did remain at liberty in the
later years of the war.

Thus there are only a few developments of interest
concerning the movement from 1941 to 1944. One of these is
the activities of its Vice-President Mustafa al-Wakil.
When the Kilani government in Iraq collapsed in late May
1941, Wakil accompanied its leaders into exile. With Hajj
Amin al-Husayni, he made his way from Iraq to Iran, then to
Turkey, Rome and eventually Berlin.[36] While ostensibly the
head of an "Islamic Institute" in Berlin, in mid-1942 Wakil
played an important role in conveying German messages to King
Faruq, and in 1943 and 1944 he served as an assistant to the
Mufti in the latter's negotiations with the Italians and
Germans.[37] Wakil was killed in a bombing raid on Berlin on
the night of March 3, 1945.[38]

In Egypt, the security services seem to have had little
difficulty in their internment of the leaders and activists
of Young Egypt in 1941, with the notable exception of Ahmad
Husayn himself. Husayn eluded arrest in May 1941 by fleeing
Cairo for the Delta, where he posed as an Azharite until
eventually apprehended in August 1941.[39] In June 1942, he
escaped from internment and was at liberty for a few months,
until he turned himself over to the Wafdist government when
he tired of the life of a fugitive.[40] These adventures,
while testifying to the ingenuity of the President of Young
Egypt, were apparently of no political significance; in none
of his later works does Husayn claim to have done anything
but concentrate on evading arrest while at liberty.

The most significant development within the moribund
movement between 1941 and 1944 was the definitive split of
Fathi Radwan from the party in 1942. Having largely withdrawn
from active participation in the party by 1939, Radwan seems
to have nothing to do with the preparations for anti-British
action which Young Egypt was undertaking in the early years
of the war. When the other leaders of the party were interned
in May 1941, Radwan spent only a few days in detention before
being released.[41] His formal resignation from the party came
in 1942. When the Wafd returned to power in February 1942
(through the medium of British intervention), Husayn sent
letters of congratulation to the Wafdist leaders, apparently
hoping to obtain his and his colleagues' release from internment through a rapprochement with the new ministry. However,
the Wafdist newspaper al-Misri published what Husayn later
claimed was an edited version of the letters, making them
appear as an outright endorsement of the ministry which had
just been elevated to power by British tanks.[42] This apparent
act of political expediency by Husayn was the cause of a public

break by Radwan with him; shortly thereafter, Radwan announced his resignation from the party.[43] Under the influence of the departure of one of the more appealing of the prewar leaders of the movement, other members of the party (most notably Nur al-Din Tarraf, a student leader of Young Egypt at the Egyptian University in the 1930's and later a Vice-President of the United Arab Republic) also disassociated themselves from the movement at the same time.

The events of 1941 and 1942 spelled the end of Young Egypt as a meaningful political movement for the next several years. The party's President and its most active members were in jail; its Vice-President was in exile, never to return; its Secretary-General had resigned, as had part of the party's membership which was still at large. It was the further misfortune of the movement that this collapse occurred at precisely the time when internal Egyptian conditions became most auspicious for the growth of the movement, had it been functioning and able to capitalize on those conditions.[44] The influx of pleasure-seeking Allied soldiers to Cairo and Alexandria, and their behavior while there; the industrial expansion of the war years and the enormous population growth in Egypt's cities; the periodic food shortages and the inflation which accompanied the war; the speculation and profiteering to which the war gave rise, along with the conspicuous consumption of the upper classes (made more galling to the vast majority of the population by their own privation); and the obvious assertion of British power over Egyptian politics and politicians during the war which demonstrated the impotence of the Egyptian parliamentary monarchy as a regime capable of asserting and maintaining genuine Egyptian independence – these wartime developments combined to create a mood of bitterness and frustration among urban-dwelling Egyptians and to provide a fertile field for the expansion of a vigorously nationalist, xenophobic and populist movement such as Young Egypt had been in the 1930's. Young Egypt was not on the scene to benefit from these circumstances, however, and so lost the opportunity to intrench itself as a mass movement.

Young Egypt/The Socialist Party
of Egypt, 1944-1952

The Egyptian political world into which Young Egypt
reemerged towards the end of World War II was one significantly
different from that of the interwar period.[1] With a monarch
widely regarded as both reactionary and degenerate, with a
Wafd weakened by its collaboration with the British during
the war as well as by increasingly serious internal differences of opinion between its conservative and liberal wings,
and with none of the non-Wafdist parties of the older
generation developing any meaningful socio-economic program
or demonstrating any great popular appeal, the establishment
which had ruled Egypt since the 1920's had undergone a
precipitous decline by the postwar period. In opposition to
these older forces playing their "game of revenge" induced
by twenty years of partisan and personal rivalry,[2] a variety
of newer movements - a surging Muslim Brotherhood which had
several hundred thousand adherents by the later 1940's;
several leftist/Marxist organizations with ties to a growing
urban laboring population and to students; and various smaller
political groups midway between these extremes - had emerged
by the war's end. Although these latter groups spanned the
political spectrum, offering radically different programs of
change for postwar Egypt, they all shared a common antipathy
to the institutions of the seemingly bankrupt parliamentary
monarchy and its ruling elite. In a sense, the Egyptian
parliamentary monarchy was dead before the military coup of
July 1952; dead because the generation inheriting it had lost
all hope in it.

It was into this fragmented political arena that Young
Egypt resurfaced in late 1944, after over three years of
suppression by the authorities. That portion of the party's
leadership which had been interned since May 1941 was
released from detention between April and September 1944.[3]
In October, the publication of Jaridah Misr al-Fatah was
resumed and a new organizational law was drafted for the
movement.[4] Local branches began to be reconstituted towards
the end of 1944.

The postwar Young Egypt was a significantly different
organization from what the movement had been in the 1933-1941
period. The "Islamic" aspects emphasized in its propaganda
in the later 1930's and early 1940's were largely abandoned
after the war, the movement calling itself "Young Egypt"

rather than the "Islamic Nationalist Party" and dropping its religiously oriented program of March 1940. With the exception of Ahmad Husayn, who remained the party's President and primary spokesman, the leadership of the party shows little continuity with that of the 1930's. Of the twenty members of the reconstituted party's Administrative Council (majlis al-idarah) in November 1944, only four had been members of that body in 1939.[5] But, although there had been considerable individual turnover in the movement's leadership, the nature of that leadership remained much the same as in the prewar period. The occupations of members of the Administrative Council in late 1944 were much the same as those which the movement's 1930's leadership had had: the bulk of the Council came from the educated and Westernized sector of Egypt's population (seven lawyers, one doctor, two civil engineers, four agricultural engineers, one merchant and one journalist - all university graduates), with only four members of more traditional backgrounds (two 'ulama and two artisans).[6] Young Egypt continued to be, after the war as before it, a movement dominated by Egypt's Westernized effendis.

The party had only a minuscule active following in the immediate postwar period, after three years of forced inactivity had given its rivals bidding for the attention of the new generation an irreversible advantage over it. Material from the party's press indicates fewer local branches of Young Egypt existing in 1944-1945 than there had been at any time in the later 1930's,[7] and the circulation of the party's journal in 1945 was reported to have been "very small."[8] Some indication of the party's limited postwar appeal may be obtained from considering its experience in the parliamentary elections of January 1945. It offered six candidates for the Chamber of Deputies, four in Cairo constituencies and two in Alexandria; all were defeated (although Ahmad Husayn forced a runoff election in his constituency before losing).[9] Young Egypt was thus unrepresented in Parliament until one of its candidates was elected in 1950.

A marginal party with a minimal following, minus much of its prewar leadership, unrepresented in Parliament, and dwarfed by new movements both to the right and left of it, Young Egypt was an unimportant element in Egyptian public life in the period from 1945 to 1949. In brief, it functioned as a minor component of the Egyptian nationalist opposition to the several ministries led by non-Wafdist parties and politicians of the late 1940's, playing a role of incitation and agitation in the successive crises over Egypt's relations with Great Britain, the Sudan, and the Palestine problem, but not being anywhere as significant as a shaper of the attitudes and actions of younger Egyptians as it had been in the later 1930's.

The dominant Egyptian political issue from the end of the war in 1945 until late 1947 was the question of Egypt's relationship with Great Britain.[10] From late 1945 onwards, a variety of nationalist elements - the Wafd (then out of office); the Muslim Brotherhood; ephemeral students and workers groups; and the socialist movements of the postwar period - agitated to force the British and the insufficiently "nationalist" Egyptian ministries of the postwar period to terminate the still-considerable British military presence in Egypt and the Sudan. Massive demonstrations aimed at the British presence occurred throughout 1946 in particular, indeed forcing the resignation of two successive ministries (that of Mahmud Fahmi al-Nuqrashi in February 1946, that of Isma'il Sidqi in November 1946), until in 1947 a new Nuqrashi ministry took Egypt's case against Great Britain to the United Nations, where an Egyptian appeal for international action against the British eventually failed.

In this turbulence of 1945-1947, Young Egypt took (as might be expected) a vehemently nationalist stance, demanding the immediate and total withdrawal of British troops from Egypt and the Sudan and calling for Egyptians to "Boycott everything that is English! Hate everything that is English!"[11] But Young Egypt had largely lost touch with the student and worker population which played the major role in the massive protests of 1946. It was not represented in the major body which coordinated protests, the "National Committee of Workers and Students" (al-lajnah al-wataniyah lil-'ummal wa al-talabah) formed in February 1946,[12] and Ahmad Husayn has admitted that his party played no role in the largest single demonstration of the immediate postwar years, that of February 21, 1946.[13] Rather, Young Egypt associated itself with the "Nationalist Committee" (al-lajnah al-qawmiyah) formed in March 1946, which was dominated by the Muslim Brotherhood and which opposed the more leftist National Committee of Workers and Students.[14] By late 1946, after Premier Sidqi had suppressed the National Committee of Workers and Students and the leftist movements in Egypt generally, Young Egypt may have played a more important part in nationalist protest than it had earlier in the year. It was one of several groups which denounced Sidqi's draft treaty with the British, and the demonstrations of late 1946 which finally toppled the Sidqi ministry show something of Young Egypt's political style (attacks on Western establishments, the destruction of symbols of European influence such as English-language books), although the dominant influence in the demonstrations of late 1946 was undoubtedly the Muslim Brotherhood rather than Young Egypt.[15] The party continued to direct the bulk of its attention to the nationalist issue

90

through 1947, Ahmad Husayn spending the period from January
to June 1947 in the United States propagandizing for Egypt
with the American public (a speaking-tour from coast to
coast; meeting with members of Congress; the placing of a
full-page editorial advertisement in the New York Times),[16]
and later in 1947 the party joined with other nationalist
groups in a campaign of non-cooperation with the British and
a boycott of British goods as long as British troops should
remain on Egyptian or Sudanese soil.[17]

By late 1947 there was another issue which came to
dominate Egyptian attention. This was the Palestine problem,
which reached its culmination with the United Nations parti-
tion of Palestine in November 1947 and the subsequent
fighting between Arabs and Jews from late 1947 to early 1949.
As had been the case in the later 1930's, Young Egypt's
sympathy for the Arab cause expressed itself partially in
anti-Jewish sentiment, the party's journal publishing
boycott-lists of Jewish merchants in Egypt similar to what
it had done in 1939.[18] But the party also participated more
directly in the struggle for Palestine: it collected money
to buy arms for the Palestinian Arabs in early 1948, raised
a volunteer group (named after its former Vice-President
Mustafa al-Wakil) which trained in Syria and which participated in the irregular warfare in Palestine which preceded the
birth of Israel and the "official" war between it and the
Arab states from May 1948 onwards, and other groups of
volunteers raised by Young Egypt fought on the Sinai-Palestine
border alongside the larger volunteer units of the Muslim
Brotherhood.[19] Ahmad Husayn spent two weeks in Palestine
under the military command of the later-dictator of Syria,
Adib al-Shishakli, but without seeing military action.[20]
Young Egypt's role in the struggle for Palestine should not
be exaggerated, however: in the agitation over Palestine in
1947-1948 the party was but one, and far from the most important, of the Egyptian nationalist groups involved.

There is little reliable evidence as to Young Egypt's
role in the crescendo of assassination and terrorism which
developed internally in Egypt in the later 1940's.[21] The only
arrests of party leaders in connection with political murder
came in 1945, when much of the party's leadership was taken
into custody because of suspected complicity in the first
major political assassination of the postwar period, that of
Prime Minister Ahmad Mahir on February 24, 1945.[22] They were
released in May 1945, however, after the investigation had
found no evidence of Young Egypt being implicated in the
crime.[23] Later in the 1940's, while the party's propaganda
contributed to shaping the climate of opinion which produced
bombings in departments stores, cinemas, and the Jewish
quarter of Cairo, neither the leadership nor the following of

Young Egypt is cited as having been involved in these attacks or in the assassinations of 1948-1949 (although many of these incidents are unresolved).[24] But Young Egypt may not have been totally blameless in the internal violence of 1948-1949. When the ministry of Ibrahim 'Abd al-Hadi (December 1948 - July 1949) undertook its repression of the Muslim Brotherhood and the Egyptian left, Ahmad Husayn is reported to have had to spend part of early 1949 hiding in the countryside, only returning to public activity after the fall of the 'Abd al-Hadi ministry.[25] While Husayn's seclusion may have been no more than a reasonable precaution against the shotgun repression of the Egyptian authorities of early 1949, it could imply some involvement by Young Egypt in the domestic terrorism of 1948-1949.

The major postwar development concerning Young Egypt occurred in late 1949. In August 1949, Young Egypt changed its name (again) to "The Socialist-Democratic Party of Egypt" (hizb misr al-ishtiraki al-dimuqrati).[26] In October 1949, the name was shortened to "The Socialist Party of Egypt" (hizb misr al-ishtiraki).[27] It was as the Socialist Party of Egypt that the movement, after almost a decade of relative insignificance in Egyptian public life, again began to play a role of considerable importance in the politics of Egypt.

The internal organization of the Socialist Party shows little change from the patterns which had been followed by Young Egypt in the past. Although a new organizational law which theoretically emphasized internal democracy and the subordination of the party's leadership to its membership was drafted for the party in March 1950,[28] in reality the Socialist Party remained much what Young Egypt had been; an organization centered about and under the firm direction of its President who, through frequent speaking tours of the provinces, through public speeches at the party's Green House (the name of which remained unchanged from the 1930's), and above all through his journalistic output continued to be the prime carrier of the party's new message of "socialism." Similarly, the party's activities show much the same pattern as had marked its earlier period of growth in the later 1930's; weekly lecture series by Husayn and other party leaders, Friday assemblies for communal prayer, and by 1951 the renewal of overnight assemblies for members at the Pyramids but now with the appellation of "socialist camps."[29]

There are two indicators which may be used to measure the growth of the Socialist Party in the early 1950's. One is the number and distribution of its local branches or shu'bahs. By the end of 1951, sixty-five local branches of the party had been reported in existence in the party's press. In terms of geographical distribution, fifteen branches were

in Cairo or its environs, four in Alexandria, twenty-eight
in cities or towns in Lower Egypt, and only twelve in Upper
Egypt (six of the shu'bahs mentioned were unidentifiable by
region or province).[30] This is a much greater number of
local branches than the party had had in the immediate
postwar period, and in all probability is larger than at any
time in the later 1940's. The regional breakdown largely
conforms to the pattern which Young Egypt had demonstrated
in the 1930's, with the movement having its greatest appeal
in Egypt's two largest cities and with it possessing
considerably more non-metropolitan support in the Delta
region than in Upper Egypt.

Perhaps the best indicator of the party's growing impact
in the early 1950's is the extent of its journalistic activities, for this provides an insight not only into the extent
of the party's active following but also into its influence
among Egyptians generally. At the start of 1950, the party
was publishing only one journal, Jaridah Misr al-Fatah.
Although technically a weekly, it appeared irregularly and
had a circulation of only a few hundred copies.[31] In June
1950, its name was changed to Socialism (al-Ishtirakiyah).
Thereafter, with the increasingly vehement attacks and exposés
which it published, it more than doubled its circulation by
the fall of 1950,[32] and by January 1951 Husayn claims its
circulation had risen to 8,000 copies weekly.[33] In April 1951
the party issued a new journal, The New People (al-Sha'b
al-Jadid), which according to Husayn began publication with
weekly sales of 15,000 issues.[34] By late 1951, when the party's
two journals together appeared three times a week, a combined
circulation of between 100,000 and 200,000 copies per week
is claimed for the Socialist Party's newspapers before
government repression struck the party and its publications
from November 1951 onwards.[35] While these circulation figures
given by spokesmen of Young Egypt cannot be checked against
independent statistics, there is no reason to doubt their
approximate accuracy:[36] in the early 1950's the party played
a greater role in Egyptian politics, and a greater popularity
for its journals would be consistent with that role.

It is the Socialist Party's place in Egyptian public
life generally which is the most important aspect of its
history in the early 1950's. For the first time since the
war years, the movement ceased to be merely a minor component
of nationalist coalitions and instead became an independent
actor with a significant input into the course of Egyptian
politics. The main approaches through which the Socialist
Party increased its influence in the early 1950's were three:
the activities of its one and only Parliamentary deputy; a
renewal of its vigorous journalism which turned the party's
fire not only on a weakened Wafd but also on the monarchy

which it had supported so ardently a decade earlier; and its
ability to function as a surrogate for the then-suppressed
Muslim Brotherhood.

The movement gained the only electoral victory it was
ever to have in the parliamentary elections of January 1950,
when its Vice-President Ibrahim Shukri was elected to the
Chamber of Deputies. From a landholding family of Shirbin in
Daqahliyah Province, Shukri had spent much of his time in
Shirbin through the 1940's, building up a position as a local
leader.[37] His electoral victory in 1950 was not a sign of any
great strength on the part of the party with which he was
affiliated, but rather the more traditional triumph of a local
notable who then gave his party a new forum which was of
importance in its subsequent growth.[38] In Parliament, he
spoke out strongly on a variety of issues, placing the
Socialist Party's ideas before both Parliament and public.
In his first parliamentary speech he introduced a bill propos-
ing his party's drastic land reform proposal; that a
fifty-faddan limit be placed on landed estates in Egypt and
that estates above that limit be purchased by the state and
then redistributed to small landholders.[39] His other legislative proposals included bills for tax relief for small farmers,
for the unilateral Egyptian abrogation of the Anglo-Egyptian
Treaty of 1936, for the revision of labor laws to allow
agricultural workers to unionize and to recognize the right to
strike of all workers, for the abolition of all titles in
Egypt, and (on a less "socialist" note, but one still indicative of the orientation of his party) for "the establishment
of an institute and a factory for nuclear research and
production."[40] In addition to his legislative proposals, the
Socialist Party's deputy took several other controversial
stands in Parliament ranging from demands for Parliamentary
debate on the legality of gambling and alcoholic beverages
in Egypt to denunciations of the wedding gifts voted by
Parliament to King Faruq on his marriage to Queen Nariman and
of the government's assumption of expenses incurred in
refitting the Royal yacht for the Faruq-Nariman honeymoon.[44]

More important in the revival of the movement in the
early 1950's was the reinvigorated journalism of its press.
The more positive aspects of the movement's "socialist"
programs and ideas will be examined in the following chapter:
here we will concentrate on the polemical aspects of its
propaganda in the early 1950's, what one knowledgeable
observer has evaluated as "perhaps the most virulent newspaper
campaign Egypt has ever known."[42]

By the early 1950's, the movement's propaganda attempted
to separate the Socialist Party from the established parties
of Egypt. Its general position was that "the Socialist Party
opposes all the old parties, equally whether they are in power

94

or in opposition, because all of them are capitalist parties composed of the classes which exploit the people and act in opposition to the people."[43] The party's propaganda repeatedly attacked the life-style of Egypt's upper classes, pictures of the "corrupt capitalists" in their private clubs being published frequently in the party's journals along with denunciations of politicians who "spend their time abroad" and who "smuggle their wealth abroad and buy palaces abroad" as insurance against the day of revolution at home.[44]

It was the Wafd and the Wafdist ministry in particular which drew the major share of the Socialist Party's fire. The ministry was "more repulsive than any previous capitalist government" in favoring the upper classes and foreign interests; it was accused of having "no goal in all of its activities except that of promoting the interests of capitalism and feudalism"; worst of all, "all of what it has done is in cooperation with the English."[45] The specifics of the charges levelled against the Wafdist ministry were many; acquiescence in the continuing British occupation of the Canal Zone, the rubber-stamp nature of Parliament and its smothering of any meaningful investigation into the Palestine arms scandal, the Ministry of the Interior's attempts to suppress press opposition to the ministry, and responsibility for the inflation of the early 1950's which was "driving the small employee to starvation."[46] The Prime Minister, Mustafa al-Nahhas, was repeatedly made the personification of the way of life of the upper classes, being denounced for his trips to Europe, for his alleged friendships with "dancing-girls and beauties," for his gambling and his spending "every evening" in night-clubs.[47] Most effective in polemical terms was the coupling of the Wafd with "feudal" interests. Thus the Ministry of the Interior was accused of favoring the rich in a dispute over land sales in Qalyubiyah Province;[48] the ministry as a whole was denounced for not taking action against the conversion of agricultural lands to the production of cotton and the resultant "starvation of the peasantry";[49] and the government was decried for having "contributed twenty million pounds to [the industrialist] Ahmad 'Abbud in tax savings."[50]

In addition to its attacks on the establishment parties and the Wafdist ministry, the Socialist Party's propaganda of the early 1950's also inveighed against the Egyptian monarchy itself. The King's advisors were relatively fair game, coming under the same sort of attack as the party was directing against Egypt's upper classes in general.[51] The King himself was only indirectly criticized through 1950, in articles ostensibly directed against the ministry for violating its constitutional powers, but articles which then implicitly chided the monarch for allowing the ministry this usurpation

of power.[52] But as time passed, the party's criticism of the
monarchy became more direct. It avowed that "we are loyal
to the monarch, but within the limits of the Constitution,"
went on to suggest the creation of a ministry of Palace
Affairs to control the excesses committed (so it maintained)
in the King's name by his advisors, and eventually extended
its criticism to the behavior of the Royal Family.[53] The
party's most dramatic attack on the King came in an issue
of al-Ishtirakiyah of September 1951: its centerfold
carried two pages of pictures of children in rags, of vaga-
bonds sleeping in the gutter, of old men emaciated with hunger,
and beneath all the caption "This is your flock, oh King."[54]

The word "revolution" (thawrah) appears frequently in
the publications of the Socialist Party in the early 1950's.
After a tour of the Delta in September 1950, Husayn warned that
"there is no doubt that revolution is coming if the present
situation continues," claiming that "talk of revolution and
its necessity is to be found in the furthest and smallest
Egyptian village."[55] An article of January 1951 stated that
the Socialist Party might be forced to "give the call for
revolution or, more exactly, kindle its flame" if democratic
methods did not succeed in reversing current political and
economic trends in Egypt.[56] In a famous article of September
1951 entitled "The Revolution - The Revolution - The Revolution," Husayn predicted that popular revolution would erupt
in Egypt in November or December 1951: "Oh you ministers
occupied with ministerial shuffles, oh you great men, oh you
deputies and senators, oh you high officials, for the last
time I say to you that you are provoking the people to revolution, for the last time I say to you that you are inciting
revolution."[57]

The third aspect of the activities of the Socialist
Party in the early 1950's which accounts for its resurgent
position in Egyptian public life was its ability to partially
serve as a surrogate for the Muslim Brotherhood. The Brotherhood had been dissolved by government fiat in November 1948,
had lost its dominant leader Hasan al-Banna through assassination in February 1949, had been severely repressed by the
authorities through most of 1949, and was only gradually
allowed to resume some public activities by the Wafdist
ministry in 1950 and 1951.[58] In effect, in the early 1950's
the future of the Brotherhood was in suspense; the charis-
matic Banna dead, his successor in doubt, and no one knowing
for sure if the movement could revive or exactly what shape
a revived Brotherhood would take. In these circumstances,
the Socialist Party (which as Young Egypt had had a program
similar in many ways to that of the Brotherhood since the
late 1930's, which had made its appeal to much the same
groups as the Brotherhood, and which had several times acted

in concert with the Brotherhood on both nationalist and reformist issues through the 1940's) seems to have conceived of itself as a possible successor to the Brotherhood. At least this is what the actions of the party through 1950 and 1951 imply: it publicly defended the Brotherhood, worked in cooperation with some of the Brotherhood's former leaders, and tailored much of its rhetoric to fit the known inclinations of the Brotherhood's following.

In its propaganda, the Socialist Party championed the cause of the dissolved Brotherhood and called for the organization to be allowed to reconstitute itself. The party took the position that "it is necessary for the Muslim Brotherhood to return to life," stated that continued government persecution would only drive the Brotherhood's adherents into further extremism, and supported the abstract principle that "if an association of Egyptians wish to form a purely Islamic party calling for the total adjustment of laws to the Quran, that is their right."[59] In April 1951, when a demonstration of Brotherhood supporters protesting a pending law of associations occurred before Parliament, it was the Socialist Party deputy Ibrahim Shukri who distributed the memorandum of the demonstrators in Parliament.[60] On the purely political level, the Socialist Party succeeded in establishing close links with Brotherhood leaders. In 1950 Ahmad Husayn developed a political alliance with one of the most important of the Brotherhood's historic leaders, Ahmad al-Sukkari, Husayn visiting Sukkari's home and the two men publicly declaring that they would collaborate politically in the future.[61] Other important figures from the Brotherhood appeared at major meetings held by the Socialist Party in 1951,[62] and by the same year one of the Brotherhood's most influential ideologues, Sayyid Qutb, was a contributor to the party's journals.[63]

The actual impact of the revivified Young Egypt/Socialist Party of Egypt upon the course of Egyptian public life in the early 1950's was considerable. Given the great increase in the popularity of its journals, it seems reasonable to assume that the party's vitriolic propaganda against the established political parties, the ministry and the monarchy played some role in the continued erosion of popular faith in the efficacy of the parliamentary monarchy in Egypt. In more immediate political terms, it was on the perennial nationalist question of Egypt's relationship to Great Britain that the Socialist Party built its most important alliances and played its most significant role in Egyptian politics in the early 1950's.

The penultimate crisis of the long Anglo-Egyptian conflict over the British position in Egypt developed during the period of Wafdist rule from January 1950 to January 1952.

Through 1950 and early 1951, desultory negotiations between
the British and Egyptian governments concerning the revision
of the Anglo-Egyptian Treaty of 1936, the future of the
British military base in the Suez Canal Zone, and the status
of the Sudan had taken place, to the accompaniment of steadily
rising Egyptian internal discontent with the failure of these
issues to be resolved in Egypt's favor. By August 1951 the
negotiations reached an impasse. Early in October, with
considerable popular pressure being directed against it, the
Wafdist ministry took the drastic step of presenting to the
Egyptian Parliament drafts of decrees for the unilateral
Egyptian abrogation of the Treaty of 1936 and the Sudan
Conventions of 1899. On October 15, Parliament passed these.
Great Britain refused to acknowledge the validity of the
Egyptian actions or to withdraw her personnel from the Canal
Zone and the Sudan, however, and so there developed in late
1951 - early 1952 another major crisis in Anglo-Egyptian
relations, a four-month "Canal Struggle" the most prominent
features of which were the withdrawal of most of the Egyptian
laborers working at British installations in the Canal Zone
and guerrilla warfare between the British Army and Egyptian
irregulars in the area bordering the Suez Canal. The struggle
ended only in early 1952, after massive demonstrations in
Cairo on January 26 had led to large-scale arson and destruction of property which allowed King Faruq to dismiss the
ministry of the Wafd and to replace it with a ministry which
clamped down on the irregular forces fighting the British.[64]
In the accelerating popular pressure of 1950-1951 which
eventually forced the Wafdist ministry into confrontation
with Great Britain, the Socialist Party played a major role.
From late 1950 the party had been calling for the unilateral
Egyptian abrogation of the Treaty of 1936 and had been
attempting to unite in a general nationalist front many of
the opposition movements and forces in Egyptian politics.[65]
It succeeded in partially achieving the latter in early 1951,
some of its meetings bringing together representatives from
groups as diverse as the Muslim Brotherhood, the Nationalist
Party, the neutralist "Partisans of Peace" movement, socialist
authors such as Ahmad Sadiq 'Azzam, and even the left wing
within the Wafd.[66] It was in the summer of 1951 that agitation
over the nationalist issue reached a level sufficient to be
of serious concern to the Wafdist ministry. Mass demonstrations against the government's foreign policy occurred on
July 11 (the anniversary of the British bombardment of
Alexandria in 1882) and on August 26 (the fifteenth anniversary of the signing of the Anglo-Egyptian Treaty of 1936).[67]
On the latter date, over 10,000 people are estimated to have
attended a meeting sponsored by the Socialist Party at which
representatives from the Socialists, the Nationalists, the

Muslim Brotherhood, the Partisans of Peace and the small
Socialist Peasant's Party all spoke.[68] The resolutions of the
meeting (which had been determined in advance by the partici-
pating groups) called for, inter alia, the abrogation of the
Treaty of 1936 and an Egyptian commercial boycott of British
firms. By September 1951 a "National Front" committee
composed of representatives from the Socialist Party, the
Nationalist Party, the Partisans of Peace and the Socialist
Peasant's Party had taken shape to coordinate pressures on
the ministry, and the Socialist Party itself began to call on
Egyptians who worked for British firms to cease work until the
British should meet Egypt's national demands.[69]

    When the Egyptian government in October 1951 did abrogate
the Anglo-Egyptian Treaty of 1936 and the Sudan Conventions of
1899, thus beginning the Canal Struggle, the Socialist Party
(like most Egyptian political groups) enthusiastically joined
in the confrontation with the British. Perhaps the party's
main contribution to the Canal Struggle was the propaganda
campaigns waged by its periodicals in late 1951 against
British interests in Egypt and against Egyptians who
collaborated with the British. The party organized a boycott
of British (and "Zionist") products, published a "black list"
of Egyptian firms which continued to have commercial contacts
with their British counterparts, arranged for pickets to
demonstrate in front of British-owned firms operating in Egypt,
and asked Egyptians to supply to the party lists of British-
made goods so that it could warn the public not to purchase
them.[70] The most famous of its propaganda activities in this
vein were a series of xenophobic attacks on specific businesses
and institutions which were either British-owned or "unpatrio-
tic." Egyptians were called upon not to patronize Barclay's
Bank ("a prop of imperialist capitalism") and generally to
boycott "companies and institutions which are cooperating with
the aggressor";[71] Egypt's leading newspapers were denounced
for continuing to carry advertisements for British-made
products;[72] and bars, cinemas, and other places of amusement
were attacked for their continued operation at a time when all
Egyptian attention should be concentrated in the great
patriotic struggle.[73]

    It was not only impersonal institutions which came under
the party's fire during the Canal Struggle. The party's journals also denounced "the despicable, dissolute minority" of
Egyptians which continued to attend the British-owned Rivoli
Cinema "at a time when the English are destroying our souls,"[74]
published license-plate numbers (gathered by the party's
"secret socialist intelligence") of autos visiting the British
Embassy and warned Egyptians to watch for these because they
transported "spies,"[75] named three individuals as British
"agents,"[76] and publicly gloated when two of the latter were

set upon and mauled after leaving the British Embassy: "being beaten with shoes will be the fate of anyone who is connected with them [the British] in any way whatsoever."[77] By early 1952, Ahmad Husayn was publicly warning the British that the repressive actions of the British military in the Canal Zone against Egyptians suspected of involvement in guerrilla warfare could lead to Egyptian retaliations against British civilians in Egypt: as a "declaration" to the British commander in the Canal Zone put it, "on your head and on the heads of your troops rests the responsibility of the extension of the zone of battle; on your head and on the heads of your troops will be the sufferings and misfortuntes which could flood this country and by which thirty thousand of your countrymen [i.e., Britishers resident in Egypt] could be inundated."[78] These attacks against the British and those Egyptians who cooperated with them were not prompted solely by the Canal Struggle; rather, they were resurrection of one of the prevalent themes of Young Egypt since its inception – its resentment against the foreign domination of Egypt, against the alien institutions and "prohibited" customs which had come to dominate Egyptian society, and against the upper-class minority who accepted this foreign hegemony of Egypt.

In terms of the military aspect of the Canal Struggle, the Socialist Party was one of several groups which sponsored the "liberation battalions" (<u>kataib al-tahrir</u>) which undertook guerrilla warfare against the British in the Canal Zone in late 1951 - early 1952. By late October 1951 the party established recruiting offices where young men could volunteer for military operations against the British.[79] The actual training of the party's volunteers began in early November at two "bases," one outside Cairo, the other near Alexandria.[80] Actual military operations by the party's units are reported to have begun by the second half of November, and consisted of the types of sabotage (the mining of roads; the cutting of telephone lines; the dynamiting of the conduits and pumping-stations supplying water to the Canal Zone) which were typical of most Egyptian irregular operations during the Canal Struggle.[81] No definite figure can be given for the number of combatants which the Socialist Party put in the field, but a report from the Sharqiyah Province Governorate on December 2, 1951, claims that the party's forward base at al-Zaqaziq, at the edge of the zone of operations, had "about 150 persons; students, farmers and workers."[82] Ahmad Husayn is reported to have devoted most of his attention in December 1951 and January 1952 to the military side of the Canal Struggle, secretly visiting Isma'iliyah and Port Sa'id, moving his base of operations to Sharqiyah Province in late December, and allegedly spending most of his time in early January in the zone of physical operations "leading and supervising the movement of jihad."[83]

After great national unity within Egypt around the government in October 1951, the nature of the Canal Struggle began to change by November. The military activities against the British of late 1951 - early 1952 had begun under the initiative of individual political organizations, not the government, and it is at least dubious if the Wafdist ministry had intended its legislative actions to lead to such physical militance. In fine, the ministry's initiative of October 1951 had put an end to the various pressures which had been building up against it, but it put the ministry in a dilemma; that independent political groups were undertaking actions which were out of the ministry's control. Placed in this position of riding the tiger of Egyptian nationalist feelings, by November the ministry began to attempt to control the various groups involved in the Canal Struggle. On November 14, the Ministry of the Interior announced its intention to bring the liberation battalions under its supervision and to oversee their finances.[84] By December, government prohibition of the meetings of political organizations had been stepped up, as had the confiscation of the journals of the most radical groups involved in the Canal Struggle. Public demonstrations were prohibited as of December 5, some schools closed for varying periods of time through December and January, and several training centers of the liberation battalions were taken over by the government, with their volunteers being disarmed or arrested.[85] The Socialist Party was definitely affected by this repression of late 1951, its party meetings coming under frequent prohibition, its journals being subject to repeated seizure, and at least one of its training-camps for volunteers being taken over by the authorities, with its recruits being disarmed.[86]

To this restriction of its own activities and of the waging of the Canal Struggle generally the Socialist Party responded by turning against the Wafdist ministry. A mid-November speech by Husayn was in effect an ultimatum to the government, demanding that it act within fifteen days on an eight-point list of suggestions for the more effective waging of the Canal Struggle or, if it did not act, "we will fight it with the twenty million of the people who are firm on their goal of total freedom. . . ."[87] When the fifteen days passed without government action, or rather with government counter-action against the Socialist Party, the party denounced the ministry for betraying the Canal Struggle: "the government has begun, under the influence of reactionary circles and under the influence of the class and interest groups of which it is composed, to turn its weapons and its force against the people themselves."[88] From early December

101

onwards, the Socialist Party's propaganda concentrated on
attacking the Wafdist ministry, "exposing" its hesitancy in
the patriotic struggle and demanding from it more vigorous
anti-British action as well as more freedom for the
irregulars fighting the British in the Canal Zone.[89] By late
January 1952, the party was irrevocably opposed to the
Wafdist ministry, with Husayn on January 20 declaring "a
battle of life and death" between his party and the ministry
and with an official party declaration of January 24 stating
that "the Socialist Party has resolved on the necessity of
the fall of the government in order to save the country from
the disorders which are about to befall it at the hands of
this government. . . ."[90]

Ahmad Husayn's declaration of a Socialist-Wafdist
"battle of life and death" and his warning of "disorders"
about to occur in Egypt, as well as his previously cited
threat to the British of possible Egyptian retaliation
against British civilians in Egypt, all preceded by less than
a week that notorious "Black Saturday" of January 26, 1952,
when much of modern Cairo went up in flames.[91] On January 25,
British troops in the Canal Zone attacked an Egyptian
Auxiliary Police barracks in Isma'iliyah, with perhaps fifty
Egyptians killed and over a hundred wounded. After news of
this massacre reached Cairo, huge popular demonstrations of
protest developed during the morning hours of January 26. The
crucial turn of events occurred about midday when, after mob
action had produced the burning of a night-club, organized and
equipped bands of incendiaries appeared and undertook the
burning of primarily "Western" premises such as bars, cinemas,
hotels, and foreign clubs. By early in the afternoon the mass
of demonstrators, taking their cue from the original incendiaries, continued arson and added looting. Order was
restored only during the course of the evening by units of
the regular Army. The toll of destruction was the greatest
of any of the days of protest which had occurred in Cairo
since the "Revolution" of 1919; some 700 establishments were
wholly or partially destroyed, with an estimated twenty-six
people killed and over five hundred injured.[92] The course of
events set in motion by Black Saturday was momentous; the
dismissal of the ministry of the Wafd, a succession of
short-lived and Palace-dominated ministries which terminated
the Canal Struggle with the British, and eventually the Army
coup of July 22-23 followed by the forced abdication of King
Faruq on July 26, 1952, exactly six months after he had allowed
his capital to be gutted.

In some of the most knowledgeable accounts of modern
Egyptian politics, it is Ahmad Husayn and his Socialists who
are singled out as the most likely candidates for having
provided the original, organized bands of incendiaries who

102

began the first acts of arson on January 26, thereby setting the destructive example which was followed later in the day by the mob.[93] It is primarily with this possible involvement of the Socialist Party in the burning of Cairo that we must concern ourselves here.

As early as the evening of January 26, the police began to arrest members of the Socialist Party on suspicion of involvement in the organized incendiarism of Black Saturday.[94] On May 12, 1952, after an intensive investigation, formal indictments were presented to a special Supreme Military Court (martial law was then in effect) against four of the party's members; Ahmad Husayn and two others for having undertaken acts of arson, the fourth for having written inflammatory articles.[95] The trial of Husayn and his colleagues was an inconclusive one. From its inception on May 18 until the July coup a considerable body of evidence was presented in spite of the obstructionism of Husayn (who undertook periodic hunger-strikes and refused to appear before the Court) and the procedural appeals made by his defense lawyers.[96] Temporarily suspended by the coup of July 22-23, the trial resumed on September 6 in an atmosphere quite different from that which had prevailed before the coup: the new presiding officer had "a perpetual beaming smile. . . which has restored tranquility to the accused," and the Court is reported to have spoken of the chief defendant as "Ahmad Husayn, the conqueror of the King."[97] On November 1, 1952, the Court released the defendants without bail, declaring the trial postponed until new evidence could be gathered.[98] Although this effectively meant the end of any attempt to prosecute Husayn and his Socialists in connection with Black Saturday, the case remained formally on the books until April 1953 when, after a series of appeals by Husayn, the Cairo Criminal Court dismissed all portions of the indictment against Husayn and his colleagues.[99]

Despite the political crosscurrents surrounding the trial of Husayn and his associates (i.e., governmental hostility to the Socialist Party prior to July 22-23, 1952, the sympathy of the new military regime after their assumption of power) and the incompleteness of the data (e.g., the official transcript of the trial is not available), some tentative observations concerning the Socialist Party's possible role in the events of Black Saturday can be made from the major formal documents issuing from the trial (the indictment presented by the prosecution; partial testimony during the first phase of the trial; and the various decisions of the courts) which are contained in Husayn's later apologia.[100]

There is little doubt that the Socialist Party and its leader bear one type of responsibility for the events of Black Saturday. The press campaign waged by the party's journals in late 1951 undoubtedly did contribute to the

103

inflaming of anti-British and anti-foreign sentiment among the
populace at large, as did the party's boycotts of "traitorous"
business firms and its picketing of "sinful" places of amusement. Such establishments ranked high on the list of structures
burned on Black Saturday. The major portion of the indictment
presented against Ahmad Husayn in May 1952 accusing him of
complicity in the burning of Cairo concerned this type of
responsibility, citing a score of articles written by Husayn
through which he was held accountable for playing an indirect
role in inciting the destruction of January 26.[101] Despite
the fact that the Cairo Criminal Court eventually held these
charges of incitation to be not subject to legal prosecution,[102]
there is no question that the press activities of the party
contributed to the inflamed climate of opinion which made
Black Saturday possible, and that for these activities Ahmad
Husayn and his party must bear a share of historical, if not
legal, blame for the burning of Cairo.

The more serious accusation levelled against the Socialist
Party concerns the question of whether the party played any
role in the first, organized acts of arson on January 26.
A strong case for the possibility of the party's involvement
in a "plot" of arson can be constructed from the party's
actions before that date. As we have seen, it had incited
popular feelings against the type of establishments which
were to be the targets of incendiarism on Black Saturday.
Ahmad Husayn's statements in the week before January 26 had
warned the British of possible Egyptian action against British
civilians, had called for the fall of the Wafdist ministry,
and had alluded to impending "disorders" in Egypt - all of
which did occur on January 26. Therefore, there is nothing
improbable about the party's undertaking violence against
foreigners and foreign property in an attempt to topple the
Wafd. As Husayn himself has recently argued (while continuing
to deny the charge), the party's public pronouncements provided the perfect opportunity to blame the Socialists for
what happened on Black Saturday.[103]

When we turn from what seems possible to the events of
January 26 themselves, however, there is a paucity of evidence
which would link the Socialist Party to any organized conspiracy. From the documents available, the outstanding feature
of the trial of Husayn and his associates was the inability
of the prosecution to offer any proof of premeditated participation by the accused in the burning of Cairo. Despite the
surveillance under which the offices and the leadership of
the party had been kept, the police informers within the
party, and the pressures which were used on members arrested
and interrogated after January 26, the prosecution was unable
to produce anyone privy to a conspiracy directed to acts of
arson. The Palace-dominated ministries of early 1952

certainly used the events of January 26 to suppress the party: yet they could manage to indict just three members of the party on charges connected with physical participation in the arson of Black Saturday, and then only on the grounds of their having been seen in the vicinity of the fires.[104] From labor intended to produce a mountain of evidence, the prosecution brought forth only a molehill.

The strongest point in the prosecution's case was the testimony of three witnesses that the automobile owned by Husayn's driver was seen coming from the direction of the Rivoli Cinema - the first "foreign" structure to be deliberately burned - at the time of its firing, and that the same vehicle was seen shortly afterwards in another area where organized arson was occurring.[105] This testimony was never challenged successfully by Husayn or his defense. However, none of these witnesses was able to identify the vehicle's occupants, and therefore the prosecution was forced to base its charge that Husayn, his driver, and his bodyguard "deliberately started fires" on other incidents later in the afternoon of January 26. In regard to these incidents the facts were well established in the investigation. According to the police agent assigned to watch his movements, Husayn remained at home until 3:30 pm on January 26, when his driver picked him up.[106] With Husayn's bodyguard, they proceeded to the center of Cairo where the major blazes of the day were already well under way. After Husayn's bodyguard had thrown an Egyptian flag on top of one of the burning heaps of material from a store, the three men dropped out of sight for the rest of the day. The basic charge of participation in the burning of Cairo against Husayn and his companions was based on these incidents of the late afternoon.[107]

In April 1953, the Cairo Criminal Court evaluated the testimony of the four witnesses to these sightings of Husayn and his companions in the vicinity of fires in the late afternoon. It found the testimony of two of the four to have been based on hearsay, that of the third to have been produced only after police proddings on the subject, and, while accepting that of the fourth witness as valid, pointed out that it contained nothing more than that Husayn and his colleagues had been seen in the vicinity of fires which were already under way.[108] The Court's conclusion was that "it is not possible to consider the first defendant [Husayn] and those with him to have been participants in the incidents which occurred on that day, either by way of conspiracy or by way of incitation. . . ."[109] As far as legal responsibility for the burning of Cairo is concerned, the court seems to have rendered the only possible decision. The prosecution was able to present no evidence of any intended or realized plan for arson on January 26, offering instead only evidence of the participation of individual members of the Socialist Party in acts of arson late in the day when thousands of Egyptians were celebrating in the ruins of cosmopolitan Cairo.[110] The unchallenged testimony of the witnesses who reported seeing the Black Citroen of Husayn's driver coming from the Rivoli Theater at the time of its firing leaves open the possibility that some members of the party, particularly ones close to the party's leader, may have been among the first incendiaries. It is only a possibility, however, and in view of the inability of the ministries of early 1952 to produce any solid evidence concerning the organized arson of January 26, the charge that the Socialist Party was behind the burning of Cairo must be regarded as dubious.

One thing is certain: even if the Socialist Party was involved in the organized arson of Black Saturday, the party did not benefit from it. From January to July 1952, the party simply ceased to function as an organized body due to the repression of the authorities. The party's Green House had its press closed in late January, and by early February eight hundred persons had been arrested in connection with the events of January 26, including much of the leadership of the Socialist Party.[111] Throughout early 1952, members of the party continued to be arrested and interrogated, the party's parliamentary deputy Ibrahim Shukri being arrested and detained (without formal charges being entered against him) in March, and as late as May several prominent figures in the party similarly being arrested and held without being charged.[112]

The military coup of July 1952 did bring a renewal of activity by the party after its suppression of early 1952, but it proved to be a short-lived one. In July and August, the party's numerous detainees (other than those four formally on trial) were released, its Green House reopened, and the party's activities resumed under the interim leadership of Ibrahim Shukri.[113] The party was a strong supporter of the new regime in late 1952, praising the forced abdication of the King, endorsing the Agrarian Reform Law of September 1952, and approving the military's ouster from the post of Prime Minister of the party's old ally, 'Ali Mahir.[114] In October, in accordance with a new regulation on political associations, the party registered its statutes with the government, reported its financial assets (the minuscule sum of £E 110), and was approved as a political organization by the government.[115] Such recognition did not last long, however: on January 16, 1953, the military regime abolished all political parties, the Socialists included. Thus ended the political life of the Socialist Party, nee Young Egypt.

The Socialism of the Socialist
Party of Egypt

By far the most significant aspect of the postwar thought
of Young Egypt are the ideas expressed by its spokesmen in the
early 1950's when the movement became the Socialist Party of
Egypt. After the eclipse of the movement through the 1940's,
the early 1950's were a period when both its following and its
impact on Egyptian politics increased considerably. It was
also a period when the movement's spokesmen did present new
interpretations of political reality and new proposals for
political and economic change in Egypt. It is therefore to
the movement's ideas in its phase as the Socialist Party of
Egypt from 1949 to 1952 that this chapter is devoted.

The particular type of socialism advocated by the
Socialist Party of Egypt in the early 1950's was a distinctly
non-dialectical form of socialism, one which consistently
disavowed any materialist philosophical basis and instead
presented itself as being based on the principles of revealed
religion. As Ahmad Husayn stated when introducing the new
name for his party in October 1949, its socialism was
". . . not derived from Karl Marx or Lenin, but rather derives
from Islam, Christianity, and the higher religions which
reconcile mankind and which preach cooperation, solidarity, and
social justice."[1] The party's propaganda spoke not in terms
of the class struggle and the dictatorship of the proletariat,
but rather claimed inspiration from ". . . early Islam, which
was pervaded by socialism and solidarity between rulers and
ruled."[2] It was a socialism "spiritual" rather than "materialist" in nature, being inspired by "the spirituality of the
East,"[3] that prevalent distinction between East and West found
in Young Egypt's thought since the movement's inception. As
such, it took as its official slogan not "Workers of the world,
unite!" or any similar internationalist and class-oriented
motto, but rather the more traditional phrase "God and people"
(Allah wa al-sha'b).[4] The Islamic and non-Marxist nature of
the party's socialism was stated in its most definitive form in
the first of the "Fundamental Principles" which served as the
party's capsule program in the early 1950's:

> Belief in and worship of God, the Creator of this
> existence, is the basis of human society. The
> worship of God manifests itself best in the
> sincere and virtuous service of the people, as

the higher religions advocate. The goal of the
people, and its watchword, is the worship of God
by way of serving the people, liberating them from
fear, ignorance, sickness, and want, and
preserving them from befalling coercion, adver-
sity, or exploitation.[5]

Thus the primary feature of the movement's socialism of the
early 1950's was a characteristic similar to Young Egypt's
driving motif in the late 1930's; a populist desire to promote the public weal on a formally religious foundation.

The second general feature of the party's socialism was
its nationalist and anti-imperialist thrust. The word "Egypt"
was included in the party's new name explicitly to express
". . . the patriotism of our movement and its independence
from other socialist movements."[6] In the years of its
existence, this uniqueness of the Socialist Party of Egypt
was repeatedly emphasized: European socialists were
denounced as "apostates who do not believe in religion"
while the followers of the party were termed "believers in
God, religion, and morals";[7] it was affirmed that Egyptians
were ". . . not in need of imitating England or Russia in
terms of the social order, for we have our religion and our
great Islamic social order";[8] and on a more practical level
connections with European socialist parties were disavowed
because these parties often supported their governments in
imperialist policies while "our patriotism makes us refuse
being a tool in the hands of Western socialism."[9] Conversely,
the centrality of Egyptian nationalist goals to the party was
consistently asserted, it being explicitly stated that "our
socialism is directed, first and foremost, at the eradication
of this odious foreign imperialism,"[10] and Husayn at one
point declaring that "when we adopted socialism as an economic
doctrine, that was only as a weapon which experience had
demonstrated to us would be useful in our continuing our
fight against imperialism."[11]

But this was not a case of the national struggle being
divorced from the internal conflict against inequality in
Egypt; rather, the national struggle and the domestic struggle
were presented as being essentially identical in the party's
propaganda. Of all the aspects of European socialist thought,
it was the Leninist coupling of capitalism with imperialism
which seems to have made the deepest impression on Ahmad
Husayn in particular by the early 1950's. Repeatedly asserting
the abstraction that "imperialism is the culmination of
capitalism,"[12] he consistently voiced the belief in an
inexorable tie between foreign dominance and internal exploitation, i.e., between British imperialism and Egyptian capitalism.
All of the political parties of the older generation were termed

"capitalist parties" which had "come to power only through the influence of a foreign power."[13] Egypt's upper classes were but the "creature" of the British who had "created this group of pashas to rule in their interest."[14] The relationship between imperialism and capitalism was in Husayn's view a symbiotic one; there was "a solid connection between the armies of the occupation and foreign capitalism on the one hand, and the forces of reaction and internal capitalism on the other."[15] But, in the bond between external and internal "exploiters," it was the former which was the primary enemy, the party whose defeat would result in the elimination of the other: "the fall of external imperialism will lead to the fall of internal imperialism."[16] Therefore, the party's socialism being directed "first and foremost" at the elimination of imperialism was the logical procedure, given this perception of the relationship between the foreign and domestic enemies of the people. Only when imperialism had ended could the internal problems of Egypt be challenged successfully.

In addition to these Islamic and nationalist emphases in its socialism, the propaganda of the Socialist Party in the early 1950's repeated many of the generalized concepts which Young Egypt had expressed previously. Its socialism was "democratic," being based on "the belief of the party in the sacred freedom of the individual"[17] and explicitly pledging loyalty to the Egyptian Constitution and its guarantees of freedom of worship, expression, and assembly;[18] its socialism was "egalitarian," holding that "the distribution of wealth should be based on the needs of individuals";[19] and it was a moralizing socialism expressing the same pious injunctions to good behavior which had been emphasized by Young Egypt in the past, maintaining that "we call for virtue and morals."[20] In fine, the attributes which had been termed "Islamic" in the late 1930's were called "socialist" in the early 1950's. The party's spokesmen themselves emphasized the continuity between the old Young Egypt and the new Socialist Party, with socialism stated to have been the implicit message of the movement since its inception: "the Piastre Plan was nothing but socialism, and the struggle of Young Egypt was based only on socialist principles."[21] Thus the socialist orientation of the movement in the early 1950's can be considered to have been primarily an instrumentality, a method for achieving the same general goals which had been those of Young Egypt since the 1930's.

Of the specific proposals found in the movement's propaganda in the early 1950's, the most famous of the measures which it advocated was its proposal in regard to the reform of land ownership in Egypt.[22] The party's stance on land reform was both drastic and simply; that a fifty-_faddan_ limitation be placed on the size of agricultural estates.

The state was to purchase all land-holdings exceeding that
limitation in exchange for interest-bearing government bonds,
and then was to distribute the lands purchased to small
farmers or tenants in exchange for payments based on the yield
of the land itself. No purchaser of redistributed land was to
be allowed to obtain an estate larger than five faddans as a
result of the land redistribution.[23]

Two points need to be emphasized about this land reform
proposal. First, although it was but one of many suggestions
for land reform made in postwar Egypt, it was among the most
radical of these, its suggested limitation of fifty faddans
being as stringent as any of the other postwar land reform
proposals.[24] Secondly, the party's proposal did not demand
the nationalization of agricultural land. Although the party
at one point had called for "the nationalization of agricultural land, making it common domain belonging to all,"[25] the
party eventually settled on the less revolutionary idea of
redistributing large landholdings to poorer peasants as their
private property. The party recognized that its goal of
"multiplying the number of landowners" separated it from
doctrinaire "Western" socialism which wished the nationalization
of land,[26] but it characteristically took pride in its alleged
uniqueness, stating that "the idea which we are presenting is
not a socialist or a communist idea but a democratic, an
Islamic, even an enlightened capitalist idea, because we wish
to make the fallahin the possessors of the land."[27] Thus even
the party's most sweeping reform proposal of the early 1950's
was viewed by it as not inspired by foreign socialist doctrine,
but rather as a measure conditioned by Egyptian traditions
("a democratic, an Islamic, even an enlightened capitalist
idea") for the solution of rural inequality in a manner suited
to Egyptian values and desires.

The specific proposals made by the Socialist Party in
regard to industry and commerce were not as radical as its
ideas in the agricultural sphere. While the party at one time
spoke of thoroughgoing nationalization of non-agricultural
properties, calling for "the nationalization of all means of
production, making them the property of all the people,"[28]
this was soon watered down to a demand for the nationalization
of public utilities and industries "connected with the economic
welfare of the people" such as communications facilities,
international trade agencies and major financial institutions.[29]
In place of sweeping nationalization in the industrial and
commercial spheres, the party advocated the idea of tightly
coordinated national economic planning. The "Fundamental
Principles of the Socialist Party" called for a six-year
comprehensive economic plan which would provide for the
construction of new factories, the "multiplying" of agricultural
output, and the increasing of hydroelectric power.[30] Although

"widespread" nationalization of industry and commerce was specifically disavowed by the party, it was emphasized that individual private enterprises would have to shape their activities to meet the public good and that it should be the state which would undertake the building of "primary industries."[31]

We have already examined the party's vehement denunciations of Egypt's upper classes, of the "feudalists and capitalists" whose economic intransigence and social degeneracy were the frequent object of the party's fire in the early 1950's. Not unnaturally, the party's specific proposals reflected this bitterness towards the circles controlling Egyptian politics and society. The party's official declarations repeated Young Egypt's older ideas that a system of progressive taxation was necessary in Egypt in order to achieve "a just distribution of wealth" and that no one's income should be allowed to exceed "a fixed limit sufficient for him to live a good life without hauteur and extravagance."[32] The party's propaganda also supported that idea rather widespread in postwar Egypt, that the right to possess private property was not unconditional but rather that private property was a "trust" to be used for the benefit of the community.[33] On a more symbolic level, one of the party's frequent demands in the early 1950's was for the abolition of titles (pasha, bey, etc.) in Egypt and the adoption of the Arabic equivalents of Mr. (sayyid) and Ms. (sayyidah) in place of terms deriving from the "feudal" past.[34] While these suggested restraints upon individual wealth and prerogative were left vague in the party's official manifestoes, they do demonstrate the advancing attitude of hostility towards Egypt's upper classes which was the party's political leitmotif in the early 1950's.

The other major specific proposals of the Socialist Party in regard to Egypt's internal life demonstrate little change from the concepts expressed by Young Egypt in the prewar period. Concerning the laboring population of Egypt, its suggested reforms are based largely on the ideas found in the 1940 program of the Islamic Nationalist Party. "Work is the right of every Egyptian";[35] the government was to have imposed upon it "the sacred duty" of finding work for any unemployed person[36] as well as the obligation to supplement incomes in order to maintain living standards;[37] and a wide variety of social security measures, from "guarantees" of food, shelter, and medical care to financial support in case of illness, unemployment, incapacity to work or old age were demanded.[38] These sweeping claims of the citizen upon the state were to be balanced by corresponding duties placed upon the individual, however: "whoever does not work shall not eat; all of the people shall work, and all of the people shall produce."[39]

For organized labor, the party advocated legislation which would eliminate the distinction between agriculture-domestic and industrial labor, make unionization allowable for all instead of just the latter, and guarantee to all labor the right to confederate and the right to strike.[40] In regard to rural life, the establishment of agricultural cooperatives for any village with more than one thousand faddans of land was proposed.[41] Some of the party's most sweeping demands were made in regard to education; compulsory and free schooling for all children through secondary school, the "right" to (although not financial assistance for) higher education for all children, and the elimination of illiteracy in Egypt within five years.[42]

On the whole, with the exception of its radical proposal in regard to land redistribution in Egypt, the Socialist Party's ideas in regard to the Egyptian economy show little change from Young Egypt's prewar demands. The bulk of "capitalist" properties outside of agriculture were guaranteed continued existence under its proposals, with only the largest (and often foreign-owned) enterprises to be nationalized. The role of the state in the economy continued to expand just as it had in the evolution of the movement's thought in the 1930's; to the state's suggested stewardship over the economic life of the country and its protection of the poorer strata of Egypt's population were now added the duty of the construction of major economic facilities and greater control and coordination of the economy through comprehensive economic planning. Thus what evolution there was in the movement's economic ideas in the postwar period was in the same direction as its thought had developed before the war; towards a greater role for the state in the economy. The resulting economic vision deserves the adjective "étatist" rather than "socialist."

One of the major areas where the propaganda of the Socialist Party voiced ideas which went significantly beyond the framework of the movement's prewar thought was in regard to Egypt's foreign relations. Through the early 1950's the party was a steady advocate of an Egyptian opening towards the Communist world, repeatedly calling for the Egyptian purchase of arms from the Soviet bloc and for Egypt to conclude a treaty of friendship and non-aggression with the states of Eastern Europe.[43] Although the party officially advocated that Egypt follow "a policy of armed neutrality" in regard to the cold war,[44] party spokesmen often expressed a preference for the Soviet Union and its allies in that struggle. Sometimes based on the emotional grounds of Egyptian resentment towards the West because of the West's domination of Egypt ("neutralism is an unnatural, unintelligible thing so long as the English are aggressing and warring on us night and day.

The natural thing is that we fight them and join their enemies in defiance of them"),[45] sometimes on the more pragmatic reasoning that closer ties with the Soviet Union would be "a sharp weapon to [bring about] evacuation of our country,"[46] the net result was the same; the idea that "Egypt cannot take a position of neutrality - the English are still in our country, and so it is necessary for us to join the side of Russia."[47] Thus "natural" Egyptian desires (after seventy years of British domination) and realpolitik (the enemy of my enemy is my friend) combined to propel the party into a pro-Soviet stance in the cold war.

But the Socialist Party's inclination towards the Soviet Union was not justified only on the legacy of the Egyptian past or the circumstances of the Egyptian present; rather, it was also rationalized on the moralistic grounds so characteristic of the movement's thought throughout its history. Thus in the same article in which he wrote of alignment with the Soviet Union as a "natural thing" for Egypt, Husayn also presented the thesis that it was the West, the United States, and "capitalism" generally which were the aggressors in the cold war and the real threat to world peace:

> If war occurs, it will be because America and England want war. They wish it not in the interests of peace and not for the defense of principles and culture, as they allege, but because they desire domination and mastery over the world for the benefit of English and American capitalists, with Jewish capitalists in the lead.[48]

The United States in particular came under attack by Husayn. On the basis of his 1947 trip to America, he denounced it as being behind the Soviet Union (which he had never visited) in regard to "family, religion, and morals," as a place where "I did not find one family intact, where I did not find religion or even partial religion," and finally for "its threatening us every morning and every evening with aggression and humiliation if we do not become slaves to the Jews and the Americans."[49] Other writings by Husayn maintained the same steadily anti-Western position, blaming the United States and Great Britain for "the Palestine tragedy,"[50] condemning the Western powers as "the aggressors" in the Korean conflict,[51] and generally holding that Britain and America were "the enemies of democracy everywhere through their support for tyrannical rulers."[52]

The obverse of this negative image of the Western powers was a more laudatory view of the Communist states. Not only was the Soviet Union held up as a more "virtuous" society than that of the United States; its actions in the

international sphere in the early 1950's, from Soviet support
of North Korea in 1950 to Soviet indirect backing (in the
United Nations) for the Iranian nationalist struggle against
the Anglo-Iranian Oil Company in 1951, drew the party's
praise.[53] Other Communist regimes were also treated favorably
in the party's propaganda. The Chinese Communist movement
came in for commendation after its victory on the mainland
in 1949, with the Nationalist regime being denounced as
corrupt, the new regime being praised for bringing stability
and honesty to China, and with the party calling for Egyptian
diplomatic recognition of the People's Republic of China.[54]
In Korea, South Korea was denounced as a corrupt "American
protectorate" whose people had been ready to revolt against
American domination before the outbreak of hostilities between
the north and the south,[55] it was asserted that "North Korea
struck before it was about to be struck,"[56] and pleasure
was taken (prematurely) in "the American defeat" in Korea
which was interpreted as proof of "the triumph of the
people's will to peace."[57]

In this anti-imperialist rhetoric of the movement in the
early 1950's, one feature in particular stands out; the
perceived sense of solidarity expressed by the movement's
spokesmen for all victims of Western imperialism and/or all
opponents of the West, regardless of their ideological
orientation. By the early 1950's, the general world surge
of anti-imperialism had produced a new awareness of bonds
beyond the more traditional ones of language and religion
which had been the dominant ones acknowledged in the movement's
propaganda in the prewar period, adding a new category of
identity to the movement's older Egyptian, Arab, and Muslim
ones; the Manichean image of "them" (the Western imperialists)
versus "us" (all other states and peoples of the world). This
sense of solidarity was felt irrespective of ideological
differences; the Soviet Union might be the most materialist
of all states in terms of its philosophical underpinnings, but
it was still termed more "virtuous" and even more supportive
of "religion" than the West.[58] This perceived unity of all
that was other than the West comes out most strikingly in a
passage in which Husayn invoked the Diety in support of the
forces of dialectical materialism: "May God grant the Korean
people and the Chinese people success in defeating Anglo-
American imperialism for the benefit of [all of] the enslaved,
advancing peoples of the world."[59] In fine, the concept of
the non-Western world was at least a mental reality to the
Socialist Party, made so by the common struggle against the
West.

Concerning the area immediately surrounding Egypt, the
Socialist Party's position was not significantly different
from that which its predecessor Young Egypt had developed

114

prior to the 1950's. The party continued to distinguish
between the Nile Valley and the Arab world, demanding the
integral unity of the former but advocating only cooperation
among the states of the latter. The party's propaganda
maintained its traditional call for union between Egypt and
the Sudan, with the major question of the Sudanese right to
self-determination in effect denied. While the party's
"Fundamental Principles" stated that the Socialist Party
"holds sacred the right of the Sudanese people to choose the
form of their government after English evacuation," the
document also stated the party's "belief that Egypt and the
Sudan are an economic and social unit and that the Nile
cannot be divided,"[60] and a speech by Ahmad Husayn made clear
that, at least as far as he was concerned, the right of
self-determination of the Sudanese meant "the freedom to
choose the form which will lead them to union with Egypt."[61]

The party's position in regard to Egypt's ties with the
Arab world was basically federative rather than unionist.
While Husayn sometimes spoke of "complete union" between Egypt
and the other Arab countries,[62] the party's official position
was the advocacy of a confederation of sovereign Arab states.
The "Fundamental Principles" gave the party's position as
follows:

> The Socialist Party of Egypt is working for the
> unification of the Arab peoples in one state, to
> be called "The United Arab States" [al-wilayat
> al-'arabiyah al-muttahidah], provided that
> every Arab continues to preserve in his own
> state his personality, his nature, and his
> independence in internal affairs, provided that
> the cooperation of all in one state is based
> on that which raises the economic and social
> level of the Arab peoples by the organization
> of production according to socialist forms, and
> provided that one army will be created by all
> to stop any aggression directed from outside
> against the Arab bloc [al-kutlah al-'arabiyah]
> or any foreign attempt of any sort to dominate
> or exploit.[63]

While this passage is internally inconsistent, the idea of a
common organization of production conflicting with "independence in internal affairs," the demand for "one army" and
the phrase "the Arab bloc" make it clear that the party's
primary concern in advocating closer Arab cooperation was the
desire for a unified foreign policy against external threats
to Arab independence. Here the Socialist Party's position,
like Young Egypt's before it, continued to be more Egyptian

nationalist than Arab nationalist in the integral, post-1958 sense. Although there were advantages to be gained by Egypt from closer cooperation with the other Arab states, Egypt itself remained the focus of the Socialist Party's nationalism. Thus we find Ahmad Husayn stating his "creed" in 1951 in terms scarcely different from those he had employed in 1933: "It is that this country which I am part of was great in the past, as great a state as the world knows today. . . . Egypt must return to her past glory and greatness, taking her place in the modern age as one of the great states of the world."[64]

In summary, the ideas expressed by the Socialist Party of Egypt in the early 1950's were not markedly different from Young Egypt's pre-World War II thought. In terms of its proposals for internal reform, only the movement's platform on land redistribution and its advocacy of state economic planning marked advances on the proposals which it had made in the 1933-1940 period. The other specifics of its ideas on internal reform - state supervision of the economy, the reduction of the foreign role in Egyptian life, and its welfare and social-reform concepts - were ideas which the movement had formulated and offered before World War II. In regard to Egypt's relationship to the rest of the world, while a new sympathy for and identification with the non-Western and anti-imperialist world demonstrated itself, nonetheless the ultimate end of Egyptian foreign policy (that Egypt should again become "a great state" uniting the Nile Valley and cooperating with the neighboring Arab states) remained substantially what it had been for Young Egypt by the late 1930's.

From a broader perspective, the leading ideas of the Socialist Party were not very different from the concepts being expressed by many of the newer (and some of the older) political forces in Egypt by the postwar period. Various individuals and parties proposed significant land reform;[65] many groups called for closer relations with the Soviet bloc as a means to break the British hold on Egypt;[66] and practically every movement in Egypt with aspirations to a mass following, from the Wafd to the Muslim Brotherhood was characterizing themselves or elements of their programs as "socialist" in the years after World War II.[67] By the postwar period, neither the Socialist Party's general concepts nor its specific proposals were unique to it alone; rather, the movement's ideas fit into what had become a generalized demand for sweeping reforms in Egypt's political and economic arrangements.

Several factors account for the relative continuity and conventionality of the Socialist Party's ideas. The circumstances of the era itself were one factor: with questions of foreign policy dominating Egyptian political consciousness for much of the postwar period, and with the increasingly

bitter and violent day-by-day political struggle between
polarized factions absorbing much of the rest of the attention
of articulate Egyptians, the movement was impelled to devote
much of its thought to issues of foreign policy (where its
ideas did evolve from its earlier conceptions) or to the kind
of concrete political attack and counter-attack which, although
it certainly added to the rancorous political atmosphere, was
by its very nature insignificant in terms of permanent
intellectual contribution.

The internal evolution of the movement by the postwar
period also contributed to its lack of originality. Many of
the individuals who had contributed to the shaping of Young
Egypt's thought in the 1930's were estranged from the movement
after the war, with a resultant diminution of the intellectual
power which it could bring to bear on ideological (and other)
concerns. To an extent which had never applied to the prewar
Young Egypt, Ahmad Husayn was Young Egypt and the Socialist
Party in the postwar period - and Ahmad Husayn simply had
little which was new to say about the solution of Egypt's
problems.

The last statement touches on the core of the movement's
intellectual stagnation in the postwar period. In essence,
Young Egypt had evolved a particular intellectual paradigm, a
comprehensive set of related views about Egypt's problems and
their solution, in the 1930's. This world-view had been the
product of several individuals, not only Ahmad Husayn; for all
its distortions and over-simplifications, it had been a plausible
fit to Egyptian reality; and it had offered detailed suggestions
about solving Egypt's problems which had been both new (in part)
and appealing (to many). As a result, a considerable amount
from Young Egypt's prewar formulations had been absorbed, in
proportions which are impossible to determine exactly, into
the thought of Egypt's younger generation generally, to
resurface in the ideas of other figures, forces and movements
after the war. With much of Young Egypt's prewar thought thus
becoming part of the main current of the thought of the Egyptian
younger generation by the postwar period, and with the bulk of
its prewar ideas still being a plausible explanation of the
world around it, the movement found little impetus to alter
its ideas. Thus Young Egypt and the Socialist Party of Egypt
suffered from a kind of intellectual inertia after the war:
it had answered (to its own satisfaction) many of Egypt's
problems in the 1930's and, because it lacked the opportunity
to put its ideas to the test of experience and because others
were offering similar solutions by that time, it clung to
most of its answers in the postwar period.

The Legacy of Young Egypt

The place of the movement known variously as the Young Egypt Society (1933-1936), the Young Egypt Party (1937-1940), the Islamic Nationalist Party (1940-1941), again the Young Egypt Party (1944-1949), and finally the Socialist Party of Egypt (1949-1952) in the life of modern Egypt was appreciable. The movement's most immediate influence was political, as an organization operating in the hurly-burly of Egyptian public life and having a definite impact – greater at some times, lesser at others – on the course of Egyptian politics from the early 1930's to the early 1950's. But the movement's deeper and more permanent importance was in the realm of ideas, where its propaganda formed part of the intellectual milieu of Egypt and where the concepts which it expressed seem to have left lasting traces in the thought of the generation of which it was a part.

In terms of its political impact over the twenty years of its existence, Young Egypt must be evaluated as having been primarily a negative force in Egyptian public life. Never actually assuming political power in Egypt (a failure common, of course, to all the newer civilian movements of the 1930's and 1940's), Young Egypt never had the chance to put its ideas and its programs into operation. Lacking this opportunity, all of the movement's activities aimed at enhancing its own position in Egyptian politics in the long run served primarily to add to the instability and eventual incoherence of the Egyptian political system. Whether in the later 1930's when it helped to erode the image of the Wafd and to promote authoritarian concepts of government centered (then) on the young King, or in the early 1950's when it again denounced the ministerial performance of Egypt's grand old party and pressured the Wafdist ministry into confrontation with Great Britain, Young Egypt's actual contribution to the course of political events was that of weakening the image and the effectiveness of the Egyptian parliamentary monarchy. To term Young Egypt's political role a negative one is not to argue that the parliamentary monarchy was a regime which should have been maintained; certainly it had its flaws, flaws which magnified themselves over time, and perhaps its passing was (as many Egyptians believe) a beneficial thing. Rather, it is merely to point out that Young Egypt's greatest contribution to the way Egyptian politics developed was in sapping the viability of the parliamentary monarchy.

But the fundamental importance of Young Egypt in Egyptian history lies not in its political actions, where it was but one of many groups whose activities in the end contributed to the demise of the parliamentary monarchy. Rather, Young Egypt's most significant role was played in the realm of ideas, in its contribution to the evolution of Egyptian thought. Its intellectual impact was greatest in the 1930's, when more than any other organization it first articulated many of the concerns being felt by younger Egyptians in what was a politically and economically depressing decade and when it propounded a variety of reformist measures designed to meet those concerns. After World War II, due to its repression during the war, to its identification with a discredited foreign model (fascism), and to the ideological advances made by rival groups (including their incorporation of many of the themes of protest originally expressed by Young Egypt), the movement's impact on the development of Egyptian thought was a much smaller one.

To maintain that Young Egypt's ideas were important is not to hold that they were of great intellectual acuity. On the whole, Young Egypt's propaganda (and the word has been used purposely) contained neither a very penetrating analysis of the contemporary Egyptian situation nor a coherent, internally consistent program for solving Egypt's problems. In their general interpretations, the movement's spokesmen viewed the world through rather simplistic spectacles which reduced complex social processes and dilemmas to matters of "spirit" or "struggle." In their detailed analyses, they all too often seized on inessential symptoms of a genuine problem or offered solutions which were little more than emotional sloganeering (e.g., the reduction of the movement's "Islamic" program to superficial reforms like the restoration of the alms-tax; the conspicuous vagueness of the movement in regard to the new political structures which should replace the corrupt parliamentary system with "sound government. . . based on the service of the people"; the shallowness of its "socialism" a decade later). In fine, the men of Young Egypt were effective publicists in many ways, capable of articulating the common problems of their generation and of striking a responsive chord in many of the members of that generation; but they were hardly political or social theorists of the first rank.

Ideological shallowness, however, does not necessarily mean ideological unimportance. On one level, one does not have to subscribe to a Gresham's Law of the intellect to admit the possibility that Young Egypt's intellectual mediocrity may have made it more representative of the "average" member of the Egyptian younger generation of the 1930's and 1940's than the more sophisticated thought of the period. While there is no way to demonstrate this definitively in

view of the absence of a record of the contemporary ideas of
the bulk of educated younger Egyptians of the period, it is
possible that in Young Egypt's romanticism, in the comprehensive and emotional tenor of its nationalism, in its disillusionment with the parliamentary system and in its confused
but insistent demands for a greater measure of social justice
in Egypt, we may have something as typical of the concerns
of educated younger Egyptians of the 1930's and 1940's as
we are likely to see through the mists of the past. Certainly
the movement's staying-power in the face of adverse circumstances would seem to imply this: in spite of the various
internal and external difficulties which the movement
experienced, it continued to linger on the Egyptian scene
and indeed was capable of rebuilding a considerable following
as late as the early 1950's, fully a decade after it had
seemed to be destroyed as a political force. If Wasim Khalid
is correct in his observation that it took much of his
generation "many years to free themselves intellectually
from this leader" (i.e., Ahmad Husayn),[1] one reason for that
may well have been that Husayn's ideas continued to mirror
and reflect the approaches of much of that generation.

More importantly, Young Egypt's temporal primacy as the
first organized political movement in the period of the
parliamentary monarchy to emerge from the ranks of youth and
to give voice to the characteristic concerns of younger
Egyptians cannot have been without its effects on other
politically inclined younger Egyptians of the 1930's and
1940's. Temporal primacy does matter, if only in the sense
that the first who articulates a problem within a given
cultural milieu thereby to some extent defines the terms in
which others in the same environment consider the issue. Once
a particular question is raised, its original formulation
cannot be ignored: even those who have a different interpretation of its nature or a different solution for its
resolution must nevertheless take account of earlier formulations which are a living part of their world. In its raising
of the problems of Egyptian political, social, and economic
development from the early 1930's onwards, Young Egypt's ideas
thus came to constitute an element in the environment of other,
later-developing groups. Its formulations had to be taken
into account by them, minimally to be rejected, maximally to
be refined, extended, and incorporated into the thinking of
those who came after it. In brief, those who grew up in the
shadow of Young Egypt were in part forced to talk its language,
even if they did not always speak the same words.

It is beyond the scope of this study to examine systema-
tically the degree to which the concepts originally articulated
by Young Egypt in the 1930's had their reverberations in all of
the various tendencies and groups which emerged out of the

Egyptian younger generation of the 1930's and 1940's. It may
be useful, however, to conclude with a brief and tentative
exploration of the possible influence of Young Egypt's particular way of looking at the world on the most important segment
of Egypt's youth population of the 1930's and 1940's; the
young men who were in secondary school in the mid-1930's when
Young Egypt began to come to prominence in Egyptian politics,
who entered the Egyptian military in the later 1930's, and who
came to rule Egypt after 1952.

   At least several of the core group of the Free Officers
movement of the late 1940's and early 1950's had been connected
with Young Egypt in the 1930's.[2] The most important of these,
Jamal 'Abd al-Nasir, was a member of the society for about two
years in the mid-1930's, joining it after witnessing one of its
demonstrations, thereafter being an active member participating
in the production of its journal, but leaving it after a few
years because (in his own words) "despite its talk and protest
meetings, it seemed to achieve nothing."[3] 'Abd al-Nasir's
successor as President of Egypt, Anwar al-Sadat, has been
reported to have been a follower of Young Egypt in the 1930's,[4]
but his participation in the movement was not recalled by former
leaders of Young Egypt.[5] Other prominent members of the Free
Officers reportedly associated with Young Egypt in the 1930's
are Hasan Ibrahim,[6] Kamal al-Din Husayn,[7] and possibly Salah
Salim;[8] the latter's brother Jamal Salim may have been
associated with Young Egypt's postwar successor the Socialist
Party of Egypt.[9] Among former military men who rose to
ministerial rank in the Egypt of the 1960's, 'Ali Zayn 'Abd
al-Din, Samir Hilmi, and Sidqi Sulayman (the last a Prime
Minister of Egypt) are reported to have been formal members
of Young Egypt in the 1930's.[10]

   An earlier association with Young Egypt does not
necessarily indicate a permanent impression by Young Egypt,
of course: men, particularly young men, change, and what once
attracted them may be quite unrepresentative of their
orientation decades later. Evidence of intellectual influence
must be sought in what men say and do, not in what they
belonged to in their youth. But here there does seem to be
evidence that the concepts which had originally been expressed
by Young Egypt in the 1930's remained a component of the
thought of leading figures of the Nasirist regime. It would
also seem that the similarities between the earlier conceptions
of the men of Young Egypt and those of the leaders of
post-1952 Egypt were fairly basic ones existing on the level
of fundamental perceptions of social reality.

   An examination of the most authoritative document of
Nasirist Egypt (and reportedly one shaped with great care by
'Abd al-Nasir himself), the "National Charter" of May 1962,[11]
indicates the extent to which many of the deeper perceptions

121

about reality which had been expressed by Young Egypt in the 1930's could also be found in the mental outlook of Egypt's leadership in the 1960's. The Charter's view of Egypt's pre-modern history, like Young Egypt's in the 1930's, extols "the Egyptian people" as "the creator of civilization,"[12] credits Pharaonic civilization with being the "foremost" source of civilized world development,[13] and attributes "the main role" in the history of Islam to the people of Egypt[14] (although the Charter also calls ancient Egyptian civilization "Pharaonic Arab civilization" and insists on Egypt being "an integral part of the Arab nation,"[15] concepts well beyond those of Young Egypt). The emotional tenor of the Charter's passages on Egypt's place in the modern world bear perhaps the greatest similarity to the earlier ideas of Young Egypt: its denunciations of "the bitter humiliation" of "the Motherland" at the hands of imperialism,[16] its portrayal of imperialism as "not merely the looting of the people's resources, but an aggression on its dignity and pride,"[17] its characterization of the Aswan High Dam as "the symbol of the will and determination of the people to fashion its life,"[18] and its peroration which asserts that "our people have a sufficiently strong faith in God and in themselves to enable them to impose their will on life in order to remodel it according to their aspirations"[19] all view Egypt's modern history with much the same emotional protest against its course and determination to reverse that course which had been Young Egypt's most deeply-felt message in the 1930's.

Although the economic ideas of the Charter show considerable variation from those of Young Egypt in terms of specifics, even here the economic goals found in it are cast in terms resembling those employed by Young Egypt earlier (including the linkage of economic justice with the freedom and autonomy of the nation):

> Our immediate aim is to do away with exploitation, and to make possible the exercise of the natural right to have an equal opportunity, to dissolve class distinctions and to end the domination of one class which constitutes a threat to the freedom of the individual citizen and even to the freedom of the whole of the country by violating the rights of the people which creates the chance of exposing the country to the lurking danger of foreign forces. . . .[20]

Finally, the Charter shows the same insistence on the congruence of its ideas with religious values which was consistently asserted by Young Egypt. From its introduction which lists "unshakable faith in God, His Prophets and His sacred messages" as one of the "guarantees" of the success of the Egyptian Revolution to its concluding paragraphs which maintain that "our people believe in the message of religions" and which praise their "sufficiently strong faith in God,"[21] the Charter, like Young Egypt's propaganda before it, insists on the religious inspiration underlying its proposals for action in the here-and-now.

Perhaps one further quotation from a spokesman of the new regime can best express the similarity between Young Egypt's 1930's conceptualization of the Egyptian condition and the outlook of Egypt's post-1952 leadership. We have already quoted from Young Egypt's strident denunciations of the injustices of the political, economic and social order in prewar Egypt and cited its belief that "force is inevitable" for the restructuring of Egypt on a more egalitarian basis. Here are Anwar al-Sadat's views of the mid-1950's on the same subjects:

> Force was inevitable in order to achieve the elimination of the following factors:
>
> Force was inevitable in order to oust the tyrannical monarchy from the country and subsequently to eliminate its concomitants.
>
> Force was inevitable in order to exterminate feudalism absolutely, in order to be able to raise the standard of living and the spirit of the people, and in order to erase from it [the people] the last vestiges of humiliation and servility, surrender and fear.
>
> Force was inevitable in order to direct the entire people in defense of its rights and its ancient freedom which imperialism had gradually robbed from it, to the point where the people had lost all hope of salvation.
>
> Force was inevitable in order to be able to stand up to the political parties which had exploited the people in order to serve their own interests and the interests of the English, to stand up against the forces of reaction which had led the people astray, diverting it from the path which its true nature had set down for it in the past, and to set its feet in the path of progress and revival.
>
> Force was inevitable in order to achieve all this, to allow the people to realize the dream for which it has aspired; that it will rule itself by the hands of its sons, and that it will be able to determine its own destiny.[22]

Not only is the slogan "la buddah min quwwah" identical with the Ten Goals of Young Egypt of November 1938,[23] but the concern and the general outline of the solution are the same — to rout imperialism, the dominant foreigner generally, and the oppressive upper classes as well, all in order to build a more equitable society in which Egyptians would again be their own masters in their own country.

Whether the similarities discussed above are found to have consistently marked the thought of Jamal 'Abd al-Nasir and "Nasserism," and perhaps Anwar al-Sadat and "Sadatism," is a matter which must be left for systematic analysis by students of contemporary Egypt. They do seem to indicate, however, an appreciable degree of continuity in both language and orientation between the Young Egypt of pre-1952 Egypt and the establishment of post-1952 Egypt. If this should prove to be the case, it would not be too surprising: Young Egypt was a major component of the world in which Egypt's later leaders came to political awareness, and it would be only natural if the movement's thought has left lasting traces in the perceptions and worldview of those who were its peers.

Notes

ABBREVIATIONS OF PERIODICALS

Periodicals of Young Egypt

JI	Jaridah al-Ishtirakiyah
JMF	Jaridah Misr al-Fatah
JSJ	Jaridah al-Sha'b al-Jadid
JWN	Jaridah Wadi al-Nil
MD	Majallah al-Diya
MS	Majallah al-Sarkhah
MTH	Majallah al-Thaghr

Other Periodicals in Arabic

JA	Jaridah al-Ahram
JB	Jaridah al-Balagh
JJ	Jaridah al-Jihad
JM	Jaridah al-Misri
JS	Jaridah al-Siyasah
MH	Majallah al-Hilal
MJJ	Majallah al-Jil al-Jadid
MLJ	Majallah al-Liwa al-Jadid
MLM	Majallah al-Lataif al-Musawwarah
MM	Majallah al-Musawwar
MR	Majallah al-Risalah
MSM	Majallah al-Shubban al-Muslimin
MSW	Majallah al-Shubban al-Wafdiyin
MT	Majallah al-Tali'ah

Western-Language Periodicals

COC	Cahiers de l'Orient Contemporain
OM	Oriente Moderno
Times	The Times, London

CHAPTER ONE

1. See Nadav Safran, Egypt in Search of Political Community (Cambridge, Mass., 1961), pp. 147-148.
2. Statistics from Jean-Jacques Waardenburg, Les Universités dans le monde arabe actuel (two vol.; The Hague, 1966), II, p. 80.
3. For representative criticisms, see Abu al-Futouh Ahmad Radwan, Old and New Forces in Egyptian Education (New York, 1951), pp. 116-129; Malcolm H. Kerr, "Egypt," in James S. Coleman (ed.), Education and Political Development (Princeton, 1965), pp. 180-184.

4. Computed from the secondary school curriculum as outlined in Russell Galt, The Effects of Centralization on Education in Modern Egypt (Cairo, 1936), pp. 127-129.

5. Bayard Dodge, Al-Azhar: A Millenium of Muslim Learning (Washington, 1961), pp. 140-142, 146-152, 211-221.

6. Statistics from Waardenburg, Les Universites, II, p. 206.

7. For example, of the seven individuals selected by Nadav Safran as the leading mature spokesmen of Egyptian thought in the 1920's and 1930's (all of whom had been educated before or during World War I), five - Taha Husayn, Muhammad Husayn Haykal, Tawfiq al-Hakim, Ahmad Amin, and 'Ali 'Abd al-Raziq - came from rural, relatively well-to-do families (Safran, Political Community, pp. 129-140). By comparison, many of the figures of the following generation who became leaders or activists in post-1930 youth politics - Ahmad Husayn and Fathi Radwan of Young Egypt, Mahmud Yunis and Yusuf Hilmi of the Wafdist Blue Shirts, Jamal 'Abd al-Nasir of several movements in the 1930's - came from an urban environment, one in which the father was usually a government functionary.

8. See Safran, Political Community, pp. 148-150, for a discussion of the civics text of the period and their idealistic approach to politics (quotations from Safran).

9. On the former organization, see 'Abd al-Rahman al-Rafi'i, Mustafa Kamil: Ba'ith al-Harakah al-Wataniyah (third ed.; Cairo, 1961), pp. 188-192. On the Nationlist youth clubs, see ibid., pp. 256-261; 'Abd al-Rahman al-Rafi'i, Muhammad Farid: Ramz al-Ikhlas wa al-Tadhiyah (third ed.; Cairo, 1961), pp. 94-96, 109, 125-126.

10. 'Abd al-Rahman al-Rafi'i, Thawrah Sanah 1919 (two vol.; Cairo, 1946), II, p. 260.

11. Salāma Mūsā, The Education of Salāma Mūsā (trans. by L. O. Schuman; Leiden, 1961), pp. 141-144.

12. On the Young Men's Muslim Association, See Georg Kampffmeyer, "Egypt and Western Asia," in H. A. R. Gibb (ed.), Whither Islam? (London, 1932), pp. 102-170; Majid Khadduri, Political Trends in the Arab World: The Role of Ideas and Ideals in Politics (Baltimore, 1970), pp. 70-73; and James Heyworth-Dunne, Religious and Political Trends in Modern Egypt (Washington, 1950), pp. 11-15. There are several monographs devoted to the Muslim Brotherhood: Richard P. Mitchell, The Society of the Muslim Brothers (London, 1969); Christina P. Harris, Nationalism and Revolution in Egypt (The Hague, 1964); Ishak Musa al-Husaini, The Moslem Brethren: Greatest of Modern Islamic Movements (Beirut, 1956); and the bulk of Heyworth-Dunne, Religious and Political Trends.

13. E.g., Ahmad Husayn and Fathi Radwan of Young Egypt. See below, p. 9.

14. Mahmud Isma'il 'Abdallah, Fihris al-Dawriyat al-'Arabiyah al-lati Taqtaniha al-Dar (multi-vol.; Cairo, 1961-), I, pp. 213-219.

15. See Nur al-Din Tarraf's memoirs of his youth, in 'Abd al-Tawwab 'Abd al-Hayy, 'Asir Hayati (Cairo, 1966), pp. 52-57.

16. On youth and the Wafd, see Ahmad Farid 'Ali, Kifah al-Shabab wa Zuhur Jamal 'Abd al-Nasir (Cairo, 1963), pp. 33-35; on the founding of the national organization, see MSW, Oct. 11, 1937, p. 12.

17. On the Liberal Constitutionalist youth groups, see Ahmad Husayn, Imani (first ed.; Cairo, 1936), pp. 66-67; JS, Sept. 1, 1929, p. 5.

18. The intellectual climate of Egypt in the interwar period is discussed in detail from differing perspectives in Jacques Berque, Egypt: Imperialism and Revolution (trans. by Jean Stewart; London, 1972), part Four, chapters Six-Eight, Ten; P. J. Vatikiotis, The Modern History of Egypt (New York, 1969), chapters Thirteen-Fourteen.

19. Raoul Makarius, La jeunesse intellectuelle d'Égypte au lendemain de la deuxième guerre mondiale (The Hague, 1960). The following observations are based on pp. 9-14 of this work.

20. See in particular Rafi'i's volumes Mustafa Kamil, Muhammad Farid, and Thawrah Sanah 1919 for this interpretation.

21. Husayn, Imani, pp. 43-44.

22. In his recollections in 'Abd al-Hayy, 'Asir Hayati, p. 55.

23. In his recollections of his youth in ibid., pp. 31-33.

24. From a speech of June 1938 as quoted in JMF, June 6, 1938, p. 6.

25. Gustave E. von Grunebaum, Modern Islam: The Search for Cultural Identity (New York, 1964), p. 264.

CHAPTER TWO

1. There is more biographical material available on Husayn than on Radwan. Husayn wrote his partially autobiographical work Imani as early as 1936, and a revised and updated edition appeared in 1946 [henceforth cited as "Imani (1936)" and "Imani (1946)"]. In the 1960's he composed three autobiographical novels which, when used with care, supplement the picture of his political career. These are Azhar (Cairo, 1963); al-Duktur Khalid (Cairo, 1964); and Wa Ihtaraqat al-Qahirah (Cairo, 1968). For Radwan, biographical articles appeared in the Cairo press after the coup of 1952 and his appointment as a

cabinet minister in September 1952: see MM, Aug. 1, 1952, p. 39; Sept. 12, p. 10; Oct. 10, pp. 15-16; MJJ, Nov. 7, 1952, pp. 4-7. Radwan also wrote a partial autobiography, Qubayl al-Fajr (Cairo, 1957), and his recent literary study of the writers of the 1919-1952 period, 'Asr wa Rijal (Cairo, 1967), contains considerable autobiographical material. In addition, I have interviewed both men.

2. While biographical accounts of Radwan give May 14 as his birthdate, Radwan claims that his birth certificate is erroneous and that he was born on May 7, 1911 (interview).

3. Interviews with Ahmad Husayn and Fathi Radwan.

4. Radwan, 'Asr, pp. 250-251, 466-468; MM, Aug. 1, 1952, p. 39; MJJ, Nov. 7, 1952, p. 6.

5. Husayn, Imani (1936), pp. 45-47.

6. Ibid., pp. 66-67.

7. As reported in JS, Sept. 1, 1929, p. 5 (italics mine).

8. Husayn, Imani (1936), p. 44; Husayn, Azhar, pp. 111-114; Radwan, 'Asr, p. 372.

9. MS, March 7, 1930, p. 2; Oct. 7, 1933, p. 1; Husayn, Imani (1946), p. 46; Radwan, 'Asr, p. 165.

10. For detailed accounts of Egyptian political developments in the early 1930's, see Berque, Egypt, pp. 435-454; Vatikiotis, Egypt, pp. 280-286; 'Abd al-Rahman al-Rafi'i, Fi A'qab al-Thawrah al-Misriyah (three vol.; Cairo, 1947-1951), II, pp. 110-197.

11. The material on the Conference and Radwan's involvement in it is taken from MJJ, Nov.7, 1952, p. 6; Radwan, 'Asr, pp. 99, 164-165, 401-402, 468, 601; Anis Sayigh, al-Fikrah al-'Arabiyah fi Misr (Beirut, 1959), p. 202; Abu al-Hajjaj Hafiz, al-Shahid Kamal al-Din Salah (Cairo, n.d.), pp. 24-25.

12. Anwar al-Jindi, al-Kuttab al-Mu'asirun (Cairo, 1957), p. 138.

13. On these economic activities, see Vatikiotis, Egypt, p. 322; Rafi'i, Fi A'qab, II, pp. 326-327; Mūsā, Education, pp. 134, 137-138; MR, Nov. 15, 1933, passim.

14. Husayn, Imani (1946), pp. 51-55; Radwan, 'Asr, pp. 90-91, 97-101, 120-121, 221, 397.

15. The following information on the Plan's first drive is taken from the press reports in JA, Jan. 2, 1932, p. 7; Jan. 3, p. 7; Jan. 7, p. 7; Jan. 26, pp. 5, 7; Feb. 1, p. 7; Feb 13, p. 7; March 1, p. 7; March 3, p. 6.

16. JA, Sept. 3, 1932, p. 7; Husayn, Imani (1946), pp. 53-55; Radwan 'Asr, pp. 100-101; Rafi'i, Fi A'qab, II, p. 326; Ahmad Husayn, al-Ard al-Tayyibah (Cairo, 1951), p. 146.

17. MH, XLI (1932-1933), p. 589; Husayn, Imani (1946), p. 53.

18. JA, March 8, 1935, p. 10; MTH, April 5, 1937, p. 4.
19. Rafi'i, Fi A'qab, II, p. 327; Muhammad Subayh, Ayyam wa Ayyam, 1882-1965 (Cairo, 1968), p. 252.
20. The program of the society as reprinted in MT, March 1965, pp. 155-157, lists the twelve founding members. Radwan originally did not sign the program because he felt it was too political for his taste (according to his biography in MJJ, Nov. 7, 1952, pp. 6-7). But he had overcome his doubts by the end of 1933.
21. Quoted in JA, Nov. 2, 1933, p. 5.
22. The material on the separation of Young Egypt's activists from the Piastre Plan is taken from JA, Nov. 2, 1933, p. 7; Jan. 8, 1934, p. 11; Jan. 13, p. 9; Jan. 14, p. 1; Husayn, Imani (1946), pp. 77, 80; Husayn, Azhar, pp. 313-315.
23. Radwan, 'Asr, p. 372.
24. According to both Muhammad Subayh (writing in JMF, Oct. 10, 1938, p. 4) and Fathi Radwan (interview).
25. The following summary of the program is based on its first published version in MS, Oct. 21, 1933, pp. 5-7. The program is also available in Husayn, Imani (1946), pp. 64-71, and in MT, March 1965, pp. 155-157.
26. MLM, June 29, 1936, p. 6; Husayn, Imani (1946), p. 74.
27. Published in MS, March 31, 1934, pp. 4, 13. Unless otherwise noted, the following information on the structure of Young Egypt is based on this document.
28. MS, Jan. 6, 1934, p. 6; Jan. 27, p. 5; March 31, p. 4.
29. Instructions on how to form a shu'bah are given in MS, Jan. 6, 1934, p. 7.
30. MS, March 10, 1934, pp. 2, 10.
31. MLM, June 29, 1936, p. 6; interviews.
32. JMF, Jan. 1, 1939, p. 8; Husayn, Imani (1936), p. 83.
33. JWN, May 1, 1935, p. 1; June 19, p. 1; Husayn, Imani (1946), pp. 171-172.
34. MS, Nov. 25, 1933, p. 2; Feb. 4, 1934, p. 2; Feb. 25, p. 3; May 6, p. 9; Sept. 2, p. 9; Husayn, Imani (1936), pp. 92-93.
35. MS, Dec. 30, 1933, pp. 1-2; Jan. 13, 1934, p. 9; Jan. 27, p. 9; Feb. 10, p. 2. The same propaganda technique was employed by the Muslim Brotherhood from the early 1930's onwards: see Husaini, Moslem Brethren, pp. 47-49, and Mitchell, Muslim Brothers, p. 15.
36. MS, Dec. 2, 1933, pp. 6, 8; Feb. 25, 1934, p. 9; March 17, p. 4; Husayn, Imani (1936), pp. 136-138.
37. MS, Jan. 27, 1934, p. 5; Dec. 27, p. 7; Jan. 14, 1935, p. 8; Jan. 21, pp. 8-11; Husayn, Imani (1936), pp. 121-139.
38. MS, Jan. 14, 1935, p. 8; Jan. 21, pp. 8-11; JA, June 24, 1934, p. 10; Aug. 27, p. 8; March 17, 1935, p. 10;

May 13, p. 8; Sept. 17, p. 8.

39. JA, June 24, 1934, p. 10: see also Husayn, Imani (1936), p. 81.

40. MS, March 3, 1934, p. 13; Jan. 14, 1935, p. 8; Jan. 31, pp. 8-9; Husayn, Imani (1936), pp. 131, 167.

41. MS, March 10, 1934, p. 2; Husayn, Imani (1936), p. 81.

42. JA, Feb. 16, 1935, p. 10.

43. JMF, Nov. 19, 1938, p. 2.

44. This is the conclusion of Rafi'i, Fi A'qab, III, p. 53, and Sayigh, al-Fikrah al-'Arabiyah, p. 196, as well as that of the movement's former leaders (interviews).

45. JA, Nov. 2, 1933, p. 7; Jan. 8, 1934, p. 11; Jan. 14, p. 1; JJ, Nov. 11, 1934, p. 4. This is also the tenor of British reports about the movement in 1934: see PRO, FO 371/17977/46 (Jan. 19, 1934); PRO, FO 371/17977/367 (April 25, 1934); PRO, FO 371/17977/129 (May 6, 1934). I am indebted to Professor Charles D. Smith for bringing these and the following references to Public Record Office materials to my attention.

46. JMF, Oct. 2, 1944, pp. 9-10, and repeated in Husayn, Imani (1946), pp. 73-74.

47. See the Wafdist 'Abbas Mahmud al-'Aqqad's attack on the society in JJ, Nov. 11, 1934, p. 4, and Ahmad Husayn's discussion of the organization's relationship to the Wafd in his Murafa'at al-Rais (Cairo, 1937), pp. 48-59.

48. Quoted from a proclamation of the society in JA, Nov. 2, 1934, p. 10.

49. JMF, June 22, 1939, p. 4.

50. JA, Nov. 16, 1933, p. 6; Dec. 4, p. 7; May 6, 1934, p. 9; MS, Feb. 25, 1934, p. 3.

51. Husayn, Imani (1946), p. 97.

52. JA, Feb. 7, 1935, p. 10; Feb. 20, p. 9; Feb. 21, p. 10.

53. MS, Jan. 14, 1935, p. 2; JA, Sept. 6, 1936, p. 11; JB, Nov. 1, 1936, pp. 1, 11. British reports also speculated that, if any political party was behind the movement, it was the Nationalists: see PRO, FO 371/17977/46 (Jan. 19, 1934); PRO, FO 371/17977/367 (April 25, 1934).

54. Report no. 505, Bulkeley, July 17, 1934 ("Communist Movements in Egypt"), United States National Archives, Microfilm series T-120 (Deutsches Auswärtiges Amt), roll 4873, frames L310544-310545.

55. MS, Dec. 30, 1933, p. 3; June 23, 1934, p. 7; Oct. 6, p. 3.

56. MS, Aug. 25, 1934, p. 5.

57. MS, Aug. 25, 1934, p. 5; Sept 1, p. 9; Sept. 8, p. 9; Sept. 28, pp. 9-10.

58. JA, Sept. 27, 1934, p. 8; MS, Sept. 28, 1934, p. 9.

59. JM, June 18, 1937, p. 12; Husayn, Imani (1946), p. 155.

60. JA, May 7, 1934, p. 8; June 24, p. 10; Aug. 27, p. 8;
    MS, Jan. 14, 1935, p. 8; Jan. 21, pp. 8-11.
61. JA, March 17, 1935, p. 10.
62. JA, May 27, 1935, p. 9.
63. MS, May 17, 1935, p. 1; Nov. 5, p. 8.
64. The developments of 1935-1936 are discussed in detail
    in Rafi'i, Fi A'qab, II, pp. 197-214; Berque, Egypt,
    pp. 451-465; H. A. R. Gibb, "The Situation in Egypt,"
    International Affairs, XV (1936), pp. 351-373; Mahmud Y.
    Zayid, Egypt's Struggle for Independence (Beirut, 1965),
    pp. 145-161; James P. Jankowski, "The Egyptian Blue
    Shirts and the Egyptian Wafd, 1935-1938," Middle Eastern
    Studies, VI, no. 1 (January 1970), pp. 77-95.
65. JA, Nov. 14, 1935, p. 12; Radwan, 'Asr, p. 221.
66. JMF, Feb. 21, 1938, p. 5.
67. JA, Nov. 14, 1935, p. 2; Dec. 6, pp. 1-2.
68. Young Egypt's announcement of the delegation as quoted
    in JA, Nov. 27, 1935, p. 9.
69. MS, Dec. 14, 1935, pp. 10, 22; JA, Jan. 7, 1936, p. 9;
    Jan. 9, p. 9; Husayn, Imani (1946), p. 199; Ahmad Husayn,
    Sab'un Yawman lil-Di'ayah fi Urubba (Cairo, 1936),
    pp. 6-18; Young Egypt Society, Egypt and Great Britain
    (London, 1936).
70. Times, Jan. 31, 1936, p. 13; Husayn, Imani (1946),
    pp. 221-223; Radwan, 'Asr, p. 299.
71. JA, Jan. 28, 1936, p. 8; Jan. 29, p. 7; Feb. 6, p. 10;
    Feb. 11, p. 9.
72. Heyworth-Dunne, Religious and Political Trends, pp. 26-
    27.
73. JA, Feb. 6, 1936, p. 10; Feb. 18, p. 7; March 22, p. 12;
    April 26, p. 12; Husayn, Imani (1946), p. 235.
74. Ibid., pp. 235-236.
75. Quotation from Husayn, Imani (1936), p. 301: see also
    JMF, June 22, 1939, p. 4.
76. JA, April 10, 1936, p. 9.
77. Speech of March 1936 by Husayn as quoted in his Imani
    (1936), p. 301.
78. Quotation from a party proclamation as quoted in JA,
    March 31, 1936, p. 12; additional data from JA, March 22,
    1936, p. 12.
79. Quoted in JA, May 20, 1936, p. 10.
80. JA, June 1, 1936, p. 10; June 3, p. 10; June 15, p. 11;
    JB, June 3, 1936, p. 6; June 4, p. 7; Husayn, Imani
    (1946), pp. 247-253; OM, XVI (1936), pp. 419-420.
81. Quoted from Nahhas's speech in JA, June 23, 1936, p. 2
    (italics mine).
82. JA, June 23, 1936, p. 2; JB, June 24, 1936, p. 1.
83. JA, June 24, 1936, p. 9; June 25, p. 9; July 10, p. 10;
    Oct. 21, p. 10; Oct. 25, p. 6; Husayn, Imani (1946),

pp. 281-284.

84. On this organization see Jankowski, "Blue Shirts," _passim_.

85. _JA_, June 27, 1936, p. 9; June 28, p. 9; June 29, p. 8; July 1, p. 11; _JB_, June 29, 1936, p. 1; _OM_, XVI (1936), pp. 419-420.

86. Quoted in _JA_, July 22, 1936, p. 12: see also _JA_, July 15, 1936, p. 9.

87. _JA_, Aug. 13, 1936, p. 11; Aug. 14, p. 10; Aug. 15, p. 10; Feb. 17, 1937, p. 9; _JB_, Aug. 13, 1936, p. 6.

88. _JA_, Aug. 13, 1936, p. 11; Aug. 15, p. 10; Aug. 18, p. 8; Aug. 21, p. 8; _JMF_, Jan. 1, 1939, p. 8; Husayn, _Imani_ (1946), p. 290; Husayn, _Murafa'at al-Rais_, pp. 134-135.

89. _Manchester Guardian_, July 21, 1936, p. 12.

90. _MD_, Nov. 29, 1936, p. 1; Dec. 6, p. 8.

CHAPTER THREE

1. _MD_, Jan. 3, 1937, p. 1.

2. The following discussion of the party's organization is based on its organizational law as published in _MD_, Jan. 3, 1937, pp. 3-4.

3. The text of the legislation is given in _JMF_, March 10, 1938, p. 3.

4. _JMF_, March 17, 1938, p. 3.

5. _Ibid._

6. The Council's membership and the educational background of all but one of its members is given in _MTH_, April 5, 1937, p. 3.

7. Interview with Fathi Radwan.

8. The close personal bond between Wakil and Husayn is discussed in Mustafa al-Wakil, _'Umar ibn 'Abd al-'Aziz_ (Cairo, 1939), pp. 3-6; Husayn, _Azhar_, pp. 456, 522, 578-580. Most of Husayn's post-World War II publications are dedicated to the memory of Mustafa al-Wakil.

9. _JMF_, March 17, 1937, p. 7.

10. _JMF_, Aug. 23, 1938, p. 2.

11. _JA_, Feb. 6, 1938, p. 10; _JB_, Jan. 27, 1938, p. 1; Feb. 5, pp. 1, 11; _JMF_, April 7, 1938, p. 2.

12. _MTH_, March 22, 1937, pp. 1, 6; April 27, p. 5.

13. _JB_, Jan. 20, 1938, p. 6.

14. Radwan, _'Asr_, p. 37.

15. For the development of the party's publishing activities in general, see _MTH_, March 22, 1937, pp. 1, 6; April 3, p. 6; April 27, p. 5; _JMF_, Jan. 31, 1938, p. 6; May 5, p. 8; May 9, p. 7; July 4, p. 7; Aug. 15, p. 8; Sept. 8, p. 8; Sept. 12, p. 9; Nov. 19, p. 2; May 8, 1939, p. 8.

16. The following information on the party's local activities

has been gathered from the page devoted to the affairs of party branches in MTH during 1937 and in JMF during 1938 and 1939.

17. JMF, July 25, 1938, p. 7; Aug. 4, p. 7; Aug. 29, p. 7; Sept. 8, p. 11; Sept. 19, p. 8; Oct. 13, p. 8; Jan. 1, 1939, p. 12.
18. JA, June 30, 1938, p. 10; JMF, May 9, 1938, p. 7; June 13, p. 7; June 27, p. 7; July 7, p. 7.
19. JA, Aug. 4, 1937, p. 12; Aug. 7, p. 12; Aug. 13, p. 11; Aug. 23, p. 9; MTH, April 24, 1937, p. 7; Aug. 4, p. 12; Aug. 23, pp. 2, 10; Aug. 30, p. 10; Sept. 2, pp. 2, 10-11.
20. JMF, May 23, 1938, p. 8: see also July 7, p. 7.
21. MD, Feb. 17, 1937, p. 6; JMF, Sept. 29, 1938, p. 7; Oct. 10, pp. 5-8.
22. JMF, May 23, 1938, p. 8.
23. JMF, July 25, 1938, p. 6; Oct. 3, p. 6; Oct. 10, pp. 5-8; July 3, 1939, p. 7.
24. JMF, June 1, 1939, p. 4; June 15, p. 7; July 17, pp. 1, 7.
25. JMF, Oct. 3, 1938, p. 7.
26. JA, Jan. 25, 1938, pp. 3, 6; Feb. 7, p. 11; April 15, p. 2; Aug. 19, pp. 7, 9; JB, Jan. 25, 1938, p. 8; Feb. 19, p. 8; March 12, p. 7; April 15, p. 10.
27. MTH, July 19, 1937, p. 4.
28. Interview with Ahmad Husayn.
29. Interview with Fathi Radwan.
30. Interview with 'Ali Fahmi.
31. MTH, Oct. 21, 1937, p. 6.
32. JMF, Oct. 27, 1938, p. 5.
33. See the reports listed in note 26, above.
34. Interview with Ahmad Husayn.
35. Wasim Khalid, al-Kifah al-Sirri Didda al-Injiliz (Cairo, 1963), pp. 16-17.
36. See below, pp. 34-35.
37. JMF, Jan. 31, 1938, p. 1; March 21, p. 4; April 28, p. 5; May 2, p. 1; Ahmad Husayn, Murafa'at Ahmad Husayn fi Qadiyah Tahtim al-Khanat (Cairo, 1939), pp. 66-67.
38. JMF, June 22, 1939, p. 6.
39. Lukasz Hirszowicz feels that "the extremist opposition" in Egypt, "such as Misr al-Fatat," may have been in contact with agents of the Nazi Party (rather than the German Foreign Office) in the later 1930's. But Hirszowicz offers no documentary evidence to back up this supposition. See Lukasz Hirszowicz, The Third Reich and the Arab East (London, 1966), p. 36.
40. Interviews with Ahmad Husayn and Fathi Radwan.
41. Muhammad Subayh, Min al-'Alamayn Ila Sajn al-Ajanib (Cairo, 1963), p. 23.
42. The quotation is by a lead article by Husayn in JMF, Sept. 29, 1938, p. 1. A similar interpretation which

blamed Germany for the Munich crisis was given in JMF,
Sept. 26, 1938, p. 6.

43. JMF, March 16, 1939, p. 6.
44. JMF, April 10, 1939, p. 1.
45. As given in JMF, Aug. 28, 1939, p. 9.
46. JMF, Sept. 2, 1939, p. 3.
47. The first charge is quoted in Husayn, Murafa'at al-Rais,
    pp. 3-4, the second in JA, March 5, 1937, p. 12.
48. MTH, April 3, 1937, p. 2.
49. Husayn, Murafa'at al-Rais, p. 10; MTH, May 31, 1937,
    p. 7.
50. JA, Feb. 27, 1937, p. 12; March 14, p. 9; May 25,
    p. 11; Oct. 1, p. 12; MD, March 19, 1937, p. 2; MTH,
    March 22, 1937, p. 2; April 1, p. 6; April 3, p. 6.
51. JA, March 19, 1937, p. 11; JB, March 18, 1937, p. 6;
    JM, March 19, 1937, pp. 9-10; MTH, April 12, 1937,
    p. 12; MSW, May 16, 1937, pp. 4-5.
52. The events of late 1937 are discussed in detail in
    Rafi'i, Fi A'qab, III, pp. 44-57; Muhammad Husayn
    Haykal, Mudhakkirat fi al-Siyasah al-Misriyah (two
    vol.; Cairo, 1951-1953), II, pp. 33-58; Philip Graves,
    "The Story of the Egyptian Crisis," Nineteenth Century
    and After, March 1938, pp. 297-313; Berque, Egypt,
    pp. 530-536.
53. MTH, Aug. 23, 1937, p. 2.; Oct. 11, p. 5.
54. For details on these incidents, see OM, XVII (1937),
    pp. 580-584; Jankowski, "Blue Shirts," pp. 88-91.
55. JA, Nov. 29, 1937, pp. 1, 9; Dec. 1, p. 9; Dec. 2,
    p. 9; Dec. 11, p. 11; JM, Dec. 1, 1937, pp. 2, 9;
    Dec. 9, p. 13; Times, Dec. 1, 1937, p. 16; Rafi'i,
    Fi A'qab, III, p. 53; Report no. 874, Cairo, Dec. 3,
    1937 ("Internal Developments in Egypt"), United States
    National Archives, Microfilm series T-120 (Deutsches
    Auswärtiges Amt), roll 4358, frames K215830-215831.
    The investigation into the assassination attempt was
    not completed until the Wafd had fallen from power,
    and was released by a ministry opposed to the Wafd.
    As such, it found Young Egypt as an organization free
    of any complicity in the attempt and brought out an
    indictment only against the would-be assassin himself.
    See "Mudhakkirah al-Naib al-'Amm," published in JA,
    Feb. 23, 1938, p. 3. 'Abd al-Qadir was found guilty
    and sentenced to ten years' hard labor in March 1939
    (JA, March 28, 1939, p. 11). In an article written
    after his release from prison in 1945, 'Abd al-Qadir
    maintained that the assassination attempt was his doing
    alone and that "none of his friends" knew about it in
    advance (MLJ, Dec. 5, 1945, pp. 18-19).
56. JMF, Oct. 13, 1938, pp. 1, 5, 9; Jan. 28, 1939,

p. 5; March 20, p. 1; April 8, pp. 4-5.

57. This propaganda campaign is discussed in detail in Elie Kedourie, "Egypt and the Caliphate, 1915-1952," in his The Chatham House Version and Other Middle-Eastern Studies (New York, 1970), pp. 177-212 (see particularly pp. 199-204).

58. JMF, June 6, 1938, p. 6.

59. JMF, Jan. 28, 1939, p. 3: see also JMF, June 19, 1939, p. 6.

60. JMF, March 7, 1938, p. 8.

61. JMF, May 9, 1938, p. 7.

62. Heyworth-Dunne, Religious and Political Trends, p. 104.

63. The interview was reprinted in JMF, May 9, 1938, p. 4; the claim about King Faruq was made in JMF, June 13, 1938, p. 6. Other rumors in this vein were reported in JB, June 13, 1938, p. 5.

64. Quotation from JMF, Aug. 4, 1938, p. 5: see also JMF, May 23, 1938, p. 5.

65. For declarations to this effect, see JA, Feb. 6, 1938, p. 10; JB, Jan. 27, 1938, p. 6; Feb. 5, pp. 1, 11.

66. See below, pp. 60-64.

67. JMF, Sept. 5, 1938, p. 3.

68. JMF, Oct. 17, 1938, p. 4.

69. JMF, Sept. 12, 1938, p. 8.

70. JMF, Nov. 5, 1938, p. 7.

71. JMF, Nov. 7, 1938, pp. 5, 7; Nov. 10, p. 10; Nov. 12, pp. 12-13.

72. JMF, Nov. 14, 1938, p. 12.

73. The publication of this list of goals in JMF began on Nov. 10, 1938 (p. 1), and continued until the latter half of 1939.

74. JMF, Nov. 14, 1938, pp. 2-3, 8-9.

75. Quotations from JMF, Nov. 14, 1938, p. 8, and Nov. 17, p. 1.

76. JA, Jan. 6, 1939, p. 11; Jan. 7, p. 12; Jan. 16, p. 10; Jan. 18, p. 11; Jan. 20, p. 10; Feb. 6, p. 11; JMF, Jan. 9, 1939, pp. 1, 7; Jan. 12, p. 7; Jan. 14, p. 7; Jan. 17, p. 4; Jan. 21, pp. 7, 9; Jan. 26, p. 9; Feb. 9, p. 7; Feb. 14, p. 5.

77. JA, Jan. 21, 1939, p. 7; Feb. 14, p. 5.

78. JA, Feb. 19, 1939, p. 11; JMF, Feb. 13, 1939, p. 7; Feb. 18, p. 4; April 6, pp. 5-6; April 8, p. 7.

79. This is discussed below, pp. 53-54.

80. JMF, July 8, 1939, p. 3.

81. JMF, July 17, 1939, pp. 6-7; July 20, p. 2.

82. JMF, Aug. 24, 1939, p. 12; Aug. 26, p. 12; Aug. 31, p. 11.

83. JMF, July 22, 1939, p. 8; July 24, p. 5; Aug. 7, p. 5; Aug. 12, pp. 9, 11; Aug. 19, p. 11; Aug. 26, p. 6; Sept. 12, p. 3.

84. Heyworth-Dunne, Religious and Political Trends, p. 36.
85. JMF, Oct. 20, 1938, pp. 3-4; May 22, 1939, p. 2; June 10, p. 12.
86. JMF, June 17, 1939, p. 10.
87. See Mitchell, Muslim Brothers, pp. 17-19.
88. Interviews with Ahmad Husayn and Fathi Radwan; for a (veiled) contemporary admission that inroads were being made into Young Egypt's following by the Brotherhood, see JMF, Oct. 20, 1938, pp. 3-4.
89. An account of the meeting at which the change of name was adopted and the full text of the new program are contained in JMF, March 18, 1940, pp. 4-8.
90. For the former, see JMF, March 18, 1940, p. 8; June 13, p. 1; for the latter, JMF, May 13, 1940, p. 1; March 13, 1941, p. 3.
91. Quoted from one indictment as given in JMF, Jan. 19, 1939, p. 1.
92. JA, Jan. 16, 1939, p. 10; April 7, p. 11; April 21, p. 10; JMF, Jan. 14, 1939, p. 6; Feb. 16, p. 1; March 23, pp. 3, 10; OM, XIX (1939), pp. 106-107, 228.
93. JA, April 21, 1939, p. 10; June 11, p. 10; JMF, June 1, 1939, p. 1; June 5, p. 7; June 12, p. 7; Jan. 1, 1940, p. 3; June 17, p. 11.
94. JMF, Jan. 17, 1939, pp. 7-8; Jan. 19, p. 7; Jan. 26, p. 9; Feb. 16, p. 8; Feb. 18, p. 3; Feb. 25, p. 2; Feb. 27, p. 7.
95. JMF, Jan. 19, 1939, p. 7; July 1, pp. 5, 8.
96. JMF, June 3, 1939, p. 7; June 15, p. 6; June 17, p. 8; June 22, p. 6; June 24, p. 11; July 1, p. 7; July 3, p. 7; July 27, p. 9; Aug. 12, pp. 9, 11; Aug. 14, p. 7.

CHAPTER FOUR

1. MS, Oct. 21, 1933, p. 5.
2. Husayn, Imani (1946), p. 15. Although page references here are to the 1946 edition, the passages were written in the 1930's.
3. Ibid., p. 19.
4. Ibid., p. 30.
5. Ibid., p. 31.
6. Ibid., pp. 31-32.
7. Ibid., p. 32.
8. Ibid., p. 34.
9. Ibid., pp. 34-35.
10. Ibid., p. 35.
11. Ibid.
12. The quotations are from two of Mustafa Kamil's speeches (the first of 1902, the second of 1907) as given in the

discussion of Kamil's nationalist thought in Charles Wendell, The Evolution of the Egyptian National Image: From Its Origins to Ahmad Lutfi al-Sayyid (Berkeley, 1972), pp. 266-267.

13. Wilfred Cantwell Smith, Islam in Modern History (Princeton, 1957), p. 117.
14. Ibid., pp. 118-119.
15. David C. Gordon, Self-Determination and History in the Third World (Princeton, 1971), pp. 129, 185-186.
16. Husayn, Murafa'at al-Rais, p. 31.
17. Husayn, Imani (1936), p. 63.
18. Ibid., p. 221.
19. Husayn, Imani (1946), p. 25.
20. From a speech by Husayn of December 1933 as quoted in ibid., p. 108.
21. From the earlier development of these attitudes towards the West, see Hisham Sharabi, Arab Intellectuals and the West: The Formative Years, 1875-1914 (Baltimore, 1970), pp. 44-45, 98-100; Wendell, Egyptian National Image, pp. 146-147.
22. Husayn, Imani (1946), pp. 46-47, from which the following quotations are taken.
23. JMF, April 21, 1938, p. 1.
24. JMF, May 19, 1938, p. 1.
25. JMF, Dec. 5, 1938, p. 4.
26. Jacques Berque, The Arabs: Their History and Future (trans. by Jean Stewart; New York, 1964), p. 42.
27. Ibid., p. 265.
28. From a speech by Husayn of April 1938 as quoted in JMF, April 14, 1938, p. 10.
29. MTH, April 5, 1937, p. 1.
30. From the party's official proclamation on the Montreux Convention as given in MTH, July 5, 1937, p. 2.
31. Ibid.
32. For examples, see Fathi Radwan writing in MH, XLI (1932-1933), pp. 1358, 1360; Ahmad Husayn writing in MS, Sept. 29, 1934, p. 9; Mustafa al-Wakil writing in JMF, April 14, 1938, p. 2.
33. From a speech of August 1938 as quoted in JMF, Aug. 23, 1938, p. 12.
34. Ibid., p. 13.
35. MS, Oct. 21, 1933, pp. 5-6.
36. JMF, March 18, 1940, p. 4.
37. See below, pp. 74-76.
38. On Egyptian attitudes towards Arab unity in the later 1930's, see Enrico Nunè, "L'idea dell'unita araba in recenti dibattiti della stampa del vincino oriente," OM, XVIII (1938), pp. 401-412.
39. JMF, May 23, 1938, p. 7.

40. Ibid.
41. From an interview by Husayn with the Giornale de Genoa as reprinted in JMF, Aug. 11, 1938, p. 3.
42. JMF, March 18, 1940, p. 4.
43. As given in JMF, April 3, 1941, p. 3. The following quotations are taken from this document.
44. MS, Oct. 21, 1933, pp. 5-6.
45. For a discussion and examples of this, see Sharabi, Arab Intellectuals, pp. 77, 93, 96-100.
46. Majallah al-Madrasah al-Khidiwiyah, December 1928, as quoted in Husayn, Imani (1946), p. 41.
47. Speech of January 1935 as quoted in MS, Jan. 14, 1935, p. 2.
48. From the program of 1933 as given in MS, Oct. 21, 1933, p. 5.
49. MS, Dec. 30, 1933, p. 9.
50. From an official proclamation of the society as cited in JA, Nov. 2, 1934, p. 10.
51. See Husayn's "Declaration to the Egyptian People" as given in MS, Dec. 7, 1935, p. 5.
52. From an article written by Husayn in May 1936 as quoted in Husayn, Imani (1946), p. 243.
53. See Husayn, Imani (1936), pp. 60, 110, 134.
54. MD, Jan. 3, 1937, p. 1.
55. See the series of articles on the Copts and the Wafd in MTH, April 1, 1937, p. 7; April 12, p. 3; April 17, p. 4.
56. The first two accusations are from a speech by Husayn of January 1938 as quoted in JMF, Jan. 24, 1938, p. 9. The demand for arrests is from a lead article by Husayn in JMF, Feb. 24, 1938, p. 1.
57. Information on this Palace gambit cam be obtained from Haykal, Mudhakkirat, II, pp. 155-160; Radwan, 'Asr, pp. 544-545; Berque, Egypt, pp. 533-536, 562-564; Kedourie, "Egypt and the Caliphate," pp. 199-204.
58. Fathi Radwan, Musulini (Cairo, 1937), pp. 157-159.
59. From a speech of March 1936 by Husayn as given in Husayn, Imani (1936), p. 315.
60. As quoted in JMF, April 14, 1938, pp. 4-5; for similar laudatory remarks about Fascism and Nazism, see Husayn's first major speech of 1938 as quoted in JMF, Jan. 24, 1938, p. 11.
61. The first quotation is from JMF, Feb. 21, 1938, p. 4; the second is from JMF, June 27, 1938, p. 4.
62. JMF, July 21, 1938, p. 5.
63. JMF, July 28, 1938, p. 2.
64. JMF, Aug. 1, 1938, pp. 1-2.
65. From an interview with a correspondent of Il Lavoro Fascista, July 29, 1938, as quoted in JMF, Aug. 1, 1938,

p. 2. For a slightly different version of this passage
from the interview, see Walter Z. Laqueur, Communism
and Nationalism in the Middle East (London, 1956),
pp. 247-248. For a partial version of the Italian
text, see OM, XVIII (1938), pp. 450-451.

66. See above, pp. 32-34.
67. From a lead article by Husayn in JMF, March 31, 1938,
    p. 1.
68. Ibid.
69. From an official party declaration as given in JMF,
    April 4, 1938, p. 2.
70. JMF, May 19, 1938, pp. 1-2. The following quotations
    are taken from this article.
71. In a speech of April 1938 as quoted in JMF, April 18,
    1938, p. 6.
72. JMF, July 18, 1938, p. 5. The following quotations
    are from this article.
73. The petition demanding a "reforming revolution" is given
    in JMF, March 21, 1938, p. 3. The quotation from
    Husayn is from a speech of April 1938 as quoted in
    JMF, April 14, 1938, p. 7.
74. As given in JMF, Aug. 23, 1938, pp. 6-8, 12-17. The
    following quotations are from this text, pp. 6-7,
    14-15, 15-16.
75. As given in JMF, Nov. 14, 1938, pp. 2-12. The following
    quotations are from this text, pp. 2, 8.
76. The first quotation is from the society's 1933 program
    (MS, Oct. 21, 1933, p. 5), the second from the pamphlet
    published by Husayn and Radwan in England in 1936
    (Young Egypt Society, Egypt and Great Britain, pp. 10-
    11).
77. MS, Feb. 17, 1934, p. 4; Dec. 24, pp. 1, 6; JA, July 15,
    1936, p. 9.
78. Husayn, Imani (1946), pp. 27, 39.
79. From a speech by Husayn of August 1938 as given in JMF,
    Aug. 23, 1938, p. 16.
80. JMF, July 21, 1938, p. 3.
81. JMF, July 21, 1938, p. 5; July 28, p. 2.
82. JMF, Aug. 1, 1938, p. 1.
83. As quoted in JMF, Aug. 23, 1938, p. 16.
84. The following material is taken from the text of the
    program as published in JMF, March 18, 1940, pp. 4-8.
85. See above, p. 30.
86. JMF, March 18, 1940, p. 6.
87. The quotation is from a speech by Husayn of August 1938
    as quoted in JMF, Aug. 23, 1938, p. 14.
88. See above, p. 17.
89. From the program of 1933 as given in MS, Oct. 21, 1933,
    pp. 5-6.

90. <u>MS</u>, Oct. 21, 1933, pp. 5-7; Dec. 9, p. 9.
91. Quotation from <u>JMF</u>, April 7, 1938, p. 4. Similar injunctions are given in <u>JMF</u>, Nov. 10, 1938, p. 1; April 3, 1941, p. 3.
92. <u>JMF</u>, March 18, 1940, pp. 4-8. The following material is taken from this document.
93. The first quotation is from the program of 1933 as given in <u>MS</u>, Oct. 21, 1933, p. 5, the second from a speech by Husayn of December 1933 as quoted in Husayn, <u>Imani</u> (1946), pp. 205-206.
94. <u>JMF</u>, March 18, 1940, pp. 7-8.
95. The demand was made in at least three of Husayn's major speeches of 1938: see <u>JMF</u>, Jan. 24, 1938, p. 10; April 14, p. 12; Aug. 23, p. 16.
96. <u>JMF</u>, Oct. 13, 1938, p. 2; Nov. 10, p. 1.
97. <u>JMF</u>, March 18, 1940, p. 7.
98. From the program of March 1940; <u>JMF</u>, March 18, 1940, p. 7.
99. From a speech of Husayn of January 1938 as quoted in <u>JMF</u>, Jan. 24, 1938, p. 10: for almost identical phrasing, see his speech of April 1938 as quoted in <u>JMF</u>, April 14, 1938, p. 10.
100. <u>JMF</u>, March 18, 1940, p. 7.
101. <u>MS</u>, Oct. 21, 1933, pp. 5-6.
102. As quoted in Husayn, <u>Imani</u> (1946), p. 109.
103. As quoted in Husayn, <u>Imani</u> (1936), p. 187.
104. See above, pp. 39-41.
105. The first phrase is from an article by Husayn in <u>JMF</u>, March 28, 1938, p. 1, the second from an interview by Husayn with the journal <u>al-Nidal</u> as reprinted in <u>JMF</u>, June 6, 1938, p. 1.
106. As quoted in <u>JMF</u>, Nov. 14, 1938, p. 8: for very similar expressions by Husayn, see <u>JMF</u>, Aug. 23, 1938, p. 13; Oct. 13, p. 9.
107. <u>JMF</u>, March 18, 1940, p. 4.
108. <u>JMF</u>, July 6, 1939, p. 1. This particular article was a lengthy "message" (<u>risalah</u>) from Husayn to Hitler. It was reprinted in pamphlet form after the war, with texts in both Arabic and English and with only one (non-essential) paragraph omitted, as Ahmad Hussein, <u>Message to Hitler!</u> (New York, 1947).
109. From an official party proclamation of November 1938 as given in <u>JMF</u>, Nov. 18, 1939, p. 1.
110. From a speech by Husayn of August 1938 as given in <u>JMF</u>, Aug. 23, 1938, p. 16.
111. von Grunebaum, <u>Modern Islam</u>, p. 35.
112. <u>JMF</u>, March 18, 1940, pp. 4-8. The following quotations and data are taken from this source.
113. Quotation from Haykal, <u>Mudhakkirat</u>, II, p. 156.
114. <u>JMF</u>, Nov. 14, 1938, p. 8.

115. <u>JMF</u>, Jan 14, 1939, p. 6.
116. <u>JMF</u>, March 18, 1940, p. 4.
117. From a speech by Husayn of August 1938 as given in <u>JMF</u>, Aug. 23, 1938, pp. 6–7.

CHAPTER FIVE

1. Egyptian politics during the war are discussed in detail in Berque, <u>Egypt</u>, pp. 564–574; Vatikiotis, <u>Egypt</u>, pp. 343–355; George Kirk, <u>The Middle East in the War</u> (vol. II of <u>Survey of International Affairs, 1939–1946</u>; London, 1952), pp. 31–41, 193–228, 255–272.
2. See above, pp. 38–39.
3. <u>JMF</u>, Sept. 16, 1939, p. 3.
4. <u>JMF</u>, Nov. 22, 1939, p. 3.
5. See <u>JA</u>, Nov. 20, 1939, p. 8; Nov. 21, p. 7.
6. <u>JMF</u>, March 18, 1940, p. 1; May 16, p. 6; June 13, p. 1.
7. <u>JMF</u>, Sept. 30, 1939, p. 3.; Oct. 14, pp. 1, 4; Jan. 15, 1940, p. 5; Jan. 25, p. 5; Jan. 2, 1941, p. 8.
8. <u>JMF</u>, Nov. 15, 1939, p. 1; Nov. 18, p. 1.
9. See above, pp. 39–41.
10. <u>JMF</u>, Jan. 1, 1940, p. 1; March 4, p. 7; April 1, p. 2; April 18, p. 9.
11. <u>JMF</u>, Feb. 29, 1940, pp. 3, 5; March 6, 1941, pp. 1–3: see also Husayn, <u>al-Duktur Khalid</u>, pp. 150–151; <u>OM</u>, XX (1940), p. 68.
12. Egyptian contacts with the Germans have been explored in detail in several works. Hirszowicz, <u>Third Reich</u>, pp. 101, 232–243, and Heinz Tillmann, <u>Deutschlands Araberpolitik im Zweiten Weltkrieg</u> (Berlin, 1965), pp. 297–299, 379–381, are based primarily on German archival materials; Mitchell, <u>Muslim Brothers</u>, pp. 20–26, and Eliezer Be'eri, <u>Army Officers in Arab Politics and Society</u> (New York, 1970), pp. 41–49, draw most heavily from Arabic-language memoir materials published after the war.
13. In addition to the major secondary sources mentioned in note 12 above and the Egyptian memoir literature which is cited in the notes which follow, this conclusion is based on an examination of the German archival material relevant to Egypt available on microfilm in the United States National Archives [notably the wartime reports of the German Foreign Ministry's State Secretary's Office and State Under-Secretary's Office; United States National Archives, Microfilm series T-120 (Deutsches Auswärtiges Amt), rolls 237, 394, 722], and on the Italian diplomatic materials published in Italy, Commissione per la Pubblicazione dei Documenti Diplomatici, <u>I Documenti Diplomatici Italiani</u>, series

eight, volumes XII-XIII, and series nine, volumes I-IV
(Rome, 1952-1960).

14. These are surveyed in some detail in the article
"Asalib al-Nidal al-Misri min Harb al-Tahrir didda
al-Ghazu al-Faransi 1798 ila al-Muqawamah al-Sha'biyah
didda al-'Udwan al-Thalathi 1956," MT, Dec. 1967,
pp. 7-55 (see particularly pp. 42-44).

15. See above, p. 39.

16. "Defence Security Office, CICI 'Iraq, Baghdad
S.405/1/2, 19th December 1944, Tel Afar Parachute
Expedition: Report 2, Appendix C; Dr. Mustafa Wakil
(Egyptian)," as published in American Christian
Palestine Committee, The Arab War Effort: A Documented
Account (New York, 1947), pp. 46-47.

17. Husayn, al-Duktur Khalid, pp. 194-195; Subayh, Min
al-'Alamayn, p. 20.

18. Husayn, Imani (1946), p. 323.

19. Husayn, al-Duktur Khalid, pp. 153-167: see also
"Asalib al-Nidal al-Misri," p. 42.

20. German Foreign Ministry, State Under-Secretary's Office,
World War II Reports, Berlin, April 21, 1941; United
States National Archives, Microfilm series T-120
(Deutsches Auswärtiges Amt), roll 394, frames 305689-
305690.

21. On Misri's wartime contacts with Young Egypt, see Ahmad
Husayn, "'Aziz al-Misri Kama 'Araftuhu," Jaridah
al-Jumhuriyah, July 1, 1965, p. 8 (from which the
quotation is taken); Ahmad Husayn, Wara al-Qudban
(Cairo, 1949), p. 39; Radwan, Qubayl al-Fajr, pp. 40-
41; Husayn, al-Duktur Khalid, p. 83. Misri's contacts
with other parties are detailed most fully in Anwar
al-Sadat, Asrar al-Thawrah al-Misriyah (Cairo, 1957),
pp. 44-46, 52-57, 68-84, 100-104 [partial translation
available as Revolt on the Nile (trans. by Thomas
Graham; London, 1957), pp. 27-42].

22. Sadat, Asrar, pp. 58-60 (Revolt, pp. 37-39).

23. Subayh, Ayyam, pp. 267, 276.

24. Alfred Sansom, I Spied Spies (London, 1965), pp. 62-69.

25. "Defence Security Office . . . Report 2," as published
in The Arab War Effort, p. 46; Majid Khadduri, Independent Iraq, 1932-1958: A Study in Iraqi Politics
(second ed.; London, 1960), p. 224.

26. Husayn, Imani (1946), p. 323; Subayh, Ayyam, p. 267.

27. "Defence Security Office . . . Report 2," as published
in The Arab War Effort, p. 47.

28. OM, XXI (1941), p. 271.

29. Husayn, al-Duktur Khalid, pp. 270-271.

30. Ibid., pp. 269-270; "Defence Security Office . . .
Report 2," as published in The Arab War Effort, p. 47;

Subayh, Min al-'Alamayn, p. 28.

31. See below, p. 86.

32. Kirk, Middle East in the War, pp. 199-200; Mitchell, Muslim Brothers, pp. 21-22; Muhammad al-Tabi'i, Min Asrar al-Sasah wa al-Siyasah, Misr Ma Qablu al-Thawrah (Cairo, 1959), pp. 302-303.

33. On his attempt at flight, see Sadat, Asrar, pp. 100-104 (Revolt, pp. 39-42); Be'eri, Army Officers, pp. 45-46; Kirk, Middle East in the War, p. 200; Hirszowicz, Third Reich, p. 152; Subayh, Ayyam, p. 270; Sansom, Spies, pp. 70-75; Mustafa Mumin, Sawt Misr (Cairo, 1952), p. 110.

34. Husayn, Imani (1946), p. 323; Husayn, Wara al-Qudban, pp. 5-10; Radwan, Qubayl al-Fajr, pp. 26-48; Muhammad Subayh, Tariq al-Hurriyah (Cairo, n.d.), p. 66; OM, XXI (1941), pp. 300, 324.

35. Subayh, Tariq al-Hurriyah, p. 66.

36. "Defence Security Office . . . Report 2," as published in The Arab War Effort, p. 47; Husayn, al-Duktur Khalid, p. 314.

37. "Defence Security Office . . . Report 2," as published in The Arab War Effort, p. 47; Husayn, al-Duktur Khalid, pp. 343-346, 427-428; Tillmann, Deutschlands Araberpolitik, pp. 379, 405; Hirszowicz, Third Reich, pp. 241-242; Subayh, Ayyam, p. 270.

38. Majallah al-Kutub al-'Arabiyah, I, no. 12, pp. 33-34; Husayn, al-Duktur Khalid, pp. 576-577.

39. Husayn, Wara al-Qudban, pp. 5-70.

40. Ibid., pp. 100-126.

41. Radwan, Qubayl al-Fajr, pp. 26-48.

42. Husayn's version is given in al-Duktur Khalid, pp. 372-375, Radwan's in MJJ, Nov. 17, 1952, p. 7.

43. Ibid.; Husayn, al-Duktur Khalid, pp. 375-381.

44. Socio-economic conditions in Egypt during the war and the frustrations which they generated are discussed in Kirk, Middle EAst in the War, pp. 35-36, 201-206, 257-259; Berque, Egypt, pp. 568-574; Safran, Political Community, pp. 185-186; Charles Issawi, Egypt at Mid-Century; An Economic Analysis (London, 1954), pp. 59-63, 141-143, 262-264; Jean and Simonne Lacouture, Egypt in Transition (trans. by Francis Scarfe; New York, 1958), pp. 99-101; Anouar Abdel-Malek, Egypt: Military Society (trans. by Charles Lam Markmann; New York, 1968), pp. 13-15.

CHAPTER SIX

1. For detailed discussions of Egyptian politics from the end of the war until the coup of July 1952, see Berque,

143

Egypt, pp. 574-582, 600-604, 652-674; Vatikiotis,
Egypt, pp. 355-373; George Kirk, The Middle East,
1945-1950 (vol. V of Survey of International Affairs,
1939-1946; London, 1954), pp. 116-147; George Kirk,
"Egypt: The Wafd and Great Britain, 1950-1," in
Peter Calvocoressi (ed.), Survey of International
Affairs, 1951 (London, 1954), pp. 260-292.

2. Vatikiotis, Egypt, p. 349.

3. COC, I (1944), p. 18; Husayn, Wara al-Qudban, pp. 126-
128; JMF, Jan. 2, 1950, p. 8.

4. The new organizational law was drafted by the Administrative Council of the party (see JMF, Nov. 6, 1944,
p. 8) and was published in JMF, Jan. 1, 1945, pp. 2,
26-27.

5. Based on the membership of the Council as given in JMF,
Nov. 6, 1944, p. 8., as compared to the membership of
the Administrative Council in 1939 as given in JMF,
Nov. 18, 1939, p. 1.

6. The occupations of members of the Administrative
Council are given in JMF, Nov. 6, 1944, p. 8. By way
of comparison, the Council four years later (1948)
showed continuity both in individual personnel (ten
of those who had been serving on it in 1944 were still
members in 1948) and in the occupational groups represented (five lawyers, five agricultural engineers, four
merchants, three teachers, one doctor, one 'alim, one
accountant, one journalist, and one "worker"); data from
a party pamphlet of 1948 as cited in MT, March 1965,
p. 162.

7. From October 1944 to May 1945, local branches of the
party are mentioned only for Cairo, Alexandria, Bani
Suwayf, al-Zaqaziq, al-Mansurah, Tanta, Asyut, Zifta,
and al-Mahallah al-Kubra (JMF, Oct. 23, 1944, pp. 4,
16; Oct. 30, pp. 8, 10; Nov. 13, pp. 4, 18; Nov. 20,
p. 18; Dec. 18, p. 16; Dec. 25, p. 11; Jan. 1, 1945,
p. 11; March 19, p. 3; May 15, p. 4).

8. COC, I (1944), p. 125.

9. On the elections of 1945, see JMF, Jan. 9, 1945, p. 4;
Jan. 29, pp. 3-5, 11; Husayn, Imani (1946), pp. 322-323;
Husayn, al-Duktur Khalid, pp. 490-493, 499.

10. For detailed accounts of the immediate postwar negotiations and protests from the British and Egyptian points
of view respectively, see Kirk, The Middle East, 1945-
1950, pp. 116-130; Rafi'i, Fi A'qab, III, pp. 178-234.

11. Quoted in Marcel Colombe, "Deux années d'histoire de
l'Égypte," Politique étrangère, May 1947, p. 207. As
an official proclamation of February 1946 put it, "there
can be no negotiations with the British after today, no
treaty, no cooperation, and no alliance, until the

evacuation of the last British soldier" (quoted in
_JA_, Feb. 10, 1946, p. 5).

12. On this organization, see Shuhdi 'Atiyah al-Shafi'i,
Tatawwur al-Harakah al-Wataniyah al-Misriyah (Cairo,
1956), pp. 98-108; Tariq al-Bishri, "'Amm 1946 fi
al-Tarikh al-Misri," _MT_, Feb. 1965, pp. 50-58; 'Abd
al-Mun'im al-Ghazzali, "Mawqif 21 Fibrayir 1946 min
al-Tarikh," _MT_, Feb. 1966, pp. 51-60.

13. Ahmad Husayn, _Wa Ihtaraqat al-Qahirah_ (Cairo, 1968),
pp. 48-50.

14. For information on the party's role on the Nationalist
Committee, see _COC_, V (1946), p. 35; Bishri, "'Amm
1946," p. 57; Ghazzali, "Mawqif," p. 59; Muhammad
Hasan Ahmad, _al-Ikhwan al-Muslimun fi al-Mizan_ (Cairo,
n.d.), pp. 84-88.

15. _COC_, VII-VIII (1946), pp. 323-325; Mitchell, _Muslim
Brothers_, pp. 48-49; Marcel Colombe, _L'évolution de
l'Égypte_ (vol. IX of _Islam d'hier et d'aujourd'hui_;
Paris, 1951), pp. 234-235.

16. Information on Husayn's trip to the United States in
1947 is contained in _JA_, Dec. 29, 1946, p. 5; _COC_,
VII-VIII (1946), p. 343; Husayn, _Ihtaraqat_, pp. 137-
209; Husayn, _al-Ard_, pp. 165-166; Heyworth-Dunne,
Religious and Political Trends, p. 91; John Roy
Carlson, _Cairo to Damascus_ (New York, 1951), pp. 55-
58; _New York Times_, May 24, 1947, p. 8.

17. _COC_, XI-XII (1947), p. 212; Heyworth-Dunne, _Religious
and Political Trends_, pp. 46-47.

18. Sayigh, _al-Fikrah al-'Arabiyah_, p. 197.

19. _JMF_, Jan. 2, 1950, p. 8; Husayn, _Ihtaraqat_, pp. 250,
282; Husayn, _al-Ard_, pp. 166-167; Sayigh, _al-Fikrah
al-'Arabiyah_, p. 197; _COC_, XIII (1948), p. 20;
Carlson, _Cairo to Damascus_, pp. 67, 144-145, 174, 201.

20. For Husayn's account of his personal experiences in
Syria and Palestine, see his _Ihtaraqat_, pp. 249-283.

21. This subject is discussed best in Mitchell, _Muslim
Brothers_, pp. 58-79.

22. The assassin, Mahmud 'Isawi, was at first thought to
be a member of Young Egypt, but later was found to have
been an adherent of the Nationalist Party: see Rafi'i,
Fi A'qab, III, pp. 152-154; Kirk, _Middle East in the
War_, p. 266; Royal Institute of International Affairs,
Great Britain and Egypt, 1914-1951 (London, 1952),
p. 81.

23. _JMF_, May 15, 1945, pp. 3-4.

24. Late in 1948, two members of Young Egypt were arrested
for possessing explosives (explosives which the party
later maintained had been intended for use in Palestine,
not in Egypt); _JI_, Jan. 26, 1951, p. 5. This is the

only instance I have found of members of Young Egypt
being arrested for possible terrorist intentions within
Egypt in the later 1940's.

25. Husayn's seclusion was discussed in a speech by his
    colleague Ibrahim Shukri in late 1949; speech reported
    in JA, Oct. 24, 1949, p. 8.
26. JA, Aug. 15, 1949, p. 5.
27. JA, Oct. 24, 1949, p. 8.
28. Its text is given in JMF, March 30, 1950, pp. 3, 9-10, 12.
29. On these camps, see JI, July 12, 1951, p. 9; Sept. 2,
    p. 12.
30. Compiled from the reports on local party meetings
    published in JMF, JI, and JSJ from January 1950 to
    January 1952.
31. Ahmad Husayn, Qadiyah al-Tahrid 'Ala Harq Madinah
    al-Qahirah (Cairo, 1957), p. 44; Husayn, Ihtaraqat,
    p. 368.
32. JI, Oct. 13, 1950, p. 4.
33. Husayn, Qadiyah al-Tahrid, p. 92.
34. Ibid.
35. Husayn gives figures of 100,000 issues per week for the
    summer of 1951 and 150,000 for the fall of that year
    (Husayn, Qadiyah al-Tahrid, pp. 172, 192). The party's
    Secretary-General Ibrahim al-Ziyadi claimed a circula-
    tion of 200,000 issues per week for the fall of 1951;
    in his introduction to Ahmad Husayn's Fi Zilal
    al-Mishnaqah (Cairo, 1953), pp. 5-8.
36. Without estimating figures, non-party observers also
    claim that the circulation of the party's journals
    increased considerably from 1950 through 1951: see
    Tariq al-Bishri, "al-Kharitah al-Siyasiyah wa
    al-Ijtima'iyah li-Thawrah 23 Yulyu," MT, July 1965,
    p. 20; Musa Sabri, Qissah Malik wa Arba' Wizarat
    (Cairo, 1964), p. 26; MT, April, 1965, p. 144.
37. On the career of Shukri, see the biographical article
    in MJJ, Jan. 26, 1953, pp. 16-17.
38. Shukri is reported to have been asked to run for
    Parliament by local people in the election campaign of
    1944-1945, but to have declined for personal reasons
    (JMF, Dec. 18, 1944, p. 21). In the campaign of
    1949-1950, a clash between Wafdists and Shukri's
    supporters on election day resulted in one death -
    perhaps an indication of the degree of local support
    which he had (JMF, Jan. 16, 1950, p. 8).
39. JMF, Feb. 6, 1950, pp. 3-4.
40. For his proposals, see JI, Dec. 6, 1950, p. 8; Jan. 5,
    1951, p. 7; JSJ, April 20, 1951, p. 3; COC, XXI (1950),
    p. 75; COC, XXII (1950), pp. 194-195 (the quotation is
    from JI, Jan. 5, 1951, p. 7).

41. COC, XXI (1950), p. 75; JSJ, June 29, 1951, p. 5;
     Husayn, al-Ard, p. 179; MJJ, Jan. 26, 1953, p. 17.
42. Issawi, Mid-Century, p. 265.
43. JMF, Jan. 16, 1950, p. 4.
44. JSJ, July 25, 1951, p. 1; JI, Sept. 23, 1951, pp. 1, 8.
45. JI, Sept. 8, 1950, p. 1.
46. JI, Sept. 23, 1951 pp. 1, 8.
47. For attacks on Nahhas, see JI, Sept. 8, 1950, p. 1;
     Sept. 15, p. 1; Sept. 23, 1951, pp. 1, 8.
48. JI, Sept. 8, 1950, p. 3.
49. JI, Sept. 23, 1951, p. 1.
50. JI, Nov. 27, 1950, p. 8.
51. See JI, July 21, 1950, pp. 3, 8; Sept. 29, p. 1;
     Dec. 8, p. 1.
52. JI, Oct. 6, 1950, p. 4.
53. See JSJ, May 4, 1951, p. 4; May 25, p. 4; June 8, p. 1;
     June 15, p. 3.
54. JI, Sept. 23, 1951, pp. 6-7.
55. JI, Sept. 15, 1950, p. 1.
56. JI, Jan. 26, 1951, p. 1.
57. JI, Sept. 23, 1951, p. 8.
58. On the Brotherhood's fortunes in 1950-1951, see
     Mitchell, Muslim Brothers, pp. 80-84.
59. JMF, Jan. 23, 1950, p. 5.
60. JSJ, April 27, 1951, p. 4.
61. JMF, Jan. 30, 1950, p. 6. On Sukkari's career, see
     Mitchell, Muslim Brothers, pp. 9, 17-18, 53-54.
62. Sukkari and Salih 'Ashmawi at a meeting on May 13,
     1951 (JSJ, May 16, 1951, pp. 4-5); 'Ashmawi and Sayyid
     Qutb at a meeting on August 26, 1951 (JA, Aug. 27, 1951,
     pp. 3, 5).
63. See JSJ, June 1, 1951, p. 6; JI, July 29, 1951, p. 1.
64. The fullest treatment of the negotiations of 1950-1951
     is that of Farag Moussa, Les négociations anglo-
     égyptiennes de 1950-1951 sur Suez et le Soudan
     (Geneva, 1955), passim. For shorter accounts, see
     Kirk, "Egypt: 1950-1," pp. 260-282; R. I. I. A.,
     Great Britain and Egypt, pp. 120-151. For detailed
     accounts of the Canal Struggle, see Kirk, "Egypt:
     1950-1," pp. 282-292; 'Abd al-Rahman al-Rafi'i,
     Muqaddimat Thawrah 23 Yulyu 1952 (Cairo, 1957),
     pp. 17-112.
65. JI, Oct. 13, 1950, p. 4; Nov. 17, p. 8; Nov. 24, p. 6.
66. JSJ, May 16, 1951, pp. 4-5; June 15, p. 1; June 29,
     p. 6; July 5, pp. 4, 8.
67. JSJ, July 12, 1951, pp. 1, 4-6, 10; Aug. 30, pp. 6-7;
     JI, Aug. 26, 1951, p. 1; JA, Aug. 27, 1951, pp. 3, 5;
     Moussa, Les négociations, pp. 227, 236-237; Bishri,
     "al-Kharitah al-Siyasiyah," p. 15.

68. <u>JA</u>, Aug. 27, 1951, pp. 3, 5 (which estimated "over 10,000" in attendance at the meeting); <u>JSJ</u>, Aug. 30, 1951, pp. 6-7.

69. <u>JI</u>, Sept. 2, 1951, pp. 1-2; Abdel-Malek, <u>Military Society</u>, pp. 392-393.

70. <u>JSJ</u>, Oct. 11, 1951, p. 5; Oct. 25, p. 6; <u>JI</u>, Nov. 4, 1951, p. 12; Nov. 11, p. 2; Nov. 25, p. 7.

71. The first quotation is from <u>JSJ</u>, Nov. 1, 1951, p. 11; the second is from the indictment against Ahmad Husayn in May 1952 on the charge of having incited the burning of Cairo (published in <u>JA</u>, May 13, 1952, pp. 1, 2, 7, and in Husayn, <u>Qadiyah al-Tahrid</u>, pp. 10-34).

72. <u>JSJ</u>, Oct. 25, 1951, p. 3; <u>JI</u>, Nov. 18, 1951, p. 9; Nov. 25, p. 7.

73. See <u>JI</u>, Nov. 11, 1951, p. 2; Dec. 11, p. 2; Dec. 18, p. 6; Dec. 23, p. 5.

74. <u>JI</u>, Nov. 11, 1951, p. 2.

75. <u>JI</u>, Dec. 11, 1951, p. 7.

76. <u>JI</u>, Dec. 23, 1951, p. 3.

77. <u>JI</u>, Dec. 25, 1951, p. 5.

78. <u>JI</u>, Jan. 20, 1952, p. 5.

79. <u>JI</u>, Oct. 25, 1951, p. 9.

80. <u>JI</u>, Nov. 4, 1951, p. 7; Nov. 11, p. 9; Nov. 25, p. 6.

81. See <u>JI</u>, Dec. 2, 1951, p. 6, and Dec. 9, p. 4, for reports on the first actions in which the party's volunteers were involved.

82. From an excerpt from the report as quoted in Subayh, <u>Ayyam</u>, pp. 394-395. By way of comparison, the same document reported the Nationalist Party as having "thirty-two armed personnel" in the same area (<u>ibid</u>.), and Mitchell gives an estimate of about 300 Muslim Brothers involved in the entire Canal Struggle as active combatants (Mitchell, <u>Muslim Brothers</u>, p. 89).

83. <u>JI</u>, Dec. 16, 1951, p. 4; Dec. 23, p. 4; Dec. 25, p. 4; Jan. 20, 1952, p. 5.

84. <u>JI</u>, Nov. 18, 1951, p. 3; Bishri, "al-Kharitah al-Siyasiyah," p. 28.

85. <u>COC</u>, XXIV (1951), p. 206; <u>COC</u>, XXV (1952), p. 47; Rafi'i, <u>Muqaddimat Thawrah</u>, p. 65; Subayh, <u>Ayyam</u>, pp. 392-396; "Asalib al-Nidal al-Misri," p. 49.

86. <u>JI</u>, Dec. 2, 1951, pp. 1, 6-7, 10; Dec. 9, p. 2.

87. As quoted in <u>JI</u>, Nov. 18, 1951, p. 10: for summaries of the speech, see <u>JA</u>, Nov. 16, 1951, pp. 2, 5; <u>COC</u>, XXIV (1951), p. 200.

88. <u>JI</u>, Dec. 2, 1951, p. 1.

89. See <u>JI</u>, Dec. 11, 1951, pp. 3-4; Dec. 16, p. 2; Dec. 18, p. 1; Dec. 20, pp. 1, 3, 7; Jan. 20, 1952, p. 3.

90. The first quotation is from <u>JI</u>, Jan. 20, 1952, p. 1; the second is quoted in Husayn, <u>Qadiyah al-Tahrid</u>, p. 206.

91. Three of the fullest accounts of Black Saturday,
    agreeing in details but differing in interpretation,
    are those in Rafi'i, Muqaddimat Thawrah, pp. 113-126;
    Lacouture, Egypt in Transition, pp. 105-122; and
    Kirk, "Egypt: 1950-1," pp. 288-292.
92. From the Public Prosecutor's report on the events of
    January 26 as cited in COC, XXV (1952), pp. 48-49.
93. Among others, see Kirk, "Egypt: 1950-1," p. 290;
    Laqueur, Communism and Nationalism, pp. 250-251; Tom
    Little, Egypt (London, 1958), p. 186; Lacouture, Egypt
    in Transition, pp. 114-122. The account of the
    Lacoutures is by far the fullest.
94. JA, Feb. 4, 1952, p. 2; COC, XXV (1952), p. 55; Husayn,
    Fi Zilal al-Mishnaqah, pp. 13-15.
95. See JA, May 13, 1952, pp. 1, 2, 7; Husayn, Qadiyah
    al-Tahrid, pp. 10-34.
96. See MLJ, July 10, 1952, p. 4; Husayn, Qadiyah
    al-Tahrid, pp. 470-471.
97. MM, Sept. 19, 1952, p. 43.
98. JA, Nov. 2, 1952, p. 4; MJJ, Nov. 3, 1952, pp. 14-15.
99. "Mahkamah Jinayat al-Qahirah, 27 Abril 1953," in Husayn,
    Qadiyah al-Tahrid, pp. 530-539.
100. E.g., his Qadiyah al-Tahrid.
101. See ibid., pp. 12-18, for the relevant portions of the
    indictment.
102. "Mahkamah Jinayat al-Qahirah, 27 Abril 1953," as
    reprinted in ibid., pp. 530-539.
103. Husayn, Ihtaraqat, pp. 454-455.
104. At the same time as indicting these three on charges
    of arson (and one other party member on charges of
    journalistic incitation), the prosecution had to
    release thirty other members of the party who had been
    in detention because of lack of evidence (JA, May 13,
    1952, p. 1).
105. From the indictment as reprinted in Husayn, Qadiyah
    al-Tahrid, pp. 27-28, 34. See also Lacouture, Egypt
    in Transition, p. 121; Sansom, Spies, p. 257; Husayn,
    Ihtaraqat, pp. 426-428, 451-452, 468-470.
106. In a letter from the officer placed before the court on
    July 21, 1952, and cited in Husayn, Qadiyah al-Tahrid,
    pp. 524-526.
107. From the indictment as reprinted in Husayn, Qadiyah
    al-Tahrid, pp. 19-23.
108. "Mahkamah Jinayat al-Qahirah, 27 Abril 1952," as
    reprinted in Husayn, Qadiyah al-Tahrid, pp. 530-539.
    An early report on the investigation into the burning
    of Cairo offers partial confirmation that government
    "witnesses" were less than definite about what they
    had seen on that hectic day: when Husayn was first

brought before some of those who claimed to have seen
him in the vicinity of fires, al-Ahram's information was
that the supposed witnesses "did not recognize him" (JA,
Feb. 4, 1952, p. 2).

109. As quoted in Husayn, Qadiyah al-Tahrid, pp. 536-537.
110. Here it should be noted that the trial had finished
hearing witnesses for the Prosecution before the coup
of July 22-23 produced a change in the government's
attitude to the trial: see Husayn, Qadiyah al-Tahrid,
pp. 470-471.
111. JA, Feb. 4, 1952, p. 2; Times, Feb. 4, 1952, p. 4;
Husayn, Fi Zilal al-Mishnaqah, pp. 13-15.
112. COC, XXV (1952), p. 55; Husayn, Qadiyah al-Tahrid, p. 349.
113. COC, XXVI (1952), pp. 159, 163.
114. MLJ, Aug. 5, 1952, p. 2; JA, Nov. 4, 1952, p. 4; COC,
XXVI (1952), pp. 163-172; Laqueur, Communism and
Nationalism, p. 251.
115. COC, XXVI (1952), pp. 170-172.

CHAPTER SEVEN

1. From a speech by Husayn of October 1949 as reported in
JA, Oct. 24, 1949, p. 8.
2. From a speech by Husayn of December 1949 as quoted in
JMF, Jan. 2, 1950, p. 4.
3. Ahmad Husayn, al-Ishtirakiyah al-lati Nad'u 'Alayha
(Cairo, 1951), pp. 9-10, 13.
4. See "Goals of the Socialist Party," JMF, Jan. 23, 1950,
p. 4, for the adoption of this motto; it continued to
be used until the party's suppression in early 1952.
5. The "Fundamental Principles of the Socialist Party"
are given in Husayn, al-Ard, pp. 173-178 (the quotation
is from p. 173).
6. From a speech by Husayn of August 1949 as reported in
JA, Aug. 15, 1949, p. 5.
7. From a speech by Husayn of January 1950 as quoted in
JMF, Jan. 23, 1950, p. 11.
8. From a speech by Husayn of December 1949 as quoted in
JMF, Jan. 2, 1950, p. 4.
9. Husayn, al-Ishtirakiyah, p. 14.
10. Ibid., p. 15 (italics mine).
11. Ibid., p. 16.
12. Ibid., p. 17. For similar expressions, see Husayn,
al-Ard, p. 170; Husayn writing in JI, Jan. 20, 1952, p. 1.
13. Husayn writing in JMF, Jan. 16, 1950, p. 4.
14. From a speech by Husayn of November 1951 as quoted in
JI, Nov. 18, 1951, p. 10.
15. Husayn writing in JI, Jan. 20, 1952, p. 1.
16. Ibid.

17. From a speech by Husayn of August 1949 as reported in JA, Aug. 15, 1949, p. 5.
18. "Fundamental Principles of the Socialist Party," in Husayn, al-Ard, p. 174.
19. "Goals of the Socialist Party," in JMF, Jan. 23, 1950, p. 4.
20. From a speech by Husayn of January 1950 as quoted in JMF, Jan. 23, 1950, p. 11.
21. Husayn, al-Ard, p. 172. For similar expressions of continuity, see JMF, Jan. 2, 1950, p. 4; March 13, pp. 1, 7; Husayn, al-Ishtirakiyah, p. 17.
22. The proposal was officially adopted by the party in March 1950, when its General Assembly (the first it had held since becoming the Socialist Party) endorsed it; see JMF, March 30, 1950, p. 6.
23. Ibid. See also "Fundamental Principles of the Socialist Party," in Husayn, al-Ard, pp. 176-177.
24. On the various land reform proposals of the postwar period, see Gabriel Baer, A History of Landownership in Modern Egypt, 1800-1850 (London, 1962), pp. 201-219.
25. "Goals of the Socialist Party," in JMF, Jan. 23, 1950, p. 4.
26. Husayn, al-Ishtirakiyah, pp. 18-19.
27. Husayn writing in JSJ, May 25, 1951, p. 4.
28. "Goals of the Socialist Party," in JMF, Jan. 23, 1950, p. 4.
29. "Decisions of the General Assembly of the Socialist Party," in JMF, March 30, 1950, p. 6: see also "Fundamental Principles of the Socialist Party," in Husayn, al-Ard, pp. 175-176.
30. "Fundamental Principles of the Socialist Party," in Husayn, al-Ard, p. 175.
31. Ibid., pp. 175-176.
32. Ibid., p. 177: see also "Decisions of the General Assembly of the Socialist Party," in JMF, March 30, 1950, p. 6.
33. In this respect, see the favorable review of Sayyid Qutb's al-'Adalah al-Ijtima'iyah fi al-Islam, in which Qutb was praised for "proving" social limitations upon property-holding in Islam (JMF, Jan. 23, 1950, p. 6).
34. The demand for the abolition of titles became part of the party's official program in March 1950 ("Decisions of the General Assembly of the Socialist Party," JMF, March 30, 1950, p. 6). By mid-1951 Husayn had gone beyond sayyid, asking his followers to refer to him by the Arabic equivalent of "comrade" (zamil); JSJ, June 22, 1951, p. 4.
35. "Fundamental Principles of the Socialist Party," in Husayn, al-Ard, p. 174.

36. Husayn, al-Ishtirakiyah, p. 21.
37. "Fundamental Principles of the Socialist Party," in Husayn, al-Ard, p. 174.
38. Ibid.
39. Husayn, al-Ishtirakiyah, p. 21.
40. For the party's demands in regard to labor, see the report on the meeting of the party's "Worker's Organization," JMF, March 30, 1950, p. 5; "Decisions of the General Assembly of the Socialist Party," in ibid., p. 6; and the "Fundamental Principles of the Socialist Party," in Husayn, al-Ard, p. 174.
41. "Fundamental Principles of the Socialist Party," in Husayn, al-Ard, pp. 176-177.
42. "Decisions of the General Assembly of the Socialist Party," in JMF, March 30, 1950, p. 6; "Fundamental Principles of the Socialist Party," in Husayn, al-Ard, p. 174.
43. For demands to this effect, see JA, May 7, 1950, p. 7; May 14, p. 7; JSJ, Oct. 11, 1951, p. 1; JI, Nov. 18, p. 10.
44. "Decisions of the General Assembly of the Socialist Party," in JMF, March 30, 1950, p. 6.
45. Husayn writing in JI, July 6, 1950, p. 6.
46. From an anonymous article in JI, July 13, 1950, p. 1.
47. From a party declaration as given in JI, Aug. 11, 1950, p. 2.
48. Husayn writing in JI, July 6, 1950, p. 1.
49. Ibid.
50. Husayn, al-Ishtirakiyah, p. 12.
51. Ibid. For similar expressions see JI, July 28, 1950, p. 1; JSJ, May 11, 1951, p. 4.
52. Husayn, al-Ishtirakiyah, p. 12.
53. The former opinion is expressed in JI, July 28, 1950, p. 1, the latter in JI, Sept. 2, 1951, p. 7.
54. See JI, July 28, 1950, p. 1; Aug. 11, p. 1.
55. JI, July 28, 1950, p. 1.
56. Ibid.
57. JI, Jan. 12, 1951, p. 4.
58. See note 49, above.
59. From a speech by Husayn of May 1951 as quoted in JSJ, May 11, 1951, p. 4.
60. "Fundamental Principles of the Socialist Party," in Husayn, al-Ard, p. 177.
61. From a speech by Husayn of October 1949 as reported in JA, Oct. 24, 1949, p. 8.
62. For expression to this effect, see ibid. and Husayn, al-Ishtirakiyah, pp. 23-24.
63. "Fundamental Principles of the Socialist Party," in Husayn, al-Ard, pp. 177-178.

64. Husayn, _al-Ard_, p. 9.
65. See note 24, above.
66. For the variety of individuals and groups calling for such by 1950-1951, see Moussa, _Les négociations_, pp. 175-182, 212-213, 236-237.
67. E.g., Marcel Colombe has estimated that some 100 parliamentary candidates were presenting themselves as "socialists" of one stripe or another in the elections of 1950 (Colombe, _L'évolution_, p. 247).

CHAPTER EIGHT

1. Khalid, _al-Kifah al-Sirri_, p. 17.
2. For only marginally different lists of the leadership group within the Free Officers movement, see P. J. Vatikiotis, _The Egyptian Army in Politics: Pattern for New Nations?_ (Bloomington, Indiana, 1961), pp. 48-49; R. Hrair Dekmejian, _Egypt Under Nasir: A Study in Political Dynamics_ (Albany, New York, 1971), p. 28.
3. The quotation is from "My Revolutionary Life: President Nasser's Own Story" (as told to David Wynne-Morgan), _The Sunday Times_, June 17, 1962, p. 25. For further information on 'Abd al-Nasir's political involvements prior to his entering the military, see 'Ali, _Kifah al-Shabab_, pp. 40-55; Georges Vaucher, _Gamal Abdel Nasser et son équipe_ (two vol.; Paris, 1959, 1961), I, pp. 68-89; Robert Stephens, _Nasser: A Political Biography_ (New York, 1971), pp. 30-37; Mohamed Hassanein Heikal, _The Cairo Documents_ (Garden City, New York, 1973), pp. 17-23.
4. Vatikiotis, _Egyptian Army_, pp. 48-49.
5. Interviews.
6. Vatikiotis, _Egyptian Army_, pp. 48-49.
7. Interviews.
8. Interviews.
9. Vatikiotis, _Egyptian Army_, pp. 48-49.
10. Interviews.
11. United Arab Republic, State Information Service, _The Charter_ (Cairo, n.d.). Where this official translation seemed awkward to me, I have altered it in light of the Arabic text as given in Hamdi Hafiz, _Thawrah 23 Yulyu: al-Ahdath, al-Ahdaf, al-Injazat_ (Cairo, 1964), pp. 285-354.
12. United Arab Republic, State Information Service, _The Charter_, p. 32.
13. _Ibid._, p. 18.
14. _Ibid._, p. 17.
15. _Ibid._, pp. 18, 94.
16. _Ibid._, p. 27.

17. _Ibid._, p. 28.
18. _Ibid._, p. 64.
19. _Ibid._, p. 104.
20. _Ibid._, p. 76; for similar expressions, see also pp. 42, 70.
21. _Ibid._, pp. 9, 104.
22. Sadat, _Asrar_, pp. 135–136.
23. See above, p. 38.

Bibliography

ARCHIVAL MATERIALS

United States National Archives, Microfilm series T-120
(Documents of the German Foreign Ministry, 1920-1945):
   Roll   237 - State Secretary's Office, World War II
                 Reports, Egypt, May 1939 - May 1943;
   Roll   394 - State Under-Secretary's Office, World War II
                 Reports, Egypt, April 1941 - October 1942;
   Roll   722 - State Under-Secretary's Office, World War II
                 Reports, Egypt, April 1941 - October 1942;
   Roll 4358 - Weekly Political Reports, Egypt, May 1936 -
                 March 1938;
   Roll 4367 - Private Materials Pertaining to Egypt,
                 May 1936 - 1940;
   Roll 4868 - Weekly Political Reports, Egypt, January 1930 -
                 .May 1936;
   Roll 4869 - Egyptian Ministries, March 1922 - May 1936;
   Roll 4872 - Journalists, Other Personalities, Egypt,
                 May 1924 - October 1933;
   Roll 4873 - The Press, Pacifism, Political and Cultural
                 Propaganda, National Socialism, Communism,
                 and the like, Egypt, October 1922 - May 1936.

INTERVIEWS

Ahmad Husayn - May 1, 1965; May 25, 1965; July 2, 1965.
'Ali Fahmi - May 22, 1965.
Anwar al-Jindi - May 17, 1965; May 25, 1965; June 14, 1965.
Farid Za'luk - May 22, 1965.
Fathi Radwan - July 19, 1969; July 28, 1969.

CONTEMPORARY PERIODICALS

Periodicals of Young Egypt

Jaridah al-Ishtirakiyah
Jaridah Misr al-Fatah
Jaridah al-Sha'b al-Jadid
Jaridah Wadi al-Nil
Majallah al-Diya
Majallah al-Sarkhah
Majallah al-Thaghr

Other Periodicals in Arabic

Jaridah al-Ahram

Jaridah al-Balagh
Jaridah al-Jihad
Jaridah al-Misri
Jaridah al-Siyasah
Majallah al-Hilal
Majallah al-Jil al-Jadid
Majallah al-Liwa al-Jadid
Majallah al-Lataif al-Musawwarah
Majallah al-Musawwar
Majallah al-Risalah
Majallah al-Shubban al-Muslimin
Majallah al-Shubban al-Wafdiyin

Periodicals in Western Languages

Cahiers de l'Orient Contemporain, "Chronique"
Oriente Moderno, "Sezione politico-storica"
The Times (London)

WORKS IN ARABIC

'Abd al-Hayy, 'Abd al-Tawwab. 'Asir Hayati. Cairo, 1966.
'Abdallah, Mahmud Isma'il. Fihris al-Dawriyat al-'Arabiyah
    al-lati Taqtaniha al-Dar. Multi-volume. Cairo, 1961-.
'Abduh, Ibrahim. Ruz al-Yusuf. Cairo, 1955.
_____. Tatawwur al-Sahafah al-Misriyah, 1798-1951.
    Cairo, 1951.
'Afifi, Hafiz. 'Ala Hamish al-Siyasah. Cairo, 1938.
Ahmad, Muhammad Hasan. al-Ikhwan al-Muslimun fi al-Mizan.
    Cairo, n.d. [1947?].
'Ali, Ahmad Farid. Kifah al-Shabab wa Zuhur Jamal 'Abd
    al-Nasir. Cairo, 1963.
'Allubah, Muhammad 'Ali. Mabadi fi al-Siyasah al-Misriyah.
    Cairo, 1942.
'Amir, Ibrahim. Thawrah Misr al-Qawmiyah. Cairo, 1956.
Anis, Muhammad Ahmad, and al-Sayyid Rajab Harraz. Thawrah
    23 Yulyu 1952, Usuluha al-Tarikhiyah. Cairo, 1969.
al-'Aqqad, 'Abbas Mahmud. Hayati Qalam. Cairo, 1964.
"Asalib al-Nidal al-Misri: Min Harb Tahrir didda al-Ghazu
    al-Faransi 1798 ila al-Muqawamah al-Sha'biyah didda
    al-'Udwan al-Thalathi 1956." Majallah al-Tali'ah,
    December 1967, pp. 7-55.
'Ashur, Sa'id 'Abd al-Fattah. Thawrah Sha'b: 'Arad
    lil-Harakah al-Wataniyah fi Misr. Cairo, 1964.
'Ata, Muhammad Mustafa. Misr bayna Thawratayn. Cairo, 1955.
'Atiyah, Ahmad Muhammad. Hariq al-Qahirah, aw Nadhir
    al-'Asifah. Cairo, 1966.
Badawi, 'Abd al-Rahman. Humum al-Shabab. Cairo, 1946.
Baha al-Din, Ahmad. Faruq Malikan!!, 1936-1952. Cairo, 1952.
Barakat, Muhammad Baha al-Din. Safahat min al-Tarikh.

156

Cairo, 1960.

al-Bishri, Tariq. "'Amm 1946 fi al-Tarikh al-Misri."
Majallah al-Tali'ah, February 1946, pp. 50-58.
_____. "al-Kharitah al-Siyasiyah wa al-Ijtima'iyah
li-Thawrah 23 Yulyu." Majallah al-Tali'ah, July 1965,
pp. 7-31.

Bustani, Salah al-Din. Ma'rakah al-Qanal Kama Shahadtuha,
1951-1952. Cairo, 1956.

al-Dardiri, Yahya Ahmad. al-Tariq. Cairo, 1952.

Fawzi, Muhammad al-Wakil (ed.). Hadhihi al-Thawrah. Cairo,
1953.

Ghali, Mirrit Butrus. Siyasah al-Ghad. Cairo, 1938.

al-Ghazzali, 'Abd al-Mun'im. "Mawqif 21 Fibrayir 1946 min
al-Tarikh." Majallah al-Tali'ah, February 1966, pp. 51-60.

Ghurbal, Muhammad Shafiq. Tarikh al-Mufawadat al-Misriyah
al-Biritaniyah, 1882-1936. Part one. Cairo, 1952.

Haddad, 'Uthman Kamal. Harakah Rashid 'Ali al-Kilani Sanah
1941. Sidon, Lebanon, n.d. [194?].

Hafiz, Abu al-Hajjaj. al-Shahid Kamal al-Din Salah. Cairo,
n.d. [1961?].

Hafiz, Hamdi. Thawrah 23 Yulyu: al-Ahdath, al-Ahdaf,
al-Injazat. Cairo, 1964.

Hamzah, 'Abd al-Latif. 'Abd al-Qadir Hamzah fi Jaridatay
al-Ahali wa al-Balagh. Part eight of his Adab al-Maqalah
al-Suhufiyah fi Misr. Cairo, 1963.

Haykal, Muhammad Husayn. Mudhakkirat fi al-Siyasah
al-Misriyah. Two volumes. Cairo, 1951, 1953.

Hijazi, Anwar. 'Amaliqah wa Ruwwad. Cairo, 1966.

Hilmi, Mahmud. Thawrah Thalathah wa 'Ishrin Yulyu 1952.
Two volumes, Cairo, 1966.

Husayn, Ahmad. al-Ard al-Tayyibah. Cairo, 1951.
_____. Azhar. Cairo, 1963.
_____. "'Aziz al-Misri Kama 'Araftuhu." Jaridah
al-Jumhuriyah, July 1, 1965, p. 8.
_____. al-Duktur Khalid. Cairo, 1964.
_____. Fi al-Iman wa al-Islam. Cairo, 1964.
_____. Fi Zilal al-Mishnaqah. Cairo, 1953.
_____. Imani. First edition. Cairo, 1936.
_____. Imani. Second edition, revised. Cairo, 1946.
_____. al-Ishtirakiyah al-lati Nad'u 'alayha. Cairo,
1951.
_____. al-Khitab al-Watani. Cairo, 1947.
_____. Murafa'at Ahmad Husayn fi Qadiyah Tahtim
al-Khanat. Cairo, 1939.
_____. Murafa'at al-Rais: Misr al-Fatah wa
al-Hukumah amana al-Qada. Cairo, 1937.
_____. Nahwa al-Majd: al-'Ilm wa al-Mal. Cairo, 1946.
_____. Qadiyah al-Tahrid 'ala Harq Madinah al-Qahirah.
Cairo, 1957.

Husayn, Ahmad. Sab'un Yawman lil-Di'ayah fi Urubba. Cairo, 1936.

_____. al-Taqah al-Insaniyah. Cairo, 1962.
_____. al-Ummah al-Insaniyah. Cairo, 1966.
_____. Ummah Tab'ath. Cairo, 1953.
_____. Wa Ihtaraqat al-Qahirah. Cairo, 1968.
_____. Wara al-Qudban. Cairo, 1949.
_____. al-Yaqazah al-'Umlaq aw Rihlah fi Asiya. Cairo, 1953.

Husayn, Muhammad. al-Ittijahat al-Wataniyah fi al-Adab al-Mu'asir. Two volumes. Alexandria, 1956, 1959.

'Izmi, Mahmud. al-Ayyam al-Miah. Cairo, n.d. [1939].

al-Jabalawi, Muhammad Tahir. Min Sahbah al-'Aqqad. Cairo, 1964.

al-Jindi, Anwar. al-Fikr al-'Arabi al-Mu'asir fi Ma'rakah al-Taghrib wa al-Tab'iyah al-Thaqafiyah. Cairo, n.d. [1961?].

_____. al-Kuttab al-Mu'asirun. Cairo, 1957.
_____. Munawarat al-Siyasiyah. Cairo, 1947.
_____. al-Sahafah al-Siyasiyah fi Misr. Cairo, 1962.
_____. Tarikh al-Ahzab al-Siyasiyah. Cairo, 1947.

Jirjis, Fawzi. Dirasat fi Tarikh Misr al-Siyasi. Cairo, 1958.

Kamil, Mahmud. Misr al-Ghad tahta Hukm al-Shabab. Cairo, 1939.

Khalid, Wasim. al-Kifah al-Sirri didda al-Injiliz. Cairo, 1963.

Khilaf, Husayn. Niqabat al-'Ummal fi Misr. Cairo, 1946.

Muhammad, Rauf 'Abbas Hamid. al-Harakah al-'Ummaliyah fi Misr, 1899-1952. Cairo, 1967.

Mumin, Mustafa. Sawt Misr. Cairo, 1951 [1952].

Qara'ah, Saniyah. Nimr al-Siyasah al-Misriyah. Cairo, 1952.

Rabi', Hasan Muhammad. Misr bayna 'Ahdayn. Cairo, 1954.

Radwan, Fathi. Akhi al-Muwatin. Cairo, 1955.
_____. 'Asr wa Rijal. Cairo, 1967.
_____. Difalira. Cairo, 1937.
_____. Hadha al-Sharq al-'Arabi. Cairo, 1957.
_____. Kifahuna al-Watani fi Nisf Qarn. Cairo, 1947.
_____. Ma'a al-Insan fi al-Harb wa al-Salam. Cairo, 1964.
_____. Muhamin Sughayr. Cairo, 1959.
_____. Musulini. Cairo, 1937.
_____. Qubayl al-Fajr. Cairo, 1957.
_____. Tarikh Ghandi. Cairo, 1932.

al-Rafi'i, 'Abd al-Rahman. Fi A'qab al-Thawrah al-Misriyah. Three volumes. Cairo, 1947-1951.
_____. Mudhakkirati, 1889-1952. Cairo, 1952.

al-Rafi'i, 'Abd al-Rahman. <u>Muhammad Farid: Ramz al-Ikhlas</u>
<u>wa al-Tadhiyah</u>. Third edition. Cairo, 1961.
_____. <u>Muqaddimat Thawrah 23 Yulyu 1952.</u>
Cairo, 1957.
_____. <u>Mustafa Kamil: Ba'ith al-Harakah</u>
<u>al-Wataniyah</u>. Third edition, revised. Cairo, 1950.
_____. <u>Thawrah Sanah 1919</u>. Second
edition. Two volumes. Cairo, 1955.
_____. <u>al-Thawrah al-'Urabiyah wa</u>
<u>al-Ihtilal al-Injilizi</u>. Second edition. Cairo, 1949.
Rif'at, Muhammad. <u>al-Tawjih al-Siyasi lil-Fikrah al-'Arabiyah</u>
<u>al-Hadithah</u>. Cairo, 1964.
Sabri, Musa. <u>Qissah al-Malik wa Arba' Wizarat</u>. Cairo, 1964.
al-Sadat, Anwar. <u>Asrar al-Thawrah al-Misriyah</u>. Cairo, 1957.
_____. <u>Qissah al-Thawrah al-Kamilah</u>. Cairo, 1957.
_____. <u>Safahat Majhulah</u>. Cairo, 1954.
Sa'id, Amin. <u>Tarikh Misr al-Siyasi</u>. Cairo, 1959.
Sayigh, Anis. <u>al-Fikrah al-'Arabiyah fi Misr</u>. Beirut, 1959.
al-Sayyid, Ahmad Lutfi. <u>Qissah Hayati</u>. Cairo, 1962.
Sayyid, Muhammad Mu'tasim. <u>Salah Salim</u>. Cairo, n.d. [1963?].
al-Shafi'i, Shuhdi 'Atiyah. <u>Tatawwur al-Harakah al-Wataniyah</u>
<u>al-Misriyah</u>. Cairo, 1956.
Shumays, 'Abd al-Mun'im. <u>Asrar al-Ahzab al-Shuyu'iyah</u>
<u>fi al-'Alam al-'Arabi</u>. Cairo, 1961.
Sidqi, Isma'il. <u>Mudhakkirati</u>. Cairo, 1950.
Subayh, Muhammad. <u>Ayyam wa Ayyam, 1882-1965</u>. Cairo, 1968.
_____. <u>Faysal al-Awwal</u>. Cairo, 1945.
_____. <u>Fuad al-Awwal</u>. Cairo, 1944.
_____. <u>Min al-'Alamayn ila Sajn al-Ajanib</u>. Cairo,
1963.
_____. <u>Stalin</u>. Cairo, 1937.
_____. <u>Tariq al-Hurriyah</u>. Cairo, n.d. [1964?].
_____. <u>Tshurshil</u>. Cairo, 1944.
_____. <u>al-Yaqazah: Khilal al-Qarnayn al-Tasi'</u>
<u>'Ashra wa al-'Ishrin al-Miladi</u>. Cairo, 1964.
_____. <u>al-Yaban: Bilad al-Shams al-Mashriqah</u>.
Cairo, 1937.
al-Sudani, Salih 'Ali 'Isa. <u>al-Asrar al-Siyasiyah li-Abtal</u>
<u>al-Thawrah al-Misriyah wa Ara al-Duktur Mahjub Thabit</u>.
Cairo, n.d. [194?].
al-Tabi'i, Muhammad. <u>Min Asrar al-Sasah wa al-Siyasah, Misr</u>
<u>Ma qablu al-Thawrah</u>. Cairo, 1959.
Thabit, Karim. "Min Dhikriyat Karim Thabit." <u>Jaridah</u>
<u>al-Jumhuriyah</u>, June 11 - July 8, 1955.
Wahidah, Subhi. <u>Fi Usul al-Masalah al-Misriyah</u>. Cairo, 1950.
al-Wakil, Mustafa. <u>'Umar ibn 'Abd al-'Aziz</u>. Cairo, 1939.
"Wathaiq: al-Ahzab wa al-Tanzimat al-Siyasiyah fi Misr;
al-Hizb al-Ishtiraki." <u>Majallah al-Tali'ah</u>, April 1965,
pp. 143-145.

"Wathaiq: al-Ahzab wa al-Tanzimat al-Siyasiyah fi Misr;
Hizb Misr al-Fatah." Majallah al-Tali'ah, March 1965,
pp. 155-162.
Zahran, Sa'd. "Harakah al-Tarikh al-Misri min Ighla
al-Mu'ahadah ila Hariq al-Qahirah (8 Uktubir 1951 -
26 Yanayir 1952)." Majallah al-Tali'ah, June 1965,
pp. 69-79.
al-Zawahiri, Fakhr al-Din. al-Siyasah wa al-Azhar. Cairo,
1945.

WORKS IN WESTERN LANGUAGES

Abdel-Malek, Anouar. Translated by Charles Lam Markmann.
Egypt: Military Society; The Army Regime, the Left,
and Social Change Under Nasser. New York, 1968.
Abul-Fath, Ahmed. L'affaire Nasser. Paris, 1962.
Alexander, Mark. "Left and Right in Egypt." Twentieth
Century, February 1952, pp. 119-128.
American Christian Palestine Committee. The Arab War
Effort: A Documented Account. New York, 1947.
Ansari, Zafar I. "Contemporary Islam and Nationalism: A
Case Study of Egypt." Welt des Islams, new series, VII
(1961), pp. 3-38.
_____. "Egyptian Nationalism vis-à-vis Islam."
Pakistan Horizon, XIII (1960), pp. 21-47.
_____. "Islam and Nationalism in Contemporary
Egypt." Pakistan Horizon, XII (1959), pp. 230-247.
Arsenian, S. "Wartime Propaganda in the Middle East."
The Middle East Journal, II (1948), pp. 417-429.
Baer, Gabriel. "Egyptian Attitudes towards Land Reform,
1922-1952." In Walter Z. Laqueur (ed.), The Middle
East in Transition (New York, 1958), pp. 80-99.
_____. A History of Landownership in Modern Egypt,
1800-1952. New York, 1962.
_____. Studies in the Social History of Modern
Egypt. Chicago, 1969.
Beeley, H. "The Montreux Conventions Regarding the Abolition
of the Capitulations in Egypt, and the Admission of Egypt
to Membership in the League of Nations." In Arnold
Toynbee and V. M. Boulter (eds.), Survey of International
Affairs, 1937 (two volumes; London, 1938), I, pp. 581-607.
Be'eri, Eliezer. Army Officers in Arab Politics and Society.
New York, 1970.
Berger, Morroe. The Arab World Today. New York, 1962.
_____. Bureaucracy and Society in Modern Egypt:
A Study of the Higher Civil Service. Princeton, 1957.
Bernard-Derosne, Jean. Farouk: la déchéance d'un roi.
Paris, 1953.

Berque, Jacques. Translated by Jean Stewart. The Arabs: Their History and Future. New York, 1964.
_____. Translated by Jean Stewart. Egypt: Imperialism and Revolution. New York, 1972.
Bilainkin, George. Cairo to Riadh Diary. London, 1950.
Binder, Leonard. The Ideological Revolution in the Middle East. New York, 1964.
Björkman, W. "Ägypten in den Jahren 1932 und 1933." Mitteilungen des Seminars für orientalische Sprachen: Westasiatische Abteilung, XXXVII (1934), pp. 65-96.
_____. "Ägypten in den Jahren 1934 und 1935." Mitteilungen des Seminars für orientalische Sprachen: Westasiatische Abteilung, XXXIX (1936), pp. 1-48.
_____. "Ägypten in den Jahren 1936 und 1937." Mitteilungen des Seminars für orientalische Sprachen: Westasiatische Abteilung, XLI (1938), pp. 53-124.
Carlson, John Roy. Cairo to Damascus. New York, 1951.
Casey, Richard. Personal Reminiscences, 1939-1946. London, 1962.
Centre d'études de politique étrangère. L'Égypte indépendante. Paris, 1938.
Chejne, Anwar G. "Egyptian Attitudes towards Pan-Arabism." The Middle East Journal, XI (1957), pp. 253-268.
Choudhury, M. L. Roy (ed.). Egypt in 1945. Calcutta, 1946.
Ciano, Galeazzo. Translated and edited by Hugh Gibson. The Ciano Diaries, 1939-1943. New York, 1945.
_____. Translated by Andreas Major. Ciano's Diary, 1937-1938. London, 1952.
Colombe, Marcel. "Deux années d'histoire d'Égypte." Politique Étrangère, May 1947, pp. 201-224.
_____. "L'Égypte et la crise actuelle de l'Arabisme." L'Afrique et l'Asie, XI (1950), pp. 31-41.
_____. "L'Égypte et les origins du nationalisme arabe." L'Afrique et l'Asie, XIV (1951), pp. 19-33.
_____. L'évolution de l'Égypte. Volume IX of Islam d'hier et d'aujourd'hui. Paris, 1951.
_____. "L'Islam dans la vie sociale et politique de l'Égypte contemporaine." Cahiers de l'Orient Contemporain, XXI (1950), pp. 1-26.
_____. "Onze mois d'evolution de l'Égypte." L'Afrique et l'Asie, XXIII (1953), pp. 4-14.
_____. "Où en est le Wafd Égyptien." L'Afrique et l'Asie, X (1950), pp. 36-44.
_____. "Où va l'Égypte." L'Afrique et l'Asie, IV (1948), pp. 29-42.
Craig, A. J. M. "Egyptian Students." The Middle East Journal, VII (1953), pp. 293-299.
Crouchley, A. E. The Economic Development of Modern Egypt. London, 1938.

Dekmejian, R. Hrair. Egypt Under Nasir: A Study in Political
Dynamics. Albany, New York, 1971.
Documents on German Foreign Policy, 1918-1945. Multi-series,
multi-volume. Washington, 1949-.
Dodge, Bayard. Al-Azhar: A Millenium of Muslim Learning.
Washington, 1961.
Douglas, Sholto (Lord Douglas of Kirtleside). The Years of
Command. London, 1966.
Dubois-Richard, M. "L'état d'esprit des étudiants égyptiens
et leur role dans la vie politique." In Centre d'études
de politique étrangère, Entretiens sur l'évolution des
pays de civilization arabe (Three volumes; Paris, 1937),
I, pp. 95-98.
al-Dusuqi, Muhammad. Hitler und der nähe Osten. Cairo, 1963.
Eden, Anthony (Lord Avon). The Memoirs of Anthony Eden:
Facing the Dictators. Boston, 1962.
_____. The Memoirs of Anthony Eden:
Full Circle. Boston, 1960.
El-Barawy, Rashed. The Military Coup in Egypt: An Analytic
Study. Cairo, 1952.
El Kholi, Loutfi (ed.). La voie égyptienne vers le socialisme.
Cairo, 1966.
Eppler, John W. Rommel Ruft Kairo: Aus dem Tagebuch eines
Spions. Gütersloh, 1959.
Galt, Russell. The Effects of Centralization on Education in
Modern Egypt. Cairo, 1936.
Ghali, Mirrit Boutros. Translated by Isma'il R. el-Faruqi.
The Policy of Tomorrow. Washington, 1953.
al-Ghazzali, Muhammad. Translated by Isma'il R. el-Faruqi.
Our Beginning in Wisdom. Washington, 1953.
Gibb, Sir H. A. R. Modern Trends in Islam. Chicago, 1947.
_____. "The Situation in Egypt." International
Affairs, XV (1936), pp. 351-373.
Gordon, David C. Self-Determination and History in the
Third World. Princeton, 1971.
Graves, Philip. "The Story of the Egyptian Crisis."
Nineteenth Century and After, March 1938, pp. 297-313.
_____. "The Egyptian Election." Nineteenth Century
and After, May 1938, pp. 579-585.
Haim, Sylvia G. (ed.). Arab Nationalism: An Anthology.
Berkeley, 1962.
_____. "Islam and the Theory of Arab Nationalism."
Welt des Islams, new series, IV (1955), pp. 124-129.
_____. "State and University in Egypt." In
Chauncy D. Harris and Max Horkheimer (eds.), Universität
und moderne Gesellschaft (Frankfort am Main, 1959),
pp. 99-118.
Halpern, Manfred. The Politics of Social Change in the
Middle East and North Africa. Princeton, 1963.

Handley, William J. "The Labor Movement in Egypt." The Middle East Journal, III (1949), pp. 277-292.

Hanna, Sami A., and George H. Gardner (eds). Arab Socialism: A Documentary Survey. Salt Lake City, Utah, 1969.

Harris, Christina P. Nationalism and Revolution in Egypt. The Hague, 1964.

Heikal, Mohamed Hassanein. Introduction by E. R. F. Sheehan. The Cairo Documents. Garden City, New York, 1973.

Hentig, Werner Otto von. Mein Leben: Eine Dienstreise. Gottingen, 1962.

Heyworth-Dunne, James. Religious and Political Trends in Modern Egypt. Washington, 1950.

_____. "Society and Politics in Modern Egyptian Literature." The Middle East Journal, II (1948), pp. 306-318.

Hirszowicz, Lukasz. The Third Reich and the Arab East. London, 1966.

Hopkins, Harry. Egypt the Crucible: The Unfinished Revolution in the Middle East. Boston, 1969.

Hourani, Albert. Arabic Thought in the Liberal Age, 1789-1939. London, 1962.

Husaini, Ishak Musa. The Moslem Brethren: The Greatest of Modern Islamic Movements. Beirut, 1956.

Hussein, Ahmad. Egypt's War Effort: A Reply to the Charges of the American Christian Palestine Committee. New York, 1947.

_____. The Episode of El Faluje. London, 1949.

_____. Message to Hitler! New York, 1947.

_____. The Story of Egypt and Anglo-Egyptian Relations. New York, 1947.

Hussein, Mahmoud. La lutte de classes en Égypte de 1945 à 1968. Paris, 1969.

Issawi, Charles. Egypt: An Economic and Social Analysis. London, 1947.

_____. Egypt at Mid-Century: An Economic Survey. London, 1954.

Italy. Commissione per la Pubblicazione dei Documenti Diplomatici. I Documenti Diplomatici Italiani. Series eight, volumes XII-XIII; series nine, volumes I-IV. Rome, 1952-1960.

Jankowski, James P. "The Egyptian Blue Shirts and the Egyptian Wafd, 1935-1938." Middle Eastern Studies, VI (1970), pp. 77-95.

Joesten, Joachim. Nasser: The Rise to Power. London, 1960.

Kampffmeyer, Georg. "Egypt and Western Asia." In H. A. R. Gibb (ed.), Whither Islam? (London, 1932), pp. 102-170.

Kedourie, Elie. "Egypt and the Caliphate." In his The Chatham House Version and Other Middle-Eastern Studies (London, 1970), pp. 177-212.

Kendall, Patricia. "The Ambivalent Character of Nationalism Among Egyptian Professionals." Public Opinion Quarterly, XX (1956), pp. 277-289.

Kerr, Malcolm H. "Arab Radical Notions of Democracy." In Albert Hourani (ed.), Middle Eastern Affairs, no. 3 (St. Antony's Papers, no. 16; London, 1965), pp. 9-40.

_____. "Egypt." In James S. Coleman (ed.), Education and Political Development (Princeton, 1965), pp. 169-194.

Khadduri, Majid. "ᶜAziz ᶜAli al-Miṣrī and the Arab Nationalist Movement." In Albert Hourani (ed.), Middle Eastern Affairs, no. 4 (St. Antony's Papers, no. 17; London, 1965), pp. 140-163.

_____. Independent Iraq, 1932-1958: A Study in Iraqi Politics. Second edition. London, 1960.

_____. Political Trends in the Arab World: The Role of Ideas and Ideals in Politics. Baltimore, 1970.

Khalid, Khalid M. Translated by Isma'il R. el-Faruqi. From Here We Start. Washington, 1953.

Kirk, George. "Egypt: The Wafd and Great Britain, 1950-1." In Peter Calvocoressi (ed.), Survey of International Affairs, 1951 (London, 1954), pp. 260-292.

_____. "The Egyptian Revolution and National Aspirations." In Peter Calvocoressi (ed.), Survey of International Affairs, 1952 (London, 1955), pp. 203-230.

_____. The Middle East, 1945-1950. Volume V of Survey of International Affairs, 1939-1946. London, 1954.

_____. The Middle East in the War. Volume II of Survey of International Affairs, 1939-1946. London, 1952.

Klingmüller, Ernst. Ägypten. Berlin, 1944.

_____. "England in Ägypten." Zeitschrift für Politik, XXI (1941), pp. 488-494.

Kotb, Sayed (Sayyid Qutb). Translated by John B. Hardie. Social Justice in Islam. Reprint. New York, 1970.

Lacouture, Jean and Simonne. Translated by Francis Scarfe. Egypt in Transition. New York, 1958.

Landau, Jacob M. Parliaments and Parties in Egypt. New York, 1954.

Laqueur, Walter Z. Communism and Nationalism in the Middle East. London, 1956.

Lenczowski, George. "Literature on the Clandestine Activities of the Great Powers in the Middle East." The Middle East Journal, VIII (1954), pp. 205-211.

Lerner, Daniel. The Passing of Traditional Society: Modernizing the Middle East. Glencoe, Illinois, 1958.

Little, Tom. Egypt. London, 1958.

Lugol, Jean. Egypt and World War II. Cairo, 1945.

Lyttleton, Oliver (Viscount Chandos). The Memoirs of Lord Chandos. London, 1962.

Makarius, Raoul. La jeunesse intellectuelle d'Égypte au lendemain de la deuxième guerre mondiale. The Hague, 1960.

Marlowe, John. A History of Modern Egypt and Anglo-Egyptian Relations, 1800-1956. Second edition. Hamden, Conn., 1965.

Marston, Ella. "Fascist Tendencies in Pre-War Arab Politics." The Middle East Forum, XXV (May, 1959), pp. 19-22, 32, 34.

Martelli, George. Whose Sea?. London, 1938.

Maugeri, Franco. Edited by Victor Rosen. From the Ashes of Disgrace. New York, 1948.

McBride, Barrie St. Clair. Farouk of Egypt: A Biography. London, 1967.

Mitchell, Richard P. The Society of the Muslim Brothers. London, 1969.

Moussa, Farag. Les négociations anglo-égyptiennes de 1950-1951 sur Suez et le Soudan. Geneva, 1955.

Mūsā, Salāma. Translated by L. O. Schuman. The Education of Salāma Mūsā. Leiden, 1961.

Nasser, Gamal Abdel. Egypt's Liberation: The Philosophy of the Revolution. Washington, 1955.

_____. "My Revolutionary Life: President Nasser's Own Story." As told to David Wynne-Morgan. The Sunday Times, June 17, 1962, pp. 25-26; June 24, 1962, pp. 21-22; July 1, 1962, p. 25.

Neguib, Mohammed. Egypt's Destiny. London, 1955.

Nune, Enrico. "L'idea dell'unita araba in recenti dibattiti della stampa del vincino oriente." Oriente Moderno, XVIII (1938), pp. 401-412.

Nutting, Anthony. Nasser. New York, 1972.

Perlmann, M. "The Egyptian Elections." Middle Eastern Affairs, I (1950), pp. 41-48.

Quraishi, Zaheer M. Liberal Nationalism in Egypt: Rise and Fall of the Wafd Party. Delhi, 1967.

Radwan, Abu al-Futouh Ahmad. Old and New Forces in Egyptian Education. New York, 1951.

Royal Institute of International Affairs. Great Britain and Egypt, 1914-1951. London, 1952.

Russell, Thomas W. Egyptian Service, 1902-1946. London, 1949.

al-Sadat, Anwar. Translated by Thomas Graham. Revolt on the Nile. London, 1957.

Safran, Nadav. Egypt in Search of Political Community. Cambridge, Mass., 1961.

St. John, Robert. The Boss: The Story of Gamal Abdel Nasser. New York, 1960.

Sansom, Alfred W. I Spied Spies. London, 1965.

Shah, Sirdar Ikbal Ali. Fuad: King of Egypt. London, 1936.

Sharabi, Hisham. Arab Intellectuals and the West: The Formative Years, 1875-1914. Baltimore, 1970.

165

Smith, Charles D. "The 'Crisis of Orientation': The Shift of Egyptian Intellectuals to Islamic Subjects in the 1930's." International Journal of Middle Eastern Studies, IV (1973), pp. 382-410.

Smith, Wilfred Cantwell. Islam in Modern History. Princeton, 1957.

Steffans, Hans von. Salaam: Geheimkommando zum Nil. Neckargemünd, 1960.

Stephens, Robert. Nasser: A Political Biography. New York, 1971.

Stewart, Desmond. Young Egypt. London, 1958.

Tillmann, Heinz. Deutschlands Araberpolitik im Zweiten Weltkrieg. Berlin, 1965.

Toynbee, Arnold, and V. M. Boulter. "Anglo-Egyptian Relations from the Breakdown of Treaty Negotiations in London on the 5th May 1930, to the Signature of a Treaty in London on the 26th August 1936." In Arnold Toynbee (ed.), Survey of International Affairs, 1936 (London, 1937), pp. 662-701.

United Arab Republic, State Information Service. The Charter. Cairo, n.d.

Vacca, Virginia. "Al-Rādyū: le radio arabe d'Europa e d'oriente e le loro pubblicazione." Oriente Moderno, XX (1940), pp. 444-451.

Vatikiotis, P. J. (ed.). Egypt Since the Revolution. New York, 1968.

_____. The Egyptian Army in Politics: Pattern for New Nations?. Bloomington, Indiana, 1961.

_____. The Modern History of Egypt. New York, 1969.

Vaucher, Georges. Gamal Abdel Nasser et son équipe. Two volumes. Paris, 1959, 1961.

Von Grunebaum, Gustave E. Modern Islam: The Search for Cultural Identity. New York, 1964.

Waardenburg, Jean-Jacques. Les universités dans le monde arabe actuel. Two volumes. The Hague, 1966.

Weizsäcker, Ernst von. Translated by John Andrews. Memoirs. Chicago, 1951.

Wendell, Charles. The Evolution of the Egyptian National Image: From Its Origins to Ahmad Lutfi al-Sayyid. Berkeley, 1972.

Wilson, H. Maitland (Lord Wilson of Libya). Eight Years Overseas, 1939-1947. London, 1950.

Woodward, E. L., and Rohan Butler (eds.). Documents on British Foreign Policy. Multi-series, multi-volume. London, 1947-.

Wynn, Wilton. Nasser of Egypt: The Search for Dignity. Cambridge, Mass., 1959.

Young Egypt Society. Egypt and Great Britain. London, 1936.

Z. N. Z. "Youth and Politics in the Middle East." World Today, VII (March 1951), pp. 102-109.

Zayid, Mahmud Y. Egypt's Struggle for Independence. Beirut, 1965.

Ziadeh, Farhat J. Lawyers, the Rule of Law, and Liberalism in Modern Egypt. Hoover Institute Publications, no. 75. Stanford, California, 1968.

Index

Abazah, Fikri, 19.
'Abd al-Din, 'Ali Zayn, 121.
'Abd al-Hadi, Ibrahim, 92.
'Abd al-Nasir, Jamal, 121-124, 126.
'Abd al-Qadir, 'Izz al-Din, 35, 134.
'Abd al-Raziq, 'Ali, 126.
Administrative Council, 26-27, 38, 89, 144.
Agrarian Reform Law of 1952, 106.
Agriculture, agricultural development, 13, 65, 68-71, 81,
    94-95, 109-110, 112, 116.
al-Ahram (newspaper), 17, 150.
Albania, 33.
'Allubah, Muhammad 'Ali, 19.
Alms-tax, 70, 72-75, 119.
Amin, Ahmad, 126.
Anglo-Egyptian Treaty of 1936, 20, 51, 78, 94, 98-99.
Anglo-Iranian Oil Company, 114.
Anglo-Italian Pact of 1938, 33.
al-'Aqqad, 'Abbas Mahmud, 11, 130.
Arabs, Arab nationalism, 39, 52-55, 83-85, 91, 115-116, 122.
Army, Egyptian, 81, 83-85, 106, 121-124.
'Ashmawi, Salih, 147.
Assassination, 35, 91-92, 134; see also Terrorism.
Aswan High Dam, 122.
Axis powers, 33-34, 81-85; see also Germany; Italy.
al-Azhar, 2, 27, 34, 39, 46, 52, 72, 76-77, 86.
'Azzam, 'Abd al-Rahman, 85.
'Azzam, Ahmad Sadiq, 98.

Bank Misr, 11.
al-Banna, Hasan, 40, 82, 85, 96.
Barclay's Bank, 99.
al-Bayt al-Akhdar; see Green House.
Berque, Jacques, 50.
al-Bilad (newspaper), 84.
Black Saturday, 102-106.
Blue Shirts, 7, 14, 19, 24-26, 34-35, 37, 44, 57.
Boy Scouts, 4.
Branches of Young Egypt, 15-16, 18, 25-26, 29-32, 37-39, 42,
    80, 88-89, 92-93, 144.

Cairo Criminal Court, 103-105.
Caliph, Caliphate, 36, 46, 58.
Canal Struggle (1951-1952), 98-102, 148.

Capitulations, Capitulatory system, 17, 50-51, 68-69; see also
   Foreigners in Egypt.
Censorship, 75, 79-81.
Chamber of Deputies; see Parliament.
China, 114.
Christianity, 45, 107.
Civilization, Eastern and Western, 46-51, 122.
Class differences in Egypt, 61-66, 71, 77-78, 87, 95-96, 108-109,
   111, 122-124.
Commerce, commercial development, 69-71, 99, 110-111.
Committee for the Boycott of Jewish Commerce, 39.
Conference of Eastern Students, 10-11.
Constitution of 1923, 3, 10, 18, 21, 37, 41, 57, 61-64, 96, 109.
Constitution of 1930, 10, 21.
Constitutionalism, 57, 61-64, 74, 109.
Copts, 57.
Council of the Struggle, 16, 26, 38.
Crusades, 46.
Czechoslovakia, 33, 66.

Dar al-Thaqafah al-'Ammah, 29.
Democracy, democratic government, 60-64, 72-73, 109.
Dictatorship, 60, 62-63.
al-Diya (journal), 25, 29.

Economic planning, 110, 112, 116.
Education, 1-4, 18, 27, 30, 65, 68, 75, 77, 112.
Egyptian University, 4, 10-11, 18, 22, 27, 31, 87.
Elections, 60-61; of 1936, 21; of 1938, 28-29; of 1945, 89, 146;
   of 1950, 94, 146, 153.
Ethiopia, 21.
Europe, Europeans, 46, 48-53, 58-60, 66, 74, 108; see also
   Foreigners in Egypt; West, Western.
Executive Committee of Students (1935), 22.

Family, 5-6, 13, 49, 67, 75-76, 113.
Faruq, King, 34-36, 39, 83, 86, 94-96, 98, 102-103, 106, 118.
Fascism, 20-21, 33-34, 58-60, 78, 119; see also Germany; Italy.
Fatimid Caliphate, 46.
Fighters of Young Egypt, 14-17, 26-27, 31, 55; see also Green
   Shirts.
Foreigners in Egypt, 13, 17-18, 34, 47-52, 57, 63-65, 68-71,
   78, 95, 100, 104, 108-109, 112, 116, 124.
France, 10-11, 33, 48-49.
Free Officers Movement, 121.
Fuad, King, 18-19.

General Confederation of Young Wafdist Committees, 5.
General Staff Council of the Struggle, 15.

German Labor Front, 59, 66.
Germany, 20, 33, 59-60, 66, 81-83, 86, 133; see also Axis powers.
Gordon, David, 47.
Great Britain, 5, 7, 9, 17, 20-22, 33, 46-48, 50-51, 79, 81-91,
    95, 98-102, 104, 108-109, 113-116, 118, 123, 144-145.
Greece, 45.
Green House, 30, 92, 106.
Green Shirts, 17-19, 21, 23-27, 34-35, 37, 57; see also Fighters
    of Young Egypt.
Grunebaum, Gustave von, 7.

al-Hakim, Tawfiq, 126.
Harb, Muhammad Salih, 83.
Harb, Tal'at, 11.
Haykal, Muhammad Husayn, 126.
Hellenistic era, 45.
Heyworth-Dunne, James, 36.
Higher Schools Club, 4.
al-Hilal (journal), 11.
Hilmi, Samir, 121.
Hilmi, Yusuf, 126.
History, views of, 6-7, 44-47, 51-52, 122.
Hitler, Adolf, 33, 59-60, 66, 140.
Hizb al-Ahrar al-Dusturiyin; see Liberal Constitutionalist
    Party.
Hizb Misr al-Ishtiraki; see Socialist Party of Egypt.
Hizb Misr al-Ishtiraki al-Dimuqrati; see Socialist-Democratic
    Party of Egypt.
al-Hizb al-Watani; see Nationalist Party
Husayn, Ahmad, 7, 9-13, 16, 19-24, 26-34, 36, 38, 41-42, 45-46,
    48-49, 51, 54, 55-66, 72-73, 77, 81-86, 89-93, 96-97, 100-108,
    113-117, 120, 126, 132, 137, 149-150.
Husayn, Kamal al-Din, 121.
Husayn, Mahmud, 9.
Husayn, Taha, 126.
al-Husayni, al-Hajj Amin, 83-84, 86.

Ibrahim, 'Ali, 11.
Ibrahim, Hafiz, 11.
Ibrahim, Hasan, 121.
Imani (book), 45.
Imperialism, 20, 47-50, 53-54, 108-109, 112-114, 122-124; see
    also Europe, Europeans; Foreigners in Egypt.
Industry, industrial development, 11-13, 53, 65, 69-71, 87,
    110-111.
Iran, 86, 114.
Iraq, 54, 83-86.
'Isawi, Mahmud, 145.
al-Ishtirakiyah (journal), 93, 96.

Islam, 13, 17, 29, 36, 38-41, 46-48, 52-53, 55, 59, 70, 72-78, 81, 88, 107-110, 119, 122.
Islamic Nationalist Party, 41, 53-55, 69, 73-75, 80-85, 89, 118.
Israel, 91.
Italy, 20-21, 24, 33-34, 58-60, 81-82, 86; see also Axis powers.
Ittihad al-Jami'ah; see Student Union.

al-Jala (journal), 29.
Jam'iyah al-Ikhwan al-Muslimin; see Muslim Brotherhood.
Jam'iyah al-Kashafah al-Ahliyah; see Boy Scouts.
Jam'iyah al-Shubban al-Muslimin; see Young Men's Muslim Assocation.
Japan, 33.
Jaridah Misr al-Fatah (journal), 29, 31, 42, 80, 88, 93.
Jews, 39, 64, 79, 91, 113; see also Zionism.

Kamil, Mustafa, 6-7, 19, 47.
Kataib al-Tahrir; see Liberation Battalions.
Khalid, Wasim, 120.
al-Kilani, Rashid 'Ali, 84, 86.
Korean war, 113-114.

Labour Party (Great Britain), 22.
al-Lajnah al-Qawmiyah; see Nationalist Committee.
al-Lajnah al-Wataniyah lil-'Ummal wa al-Talabah; see National Committee of Workers and Students.
Land ownership, 65, 70-71, 94, 109-110, 112, 116.
League of Nations, 22.
Lebanon, 10-11.
Lenin, Vladimir, 107-108.
Liberal Constitutionalist Party, 5, 19, 32.
Liberation Battalions, 100-101.
Libya, 20.

Mahir, Ahmad, 91.
Mahir, 'Ali, 19, 21-23, 27, 32, 35-36, 40, 83, 85, 106.
Mahmud, Muhammad, 5, 9, 19, 32, 35, 41.
Majlis Arkan Harb al-Jihad; see General Staff Council of the Struggle.
Majlis al-Idarah; see Administrative Council.
Majlis al-Jihad; see Council of the Struggle.
Makarius, Raoul, 5.
Maktab Shuun al-Kharijiyah; see Office of Foreign Affairs.
Mamluks, 46.
Martial law, 79-81.
Marx, Karl, 107.
Marxism, 88, 107.
Masaryk Institutes, 66.
Mashru' al-Qirsh; see Piastre Plan.

Mecca, 81.
Membership of Young Egypt, 14, 17-18, 30-32, 40, 42, 85, 87, 92-93.
al-Misri (newspaper), 86.
al-Misri, 'Aziz 'Ali, 40, 83-85.
Mixed Courts, 17, 68-69.
Montreux Convention, 50-51, 78.
Muhammad 'Ali, 46-47.
Mujahid; see Fighters of Young Egypt.
Muslim Brotherhood, 4, 14, 23, 39-42, 44, 52, 76, 80, 82-83, 85, 88, 90-92, 94, 96-99, 116, 148.
Mussolini, Benito, 20, 58-60.
Mutamar al-Talabah al-Sharqiyin; see Conference of Eastern Students.
Mutran, Khalil, 11.

Nadi al-Madaris al-'Ulya; see Higher Schools Club.
al-Nahhas, Mustafa, 24-25, 32, 35, 95.
Nariman, Queen, 94.
Nasser; see 'Abd al-Nasir, Jamal.
Nassim, Tawfiq, 21.
National Charter, 121-123.
National Committee of Workers and Students, 90.
Nationalism, 13, 44-55, 69, 76-78, 89-90, 97-98, 108, 120.
Nationalist Committee, 90.
Nationalist Party, 4-5, 19-20, 98-99, 148.
Nazism, Nazi Party, 59-60, 66, 133; see also Fascism.
New York Times (newspaper), 91.
Nietzsche, Friedrich, 56.
North Korea, 114.
al-Nuqrashi, Mahmud Fahmi, 35, 90.

Office of Foreign Affairs, 36.
Office of Propaganda, 37.
Ottoman Empire, 46.

Palace, Egyptian 10, 13, 18-19, 21, 23, 27, 32, 34-36, 39-40, 58, 76, 81, 83, 85, 95-96, 102, 104-105; see also Faruq, King; Fuad, King.
Palestine, Palestinian Arabs, 39-40, 52-53, 79, 83, 91, 95, 113.
Paramilitarism, 14-15, 17, 26-27, 29, 55; see also Fighters of Young Egypt; Green Shirts.
Parliament, parliamentary government, 24, 28-29, 36-37, 41, 56-58, 60-64, 88-89, 94-95, 97-98, 118-120.
Partisans of Peace, 98-99.
Peasantry, 23, 29, 34, 51, 63, 65, 67-68, 70-71, 78, 110.
Pharaohs, Pharaonic Egypt, 45-46, 122.
Piastre Plan, 11-12, 14, 16, 109.
Poland, 33.

173

Political parties, 5, 14, 25-26, 47-48, 56-58, 60-61, 79, 88, 94-95, 123.
Prayer, 29, 75, 92.
Pyramids, 17, 80, 92.

al-Qumsan al-Zarqa; see Blue Shirts.
Quran, 29, 72-74, 97.
Qutb, Sayyid, 97, 147, 151.

Rabitah Lijan al-Shubban al-Wafdiyin al-'Ammah; see General
    Confederation of Young Wafdist Committees.
Radwan, Fathi, 9-13, 16, 19, 21-22, 27-28, 30-31, 58-59, 62,
    86-87, 126, 129, 137.
al-Rafi'i, 'Abd al-Rahman, 19.
Religion, 72-78, 107-108, 114, 122-123; see also Islam.
Revolution, views of, 38, 60, 63-64, 96.
Revolution of 1919, 7, 47, 102.
Revolution of 1952, 103, 106, 121-124.
al-Risalah (journal), 11.
Rivoli Cinema, 99, 105-106.
Rome, Roman Empire, 20, 45.

Sacred Law, 3, 38, 54, 73-74, 76-78.
al-Sadat, Anwar, 83-84, 121, 123-124.
Sa'id, 'Abd al-Hamid, 19.
Saladin, 46.
Salah; see Prayer.
Salah, Kamal al-Din, 10-12.
Salim, Jamal, 121.
Salim, Salah, 121.
Sansom, Alfred, 84.
al-Sarkhah (journal), 10, 16-17, 19-21, 25.
al-Sha'b al-Jadid (journal), 93.
Shari'ah; see Sacred Law.
Shawqi, Ahmad, 11.
Shi'ah, Shi'ism, 46.
al-Shishakli, Adib, 91.
Shu'bah; see Branches of Young Egypt.
Shukri, Ibrahim, 94, 97, 106, 146.
Shubban al-Ahrar al-Dusturiyin; see Youth of the Liberal
    Constitutionalists.
Sidqi, Isma'il, 10-11, 13, 90.
al-Siyasah (newspaper), 9, 19.
al-Siyasah al-Usbu'iyah (journal), 11.
Smith, Wilfred Cantwell, 47.
Social Darwinism, 55-56.
Social security measures, 67, 111.
Socialism, socialist movements, 72-74, 76, 88, 90, 107-109,
    112, 115-116, 119, 153.

Socialist Party of Egypt, 1, 28, 92-118, 121.
Socialist Peasant's Party, 99.
Socialist-Democratic Party of Egypt, 92.
Society of Liberal Youth in Support of the Treaty, 9.
South Korea, 114.
Stohrer, Eberhard von, 20.
Student Union, 4, 31.
Students, 1-4, 7, 11-13, 22, 30-32, 51, 90; see also Youth.
Subayh, Muhammad, 12, 33, 82, 84.
Sudan, 13, 17, 55, 89-91, 98, 115.
Sudan Conventions of 1899, 98-99.
Suez Canal, 69, 95, 98, 100, 102.
al-Sukkari, Ahmad, 85, 97, 147.
Sulayman, Sidqi, 121.
Supreme Military Court, 103.
Switzerland, 50.
Syria, 10-11, 54, 91.

Tarraf, Nur al-Din, 7, 12, 22, 87.
Taxation, 70-71, 94, 111.
Territorial Army, 85.
Terrorism, 91-92, 145-146; see also Assassination.
al-Thaghr (journal), 29.
Titles, 94, 111, 151.
Turkey, 10, 86.

'Ulama, 89.
Union of Soviet Socialist Republics, 108, 112-114, 116.
Unions, unionization, 30, 68, 71, 94, 112; see also Workers.
United Nations, 90-91, 114.
United States, 91, 113-114.
Usury, 74-75.
'Uthman (Caliph), 46.
'Uthman, Radwan, 9.

Wadi al-Nil (journal), 16.
Wafd, 5, 7, 10-11, 18-19, 21, 23-25, 27, 31-32, 34-35, 42, 44,
    57-58, 86, 88, 90, 93, 95-98, 101-102, 104, 116, 118, 126,
    134, 146; see also Blue Shirts.
al-Wakil, Mustafa, 27-28, 40, 62, 77, 82, 84-86, 91, 132, 137.
Waqf, Awqaf, 75.
West, Western, 47-52, 76, 90, 110, 112-114; see also Europe,
    Europeans; Foreigners in Egypt.
Women, 75-76.
Workers, 23, 29-30, 34, 40, 59, 63, 65-68, 78, 90, 94, 111-112;
    see also Unions, unionization.
World War II, 1, 5, 27, 33-34, 39, 41, 79, 81, 88, 116, 119.

Y. M. C. A., 4

Y. M. M. A.; see Young Men's Muslim Association.
Yahya, 'Abd al-Fattah, 13, 19.
Young Men's Muslim Association, 4, 14, 19, 23.
Youth, 1-8, 11-13, 14, 16-17, 23-24, 30-31, 42, 44, 119-121;
    see also Students.
Youth of the Liberal Constitutionalists, 5, 9-10.
Yunis, Mahmud, 7, 126.

Zakah; see Alms-tax.
Zionism, 39, 53, 99; see also Jews.
al-Ziyadi, Ibrahim, 146.